J G MERQUIOR, born in 1941, first trained in law and philosophy, studied literature at the Sorbonne and social theory at the London School of Economics. Once a visiting professor at King's College, London and in Brazil, his native country, he was for five years a member of Claude Lévi-Strauss's seminar at the Collège de France. Several of his books deal with the history of French thought: *Rousseau and Weber* (London 1980), *L'Esthétique de Lévi-Strauss* (Paris 1977), the Fontana Modern Masters *Foucault* (1985), *Western Marxism* (London 1986). He has also written extensively on Georges Sorel, Raymond Aron and the influence of Comte's positivism outside France. He is at present working in the philosophy of history, concentrating on the issue of the nature of modernity.

From Prague to Paris

A Critique of Structuralist and Post-structuralist Thought

◆

J. G. MERQUIOR

Plato thought nature but a spume that plays
Upon a ghostly paradigm of things.

Yeats

VERSO

London · New York

British Library
Cataloguing in Publication Data

Merquior, J. G.
   From Prague to Paris: a critique of
   structuralist and post-structuralist thought.
   1. Structuralism — History
   I. Title
   149'.96'09   B841.4

First published 1986
© J G Merquior 1986
Second impression 1988

Verso
UK: 6 Meard Street, London W1V 3HR
USA: 29 West 35th Street, New York, NY 10001-2291

Typeset in Times by
Cover to Cover, Cambridge

ISBN 0-86091-129-2
ISBN 0-86091-860-2 Pbk

Printed in the USA

Contents

For Stella and João Cabral de Melo Neto

Foreword

'The highest thing would be so to grasp things that everything factual was already theory.' When one thinks of structuralism and its progeny, it is tempting to read this jewel, no. 575 of Goethe's *Maximen und Reflexionen*, as if the Weimar sage had been engaging in an exercise of prophetic irony. For many regard the structuralisms that have conquered academic strongholds in Anglo-Saxonland as Gallic theory with a vengeance, in all its Olympian contempt for the untidy mess of the empirical. As the German idealists used to say: 'so much the worse for the facts'.

Or is such a charge, to a large extent, a caricature? How do the different brands of structuralism fare in this respect? Which of them come to grips with cultural reality—and if so, how—before the post-structuralist attempt to undermine the very legitimacy of factual questions? This and other important issues are seldom faced. The literature on structuralism and post-structuralism continues to grow, though there are signs (nowhere more visible than in France) of their decline as intellectual fashions. Yet most discussions are written in a vein of uncritical acceptance, the experts here tending to act as votaries. The present book, whose author is a one-time disciple taught in the heartland of the faith by some of its high priests, proposes to redress the balance. It is intended as a critical study, an analysis incorporating, expanding and complementing previous criticisms levelled at the structuralist enterprise and the post-structuralist adventure.

x

Without offering a linear chronicle, much less a panorama, I have tried to work in that honourable but now much maligned discipline, the history of ideas. If the result may often sound like outright (though hopefully high) polemic, structuralisms are so often an object of donnish deference that there should be no harm in trying to rock the boat a little. Nevertheless, an earnest effort has been made to present the views of the various thinkers before assessing their cognitive value, and I have therefore devoted whole sections to sheer exposition, as jargon-free as possible. The book is by no means addressed only, or even chiefly, to the reader already familiar with structuralese or the post-structuralist idioms. In any event, I hope the general reader can profit from my description even when rejecting my judgement; in other words, that he or she can trust the tale if not the teller.

From Prague to Paris is primarily a critique of French structuralism, its fate and its determinate negation in post-structuralism. However, structuralism had already evolved significantly prior to its French incarnation, in ways that often foreshadowed major problems inherent in Parisian structural or post-structural theory. Hence the discussion in chapter 2 of a contrasting pair of Slav theorists from the interwar period: Jakobson and Mukařovsky. For, far from being the straightforward methodological highway we are often invited to think it was, the intellectual road from Prague in the thirties to Paris in the sixties was marked with many a philosophical choice and an ideological bias. Hence, too, my title, which I can only hope won't be mistaken for a travel guide or the biography of one of my favourite novelists, Milan Kundera. Still, prewar 'Prague' is just a strategic background; the real location of the story is the *haute culture* milieu of modern Paris.

Three French theorists have been singled out for extensive discussion: Claude Lévi-Strauss, Roland Barthes, Jacques Derrida. Insofar as the first two have a larger output dealing with a given corpus of interpretable data (myths or literary texts), their work has been given a more comprehensive coverage.

Of course other prominent French thinkers since the 1960s could have been chosen with equal justice: Jacques Lacan, Louis Althusser, Michel Foucault readily come to mind. But since I have already written on Foucault[1] (who never admitted to being a structuralist anyway) and more than once on Althusser,[2] and since I share with most of the rest of mankind a persistent inability to understand what the devil Lacan meant, I thought there was as good a case as any to stick to my chosen triad. After all, it fits ideally my main theme: the rise, change and dissolution of the structuralist idea. Lévi-Strauss remains the master of classical structuralism, Barthes its most distinguished apostle, and then apostate, in literary criticism, and Derrida currently leads the most influential revolt against the main assumptions of classical structuralism.

As for other figures—Benveniste or Lacan, Mauss and Dumézil, Bataille and Blanchot, Klossowski or Levinas—they have been touched upon as key sources in the genealogy of the Saussurean disaspora, rather than in their own right as important authors. They are as it were snapshots, not true portraits, in my structuralist album.

Part of the Barthes chapter appeared in *Portuguese Studies* (a journal published by the Modern Humanities Research Association for King's College, London), vol. 1 (1985). Parts of the argument have greatly benefited from critical suggestions made by Ernest Gellner, John A. Hall, Perry Anderson and Helder Macedo, none of whom is held responsible for the final outcome. My wife transformed a rambling screed into a neat typescript, to which my daughter added a large bibliography. I owe Neil Belton a vastly improved text. And I am very grateful to him and, once again, Perry Anderson for the warm and unprejudiced hospitality I was given at Verso.

JGM
London, September 1985.

[1] Cf. J. G. Merquior, *Foucault*, London 1985.
[2] Cf. J. G. Merquior, *Western Marxism*, London 1986.

1

The Rise of Structuralism

*Nous sommes . . . profondément con-
vaincu que quiconque pose le pied sur
le terrain de la* langue *peut se dire qu'il
est abandonné par toutes les analogies
du ciel et de la terre.*

Ferdinand de Saussure

Down with the Cogito

'Structuralism' is, I suspect, a word that suggests more than one
thing to the average reader. But in terms of the history of ideas
it now seems to refer to the work of a bunch of crabbed
academic pundits, mostly French, active in social science,
philosophy and the humanities. More precisely, it is increasingly acknowledged that 'structuralism' means a trend of
thought in the humanist wing of academe, stemming from
modern linguistics and flourishing in France mainly in the
1960s. Indeed, it appears so French a phenomenon that some
like to retain the French noun—*structuralisme*—when commenting on it, if only in order to avoid confusion with previous
trends, often also named 'structuralism', in different disciplines
(such as biology) or even in social science itself (as in the
anthropology of Radcliffe-Brown or the sociological theory of
Talcott Parsons). French structuralism has been losing momen-
tum for almost a decade. At any rate, it has never percolated
through the general ideological atmosphere in a way compar-
able to the previous Gallic vogue: Sartrean existentialism.

In its heyday, the stars of French structuralism were the
anthropologist Claude Lévi-Strauss (b. 1908), the literary critic
Roland Barthes (1915–80), the philosophers Michel Foucault
(1926–84) and Louis Althusser (b. 1918), a Marxist, and the
psychoanalyst Jacques Lacan (1901–82). So wide a range of

intellectual areas explains why structuralism, for all the family resemblance among the theories of its founders, is actually less than a unified movement, let alone a school. Rather it is a *style of thought* on the humanist side of knowledge.

This book attempts a critical discussion of structuralism and its prolongation and denial in post-structuralism. The discussion has three main steps: (a) a brief recapitulation of the main foundations of structural theory in linguistics, literary criticism and social science (chapters 1 and 2); (b) a more extended analysis of the work of the originator of classical French structuralism, Lévi-Strauss (chapter 3) as well as of a pivotal theorist in its self-supersession: Barthes (chapter 4); and finally (c) an examination of the post-structuralist scene in French thought (chapter 5), where the chief thinker in focus will be Jacques Derrida (b. 1930).

To return to the notion of a style of thought: much as one can tell one style from another in, say, poems or novels by looking at different general patterns of form rather than at the specifics of plot or lyrical content, we can isolate some common habits of mind in structuralist thinking, quite apart from the specific tenets of each particular structuralism. And as often happens with style in art and literature, the rise of the new form of thought is best realized in terms of its polemical departure from prior standards and directions of inquiry. Historians of ideas are bound to agree with Spinoza: every determination implies negation. Intellectual trends often seem to achieve their own identity by dint of a strategy of blunt refusal—the strident negation of previous conceptual moulds.

Accordingly, the spread of structuralism as a new Parisian intellectual fashion in the early and mid-1960s came as an onslaught on the frame of mind associated with existentialism. French philosophy since the war had been largely dominated by existentialist philosophy, especially its atheistic variety, with Jean-Paul Sartre (1905–80) and Maurice Merleau-Ponty (1908–61) as commanding figures.

Now as a whole, existentialist thinking had two keynotes: humanism and historism. It dwelt on the peculiarities of the human condition. 'Existentialism is a humanism', as Sartre famously put it. A character in his play *Le Diable et le Bon Dieu* (1952) goes as far as to state that 'only human beings really exist'.

In addition, when structuralism began to rise, existentialism became much more historically minded. Sartre held that 'existence precedes essence'. But existence, though defined by the most uncompromising freedom from the past (to such an extent that Sartre's treatise, *Being and Nothingness*, actually amounted to a copious rhetoric of absolute freedom), was held emphatically to be *situated* within history. Sartre's later evolution towards Marxism pushed existential philosophy into the orbit of modern historism in the broad sense of the word, that is the prospensity to view human experience in a context of historical change.

In any event, Marxisant beliefs loosely combined with existentialist tenets were the dominant feature of French philosophizing at the time, and therefore humanism tended to go hand in hand with historism and/or historicism. Now the two main targets of structuralism, or of a critique of existentialist ideology, would be precisely the joint themes of humanism and historism; structuralism asserted itself in the intellectual climate as both an anti-humanism and an anti-historism.

But why did structuralism challenge humanism? Because humanism, in philosophy as in social science, implied the primacy of consciousness, or, in more philosophical jargon, of the *subject*. Technically speaking, existentialism derived from the phenomenology of Edmund Husserl (1859–1938); and like phenomenology, it began with a theory of consciousness—a latter-day version of the doctrine of the cogito, a modern edition (with corrections) of Descartes's 'thinking substance'. As a highly literary mode of philosophizing, nourished since its inception in the work of Martin Heidegger (1889–1976) by quasi-religious needs expressed in the idiom—and with the pathos—of a lay theology, existentialism strikingly *romanticized* the modern cogito.

How? To put it in a nutshell, it happened as follows:

Act I: phenomenology claims (against classical idealism) that the cogito is always *intentional*; no cogito without a cogitatum—and therefore, no subject without an object.

Act II: Sartre *dramatizes* this very correlation of subject and object. The Sartrean subject, the *pour-soi*, is pure negativity: its sole task consists in transcending each of its own states by a relentless annihilation of each of its objects (the *en-soi*). The *pour-soi*, insofar as it gives us a philosophical translation of

Sartrean man, amounts to a straight antithesis of the Christian God: 'whereas God creates the world out of nothing, the *pour-soi* creates nothingness out of the world.'[1]

Whenever the *pour-soi* slackens tension and dwells on the *en-soi*, the ugliest sin in Sartrean morals arises: bad faith. For the subject as *pour-soi*, in its craving for self-transcendence, can never find a satisfying object, any more than it can bear a peaceful relation with other consciousnesses. That is why the self's infinite play of negativity exudes a strong smell of nihilism —the gloom of empty freedom that pervades Sartre's philosophical treatise, *Being and Nothingness* (1943) and leaves everything as meaningless as the viscous world of his archetypal existentialist novel, *Nausea*. Liberty is real but irredeemably absurd; man, 'a useless passion'; and the new cogito a compulsive bungler. The Sartrean subject is the Flying Dutchman of metaphysics: he is nowhere at home with the world or at peace with himself.

Now Lévi-Strauss will have none of this litero-philosophical melodrama. He calls the phenomenological subject (the epistemological stuff beneath all the pathos in *Being and Nothingness*) an *'enfant gâté'* of reflection, getting in the way of a serious search for mental structures which are by definition beyond the purview of consciousness. Nor does it get any better if we replace Sartre's stark dichotomy of humans and things, *pour-soi* and *en-soi*, with a more worldly subject, like Merleau-Ponty's perceptual cogito, which relishes its own entanglement with the Other, be it human or physical. For structures cannot possibly be 'lived' in any state of awareness—they are just experienced, 'undergone', without ever becoming objects for the conscious mind. Therefore neither the Flying Dutchman of the *pour-soi* nor the cosy self enmeshed in the world can save the cogito; from the viewpoint of a theory of structures, both are simply worthless.

Later assessments of the intellectual wars of the 1960s saw it all as a struggle between the philosophy of cogito and a more 'combinatorial' mode—a battle between the rival heritages of Descartes and Leibniz.[2] In a deep historical sense, this account of things is quite accurate. For if one takes Sartre as the

---

[1] Norberto Bobbio, *Existentialism*, Oxford 1948, appendix.
[2] Cf. Jean-Marie Benoist, *La Révolution structurale*, Paris 1976.

epitome of the outlook rejected by the rise of structuralism, then one might well see him as belonging to something very French in Western philosophy: the time-honoured concern with *consciousness*. Indeed, his loyalty to it underlies a crucial difference between his own existentialism and that of Heidegger, despite their sharing a mood of anguish and a quest for 'authenticity'. Like Heidegger's, Sartre's work both derives and diverges from Husserl's phenomenology—but the actual direction of his divergence is the opposite of Heidegger's. Whereas the German thinker replaced the Husserlian concept of a transcendental consciousness with the far more *ontological* notion of *Dasein*, the gateway to Being, thereby fastening existentialism to the framework of a 'fundamental ontology', Sartre got rid of the selfsame transcendental ego precisely in order to strengthen the element of *consciousness*. He dropped the ego because it was still an object within consciousness, fully transparent to itself. That places Sartre firmly with Descartes, Maine de Biran and Bergson—a three-century old tradition of *'philosophie de la conscience'*.[3]

Yet to structuralism the sovereignty of consciousness was a nuisance. However speculative it may seem by the more empirical criteria of Anglo-Saxon theories of knowledge, in French academe during the sixties structuralism meant 'rigour'. But more rigorous analysis entailed an abandonment of the focus on intentional, even conscious action, for the sake of identifying hidden springs of human conduct.

At the same time, structuralism also relinquished the old anti-positivist custom of defining social science against 'hard' science—a ritual notoriously reinforced under the long sway of phenomenology and existentialism. Taken together, cogito-bashing and the subsidence of anti-scientism shaped the anti-humanist stance of most structuralisms. Generally speaking, the latter shared both a fascination with the death-of-the-subject theme and, at least originally, a strong scientistic leaning.

So much for anti-humanism. What of the other big negative element—anti-historism? Here the chief motivation seems to have been more conspicuously ideological. Since Sartre's espousal of Marxism in the fifties, mainstream existentialism in

---

[3] On this point, see Pierre Thévenaz, *De Husserl à Merleau-Ponty: Qu'est-ce que la Phénomenologie*, Neuchatel 1966, ch. 3, section 1.

6

France had evolved from *historism* into *historicism*—from a
sense of situation to a belief in the logic of history and in
liberation through history. In point of fact, Sartre, in his Marxist
magnum opus, the *Critique of Dialectical Reason* (1960), never
managed to suppress the pessimistic, nihilistic overtones of his
erstwhile existential creed. Nevertheless, in the main, Marx-
izing existentialism—the lingua franca of the French humanistic
intelligentsia at the time—conveyed the faith in history characteristic of more conventional Marxism.

Significantly, the cogito, that conceptual hero about to become a villain, once again played an important part. For what
were the smug certainties of the Eurocentric left but a kind of
cogito writ large, a self-righteous History-man, a socialist subject speaking in the name of History—and all the more blind to
the gaps and limits of western experience in those days of the
'affluent society'? Soon, as we shall see, Lévi-Strauss was to
chide Sartre's *pour-soi*, Marxified as a 'group-in-fusion',
as exemplifying the crypto-colonialism of his radical progressivism—and Sartre did not find a way to reply.

It was as though the Algerian war crisis and the rise to power
of the right under de Gaulle had shaken the intellectuals' faith
in historical progress and made them suspicious of philosophical
concepts traditionally linked to it. As a result, a disillusioned
and disheartened left turned towards primitive peoples, not in a
quest for origins (which would only have reinstated the historical approach) but for the truth about humankind.[4] The hour of
radical theoretical anthropology had struck.

Old and New Structuralisms

Up to now, all we have sketched is a negative picture, showing
that structuralism as a style of thought was born from a revulsion against the existentialist cast of mind. But why did such a
dissatisfaction with existential thinking take the form of *structuralism*? Why was it that 'structure' seemed so apt to supersede the alternative conceptual clusters of existentialism?

There are of course several meanings attached to the word

[4] François Furet, 'Les Intellectuels français et le Structuralisme,' *Preuves*,
February 1967.

'structure'. The term can be understood: (a) in the *architectural* sense, denoting an arrangement of parts, so that everything holds together, literally (as in buildings) or metaphorically; (b) in the organic sense, stressing that components are actually linked to each other, as in bodies and other living forms; and finally (c) in the *mathematical* sense, meaning a set of abstract relations defined in a *formal* manner and implying a *model* that holds good for several different contents, the latter said to be *isomorphic* precisely because they share the same structure. Structuralism purports to be a theory of structure in the third, formal sense—which explains why the structures of structuralism are generally subsumed under a model, a master structure explicated by analysis as the basic 'mechanics of meaning' obtaining in any given area of social life.

The first structuralists—the linguists of the Prague Circle—believed that their methodological breakthrough in phonology, which was to become the paradigm for the rise of structuralism in social science and the humanities, was part and parcel of a broad scientific trend. Half a century ago, the founder of structural phonology, Nicolai Trubetzkoy (1890–1938) pointed out the epistemological assumptions of their work. He wrote: 'the age in which we live is characterized by the tendency in all the scientific disciplines to replace atomism by structuralism. . . . This tendency can be observed in physics, in chemistry, in biology, in psychology, in economics, etc.'[5] Within this general drive towards structure, however, some disciplines were more equal than others. The late Roger Bastide noticed that in the 1930s—the *Gründerzeit* of structuralism in linguistics—there occurred a shift in the concept of structure from a biological to a mathematical view, a change fostered by the prestige of Gestalt theory in psychology.[6]

To the psychologist Jean Piaget, the triumph of the formal idea of structure, spreading the sense of system in so many disciplines, implied three key concepts: the notion of wholeness;

---

[5] N. Trubetzkoy, 'La phonologie actuelle', in *Psychologie du Langage*, Paris 1933, p. 245. Trubetzkoy's epistemological overview became a classic reference point for linguistics: for example, E. Benveniste, *Problems in General Linguistics*, Miami 1971, chapter 8) and non-linguistics (C. Lévi-Strauss, *Structural Anthropology*, New York 1963, chapter 2) alike.

[6] R. Bastide, ed., *Sens et Usage du Mot Structure*, The Hague 1962, p. 13.

that of self-regulation; and that of transformation.[7] Piaget's own enumeration actually ends and culminates with self-regulation, but I have altered his order because whilst self-regulation plays a crucial role in his biological approach to cognitive psychology, it has a more dubious status in other domains scanned by structural analysis, such as Lévi-Straussian anthropology. By contrast, our third element—*transformation*—is a defining trait in all genuinely structuralist research. It is also the element most obviously linked to an ideally mathematical notion of structure—the sense of structure Bastide correctly identified as the dominant one in the structuralist movement.

The shift from the biological to the formal idea of structure provides a neat way of distinguishing old structuralism in social science (the Radcliffe-Brown or Parsonian variety, widely known as structural-functionalism) from the French dispensation. For Radcliffe-Brown saw social structure, and Parsons the social system, in terms that owed nothing to the transformative capacity of a structural model. Lévi-Strauss blamed British anthropological theory, especially in its Oxford branch, led by Radcliffe-Brown, for its empiricism;[8] but the same criticism could hardly be levelled at Parsons's structural-functionalism, whose ponderous conceptual weaponry is anything but close to social empiria. Both Radcliffe-Brown and Parsons, however, were far from thinking of structure in a formal, ultimately universal sense. They thought of structure mainly in terms of practical categories (like the relation between social functions and collective needs) and picked up their analogies from biology and cybernetics, with a keen eye on homeostatic processes (Piaget's self-regulation) but ignored the possibility of equivalence between differently structured units or systems.

Perhaps this major difference between what might be called *palaeo-structuralism* in social theory and the much more formal viewpoint of modern structuralism is not unrelated to their dissimilar subject matter. This was quite conspicuous in anthropology. The stuff of Oxford anthropologists under palaeo-structuralism was social structure as opposed to culture—the hardware of society, so to speak; whereas its software, the frills of art and mores, was left to the rickety psychologism of

[7] J. Piaget, *Structuralism*, New York 1970, p. 5.
[8] Lévi-Strauss, *Structural Anthropology*, ch. 15, III.

German-American culture theory.[9] Modern structuralism, on the other hand, mainly deals with culture, not 'social structure': its normal business has always been the decoding of language and myth, art and ritual—the symbolic heartland of culture. Ernest Gellner first put his finger on this discrepancy between the two anthropological structuralisms, old and new, by building on a shrewd analogy with the famous Lockian distinction between primary and secondary qualities. In Gellner's picture of it, palaeo-structuralism features as a theory of primary social qualities—of economic and power relations; new structuralism, on the other hand, focusses on secondary, or surface, social qualities: the cultural codes.[10] While acknowledging that Lévi-Strauss's remarkable work on kinship systems does not chime with such a division of labour between the old and the new structuralisms, Gellner claims that in the main the general difference stands, since at any rate modern structuralism has been so vocal in asserting the centrality of culture (and suggesting its autonomy) and so reluctant to accept any talk of 'hard' infrastructural determination of the cultural realm.

The gist of the matter is that modern structuralisms conceive of their structural models as the infrastructure of culture at large. In other words, they keep looking for primary, determining qualities, as it were; but they find them *at the level of surface itself.*[11] That is why it makes little sense to claim seminal figures like Marx and Freud as structuralists (or proto-structuralists) on the grounds that they share with the progeny of Saussure—the official structuralists—the conviction that surface phenomena are to be explained by other phenomena operating below the surface.[12] A sense of depth is not enough to make an analysis structuralist: it all depends on where one places one's deep

[9] On the Teuto-anthropological concept of culture, in the tradition stretching from *Historismus* to ethos theory, that is, from Herder to Kroeber, see J. G. Merquior, *The Veil and the Mask: Essays on Culture and Ideology*, London 1979, chapter 2, section I.

[10] E. Gellner, 'What is structuralisme?', *Times Literary Supplement* 31 July 1981; reprinted in E. Gellner, *Relativism and the Social Sciences*, Cambridge 1985, pp. 128–57.

[11] As fully recognized by Gellner in *Cause and Meaning in the Social Sciences*, London 1973, chapter 10.

[12] This mistake was committed in one of the first American readers: Richard and Fernande DeGeorge, eds., *The Structuralists from Marx to Lévi-Strauss*, Garden City 1972.

mechanisms. Hardware depth, such as Marx's technological forces and relations of production, or Freud's instinctual drives, will not do. Software depth will suffice, be it phonological laws in a natural language, taxonomic grids, patterns of myth transformation or hidden rules of exclusion in each age's modes of discourse. In order to be 'structuralist', a structure must qualify on at least two accounts: (a) it must be formal and transformational, rather than just an empirical metaphor of buildings or organisms; and (b) it must be located on the 'proper' level of the social whole. Taken together, they help one realize why the example of modern linguistics was bound to become a true compass for the founding fathers of structuralism in social science.

The Linguistic Paradigm

According to Lévi-Strauss, three conditions must be met for the human sciences to reach scientific maturity: (a) their object should be universal, that is to say, present in all known societies; (b) their method must remain homogeneous, regardless of the diversity of their areas of application; and (c) they must enjoy a consensus of experts on the validity of the basic assumptions underlying their method.[13] The first—perhaps the only—human science to meet such requirements was linguistics, thanks to the foundation of phonology before 1930. Trubetzkoy's brainchild did in fact evince a universal object and a homogeneous method (one applicable to all phonemic systems) blessed by all the relevant scientific community.

Now Trubetzkoy himself, in the article quoted above (see p. 7), claimed that his phonological method (a) analysed *relations between terms* rather than taking the latter in isolation; (b) it *demonstrated*, instead of simply asserting, the systemic character of phonological data; and (c) it pursued *general laws*, valid for all such systems.

Naturally, the world of phonemes is ideally suited to this kind of analysis. Not only the highest coded unit to be scrutinized, the sentence, lends itself easily to analysis, but linguistic objects

[13] Lévi-Strauss, *Structural Anthropology II*, New York 1976, chapter 16 (originally a 1964 essay commissioned by Unesco's journal of social science).

in general allow, far better than other social phenomena, an abstraction—for the purposes of analysis—from their diachronic or historical dimension.

The rise of phonology marked an epoch in the history of linguistics because it made truly operational a kind of Copernican revolution in the way we look at language. This was derived from the teaching of someone already mentioned in passing: the Swiss scholar Ferdinand de Saussure (1857–1913) whose *Course in General Linguistics* (1916) was posthumously edited, Aristotle-wise from the notes of his pupils, exactly a century after Franz Bopp fathered linguistics as a science in the form of a full-fledged comparative grammar. Nowadays, it is rightly deemed the theoretical fountainhead of modern structuralism.

Saussure never employed the word 'structure', any more than Darwin spoke of 'evolution' or Mendel of 'genetics' (or Marx, for that matter, of 'dialectical materialism'). Today, without ignoring the value of his theoretical breakthrough, we begin to realize that in more than one respect he was a developer rather than the author of certain decisive insights into the nature of language. He stands at the apex of a long chain of philosophical thinking on language which, from Locke and Condillac to Humboldt and Taine, firmly denied that language could be conceived of as just a nomenclature. This stance, as a harbinger of the systemic view of language, foreshadowed the great achievement of Saussure.

Recent research by Hans Aarsleff has shown how key concepts in Saussure's seminal *Course* were already present in the theoretical writings of Hippolyte Taine (1828–93). In the opening book of his treatise *De l'Intelligence* (1870) Taine drew the vital distinction between signified and signifier (without, however, using the last term), the difference, that is, between the two faces of the linguistic sign, roughly corresponding to sense and sound. Elsewhere he suggested Saussure's own synchronic/diachronic dichotomy by contrasting the study of 'the connection between things simultaneous', inspired by the approach of the naturalist Cuvier, with the focus on 'the connection of successive things', in the evolutionist fashion of Cuvier's great opponent, Saint-Hilaire. Again, another outstanding French scholar of the late nineteenth century, the linguist Michel Bréal (who actually sponsored the young Saussure's teaching at the Paris Ecole des Hautes Etudes during the 1880s) used concepts like language (*langue*), discourse (*parole*) and 'value' —the very cornerstones of Saussure's *Course*. [14]

Today the single notion most generally credited to Saussure is the idea of the *arbitrariness* of the sign: the independence of linguistic signs from non-verbal reality. The concept of the arbitrary sign is something of which structuralism has made heavy, and indeed heavily ideological, use. Yet Saussure did not at all assert the arbitrariness thesis as a novelty. At most, he presented this view as a radicalization of the position of a previous linguist, William Dwight Whitney, whose book, *Language*, was published in 1867. In the 1930s, well known linguists such as Otto Jespersen deemed Saussure's claims about the arbitrariness of the sign as endorsement of prior theorists such as Johann Nicolai Madvig (1842) and Whitney. Moreover, without the use of the term 'arbitrary', the same idea was already present in Russian linguistics, especially in the work of Baudouin de Courtenay (1893), one of Saussure's acknowledged forerunners.

What is more, the term 'arbitrary' itself, applied to language, was commonplace in the eighteenth century, and was also employed during the previous century. Eugenio Coseriu (1967) has listed several authors who wrote of language as something arbitrary in relation to reality. They include Hobbes (1655), Locke (1690), Leibniz (1703), Wolff (1719), Berkeley (1733), Breitinger (1740), Condillac (1746), Turgot (1751), Lessing (1766), D. Stewart (1792), Fichte (1795) and Hegel (1817).

At any rate, the notion that names do not reflect the nature of things was quite familiar to classical antiquity, as can be seen in Plato (*Cratylus*) and Aristotle (*De Interpretatione*). Studies by A. Pagliaro (1957) and Coseriu show that since Aristotle there had been a shift, beginning with Boethius in the early sixth century, from the pure idea of arbitrary signs *unmotivated* by the nature of their signifieds to an insistence on a genetic viewpoint: from the scholastics to Hobbes and Locke, authors continued to regard the linguistic sign as an arbitrary institution, but instead of concentrating on this they became more interested in explaining how such institutions were brought about. The primacy of a functional, that is, non-causal and non-genetic

---

[14] Cf. H. Aarsleff, *From Locke to Saussure: Essays on the Study of Language and Intellectual History*, Minneapolis 1982, pp. 356–71 and 382–98.

perspective, though adumbrated by Leibniz, was eventually recovered by Locke's greatest French disciple, the abbé de Condillac, in his enormously influential *Essai sur l'origine des connaissances humaines* (1746). In the early nineteenth century, the idea of non-motivation was reinforced by the distinction drawn by Hegel between sign and symbol (*Enzyklopaedie*, 1817, p. 458): in symbols, says Hegel, there is a direct relation between meaning and its vehicle; in signs, by contrast, there is no such relation. The Hegelian distinction was then appropriated by the Dane Madvig, who handed it over to the later Russian school of linguistics. Whitney, for his part, asserted the same concept by harking back to the evolution of linguistic theory within the empiricist tradition. Thus Saussure inherited the tenet of linguistic arbitrariness from both his acknowledged precursors, Whitney and Baudouin de Courtenay.

Structuralists often hailed Saussure's subscription to the arbitrariness of the sign as an epoch-making 'discovery', extolling the 'declaration of independence of the sign' as the *fons et origo* of the 'structuralist revolution' in social science. However, in view of what has just been recalled, such an attitude does not recommend itself as a token of theoretical culture on the part of the self-appointed revolutionaries. On the other hand, none of these striking anticipations, be they of the arbitrary sign or of other key Saussurean concepts, detracts from the significance of Saussure's own labours. After all, he alone wove together all these strands of thought: the unmotivated nature of the verbal sign; the difference between signified and signifier; the principle of the primacy of synchronic analysis; the need for distinguishing the structure, or 'code', of a given language (*langue*) from the boundless wealth of its infinite messages, uttered and as yet unuttered; and, last but not least, the concept of 'value', pointing as it did to the fact that language as a working system rests on a complex network of differences—differences between units as well as between lower and higher levels of units (lower units like phonemes, higher ones like morphemes). Such were the main analytical tools assembled by Saussure under his master concept: the injunction to regard language *as a system*.

Phonology represented a truly operational breakthrough because with it, for the first time, the Saussurean way of tackling language proved quite fruitful. Thanks to the Saussurean guidelines for the phonological method, it began to dawn upon linguists that—as stressed by Saussure's chief successor, the Danish Louis Hjelmslev (1899–1965)—it was possible to elicit the permanent structure of natural languages beneath their myriad of actual manifestations: a permanent structure composed of a limited number of elements and of a sum, equally limited, of their meaningful combinations.[15]

Let us cast a quick but closer glance at the basic procedure followed by modern linguistics in the pursuit of structure. The first thing to do, said the late Émile Benveniste (1902–76), one of structural linguistics' best interpreters, is to divide up a given piece of language, no matter how large, into smaller and smaller parts until one reaches elements that cannot be further decomposed. At the same time, one has to identify these ground elements by means of the *substitutions* they allow. So the method defines each element by the sum of its environments along two axes of relations: those obtaining between the element and all the others also present in the same bit of language (thus forming the *syntagmatic* axis) and those relations obtaining between the same given element and others that are absent from it, but are mutually replaceable (the *paradigmatic* axis).[16] Take for instance the word 'reason'. Its first phoneme, /r/, will be defined: (a) against the other phonemes present in the same word; and (b) against the set of possible (that is, meaningful) replacements of /r/, such as /s/ in 'season'—and so on.

Clearly, this kind of analysis has a general premise—*meaning*. For meaning is what determines the range of possible replacements. This amounts to saying that each phoneme can be defined only when envisaged as a legitimate component of a unit of a higher level, the morpheme, which in turn depends on a still higher level, that of the sentence. Note that these levels of meaning *have nothing to do with semantics* in any serious analytical sense. They are just a 'horizon' enabling us to distinguish what is functional in a given language from what is not. Thus we can think of /s/, but not /l/, as a possible replacement for /r/ in 'reason' because English contains the word 'season', but not the word 'leason'. Consequently, Benveniste is right in calling meaning, in such instances, just a tool (*'un opérateur'*).

---

[15] Cf. Hjelmslev 1953, p. 9.
[16] E. Benveniste, *Problems in General Linguistics*, Miami 1971, chapter 10.

Meaning used to spot difference as the diacritic support of
structure, difference equated with sense: this delicate balance
between form and meaning lay at the core of the structuralist
enterprise, as it came to fruition in the study of language. Now
the question is: was this subtle play of system and difference
capable of yielding similar results in other spheres of culture?

From Language to Culture

Benveniste was an immensely learned scholar who concealed
his gigantic erudition under an exceedingly self-effacing mod-
esty. A worthy pupil of Saussure's greatest disciple, Antoine
Meillet, he died poor, granted the respect of his peers but
utterly bypassed by the slightly meretricious fame enjoyed by
the structuralist gurus. (I still recall how we were awestruck into
silence as we passed by the door of his office on our way to
Lévi-Strauss's crowded seminar at the Collège de France.) The
same year illness forced him to leave his chair of *'grammaire
comparée'*, he published a masterpiece of insight, in which the
best qualities of the philological tradition went hand in hand
with the keenest structuralist acumen: the *Vocabulaire des
Institutions Indo-Européennes* (1969), a treasure-house of interpretations and aperçus disguised, as always with him, behind
a most unassuming title.

Benveniste wrote cogently and authoritatively on problems
of linguistic theory per se. But structural linguistics also helped
him solve several puzzles bequeathed by pre-Saussurean philology, in a way that was highly instructive about the explanatory
potential of structural perspectives. I shall restrict myself to a
single instance of it. One of the fascinating little mysteries in
Indo-European semantics revolved around the meaning of the
ancient word represented in classical Greek by *pontos* (sea) and
in Latin by *pons* (bridge).[17] The same word means, in Indo-
Iranian (Benveniste's speciality), Slav and Baltic, 'way'. Before
the spread of Saussurean ideas (which Benveniste imbibed
through Meillet), comparatists often thought that in such cases
of semantic divergence everything hinged upon a primeval
meaning, generally preserved in the oldest language but lost in

[17] Ibid., chapter 24.

its younger relations. Philological reasoning showed a strong bias towards explanation in terms of origins. Thus, as Indo-Iranian was the oldest, it was assumed that the original meaning in our case was 'way', turned somehow figurative in Greek and modified in Latin owing to the mesological pecularities of the Roman heartlands.

Unfortunately, however, in ancient Vedic (the old form of Sanskrit), *panthah* does not mean just 'way', but 'a painful way'—a way difficult to cross. Now a more synchronic, less origin-obsessed, *structural* perspective shows that the Greek and Latin forms can be construed as variations on this theme. As it is easy to see in 'Hellespontos', *pontos* originally meant sea in the sense of a dangerous crossing between two shores. Similarly, 'bridge' (Latin *pons*) connotes an obstacle to cross. Naturally, Greek sailors and Roman bridge-builders did play a part in the social background of such semantic variations. But the point is that a structural approach helped solve the puzzle by getting rid of the fetishism of origins that plagued much of traditional philological research.

Lest one think such a result too meagre, it should be said that traditional philology bristles with problems of this kind. Moreover, true philology never proceeds by sweeping discoveries, as though it were a sensationalist archaeology, but by the patient identification and elucidation of often minute, yet quite revealing details from dead alien cultures or our own remote past. Benveniste's masterly renewal of philological exegesis with the aid of structuralist strategies presents structuralism in its wisest, least whimsical or arbitrary guise.

This positive impression is further reinforced when one turns to the work of a man justly considered to be one of the main forerunners (acknowledged by Lévi-Strauss himself) of the structural analysis of myth: Georges Dumézil (b. 1898), the Indo-European scholar. Instead of interpreting the religion of the several Indo-European areas in terms of isolated deities or bits of creeds, as in the comparative religion studies of Mircea Eliade, Dumézil opted for a different, pathbreaking approach. He did not compare each Indian god to its Greek or Roman counterpart. Rather, he compared each Indo-European pantheon with another, concentrating on sets of relations instead of working on separate elements. Next, underneath the homologies between these kindred polytheistic systems, he identified a set of functions—like sovereignty, war and fertility, embodied in ancient Roman religion by the Jupiter/Mars/Quirinus triad—amounting to a common pattern of belief. He then correlated this same sacred division of labour with the Indo-European ideology of social order: priests, warriors and peasants.

This last move brings to mind the later study of feudal representations undertaken by the medievalist Georges Duby (b. 1919)—a historian with avowed structuralist leanings. Indeed, Duby opens his book *Les Trois Ordres ou l'Imaginaire du Féodalisme* (1978) with an explicit reference to Dumézil's work as an intellectual pedigree. However, he immediately stresses that in the feudal case the doctrine of the three functions performed by the three social orders was an ideology, a 'polemical' belief aimed at making an ideal come true by exercising power over a given type of society: as his research shows, it was when the 'feudal revolution' was still in the making, in the early eleventh century, that the idea of three orders was developed.[18] Duby's ability to combine a focus on meaning and an awareness of the economic and social base of historical change established an undogmatic structural approach as a sharp instrument for coming to grips with ideology.

If things could be left at that, structuralism would be best described as a hygiene of explanation—a clever way of unravelling philological and historical problems by rephrasing questions long entangled in a mire of historist or historicist misconceptions. Besides greatly advancing the anatomy of natural languages, structuralism held a promise of sharpening and enhancing historical knowledge, at least in the history of culture and ideology.

---

[18] G. Duby, *Les Trois Ordres ou l'Imaginaire du Féodalisme*, Paris 1978, p. 17 and especially pp. 183–205.

Mukařovsky (1891–1975), blended a new awareness of the linguistic sign with a new sense of the social context of literature.

Jakobson left Russia for Prague in 1920, and his meeting with Vilém Mathesius was decisive for the foundation, in 1926, of the Prague Linguistic Circle—the very cradle, as we know, of the structuralist movement in modern linguistics. The most gifted and creative of Trubetzkoy's disciples, he was twice crucial to the development of structuralism: first, in the twenties, he inspired the launching of the Prague Circle (structuralism in linguistics); then, in the forties, in America, he was the determining influence on Lévi-Strauss (structuralism in social science). Yet his place in the history of modern criticism is not merely a consequence of his stature as a linguist. Long before the war, Jakobson was a linguist and a literary theorist in his own right. Before he became the second great phonologist after Trubetzkoy, he had been the main formalist critic associated with Victor Shklovsky (b. 1893). Actually, Russian formalism had two bases: the Moscow Linguistic Circle, started in 1915 by Jakobson, and the Society for the Study of Poetic Language (*Opoyaz*), founded in 1916 in Petrograd and led by Shklovsky. Jakobson thus found himself at the roots of revolutionary trends in both linguistics and literature.

Before the war, Jakobson as a critic, for all his scientific training, was not strictly speaking a structuralist but a *formalist*. What is the difference? We shall try to show that it meant a great deal, at least in the foundation (if not the development) of structuralist thought in the humanities. With the benefit of hindsight, one is bound to acknowledge that formalist and structuralist criticism have much in common, as can be seen from the fact that some central fetishes of the latter sound, as we shall see later, like a belated reprise of formalist beliefs. But there are also important ways in which structuralism departed from formalism. If we take formalism to mean neglect of content in art and symbolism in general, then the plain historical truth is that structuralism reacted against it almost from the outset. We will discuss a classic instance of this reaction, Lévi-Strauss's 1960 critique of Propp, in the next chapter. But a quarter of a century earlier the founder of structuralist aesthetics, Jan Mukařovsky (1891–1975), was already thinking in terms of a *supersession* of formalism. Indeed he was apparently the first to employ (in 1934) the term 'structuralism' in the humanities.

Clearly there seems to be some advantage in spelling out the discrepancy between Russian formalism and Czech structuralism. Let us start by recalling one or two essentials about the former.

No sooner had Jakobson settled in Prague than he published the second edition of his influential pamphlet *The Newest Russian Poetry* (1919). His first major statement as a critic,[1] it was a spirited defence of avant-garde poetry, and more specifically of the verse of Velemir Khlebnikov (1885–1922). Khlebnikov was, along with the now better-known Mayakovsky, the main voice of Slav futurism. The futurists formed a sect striving to revolutionize literature not only in content but especially in technique, even to the point of a complete break with sense (as in Khlebnikov's own usage of 'zaum' or 'transrational' language, a radical application of Marinetti's motto, 'words at liberty').

Launched by Marinetti (1876–1944) in Paris (and in French) in 1909, futurism seethed with a Nietzschean revolt against 'decadent' culture. Russian futurism, dating from as early as 1910, ignored the Marinettian celebration of war and modern machinery and was far more *primitivist* than its Western counterpart. Above all, it challenged symbolism. The symbolist school had given Russia splendid poetry, as shown in the work of Alexander Blok (1880–1921); but its sophisticated verbal artistry, the hieratic demeanour of its highly allusive poetics, ever plunged in a quest for transcendence, became the favourite target of futurist 'barbarism'. Unlike more sober modernists (for instance the 'acmeist' movement of Osip Mandelstam and Anna Akhmatova), the futurists were not content to get rid of the symbolist vision; they liked to pose as a 'Scythian' horde blatantly defying literary decorum.[2]

Shklovsky masterminded 'the formal method' (as formalism called itself) as a revolution in literary theory in league with the futurist avant-garde. His nimble manifesto-essay of 1917, 'Art as a Device', struck a sharp blow at symbolist pieties. It was written in open polemic with the ideas of Alexander Potebnya

[1] Most of Jakobson's essay is translated in E. J. Brown, ed., *Major Soviet Writers*, Oxford 1973, pp. 58–82.

[2] See the excellent analysis of G. M. Hyde in Malcolm Bradbury and James McFarlane, eds., *Modernism 1890–1930*, Harmondsworth 1976, pp. 259ff.; on Jakobson and Khlebnikov, pp. 268–71.

(1835–91), a chief source of symbolist poetics. To Potebnya, art was 'thinking in images' with a view to grasping the Unknown. Against this, Shklovsky asserted art's right to offer things not as they are known but as sensuously *perceived*. Instead of the Unknown, he extolled the 'sensation of life' through the life of sensation, *regardless of content*. In order to recover the sensation of life, art had to *defamiliarize*, to make objects unfamiliar by making forms difficult, shattering the layer of custom on our humdrum perceptions; and defamiliarization, in turn, had to be achieved through the constant use of unmotivated formal *devices* (hence the title of his essay) invariably based on *deviation* from established norms of language and style.[3]

None of Shklovsky's key concepts—device (*priem*), deviation, defamiliarization (*ostraneniye*) and 'literariness' (*literaturnost*) had anything in common with the Saussurean categories of structural linguistics (if anything, they were close to Brecht's 'alienation effect', although Brecht would of course never have dreamt of upholding such an art-for-art's sake notion as 'literariness'). Jakobson's *Newest Russian Poetry* derived from Shklovsky's views—indeed, it was a vindication of Khlebnikov with the help of Shklovskyan concepts. Jakobson justified the new, subversive poetry of the futurists, most vigorously embodied in Khlebnikov's playful verse, by referring to the primacy of artifice (device), the need for deviation and the positive effects of defamiliarization. On top of this, he criticized Marinetti—a popular pastime among Russian futurists, who were rather irked by the Italian's proto-fascism (Marinetti's visit to Russia, like his trip to Brazil in the next decade, turned out to be a fiasco). The founder of futurism held to a 'reportage theory' of literary change, ascribing the rise of new poetic forms to alterations in the social patterns of experience. For Jakobson, on the contrary, poetry changed *from within*, by dint of a strictly literary-linguistic dynamic.

As a critic, then, the young Jakobson was a staunch formalist. Would the picture change in the 1920s, when phonology was in the making, and he committed himself fully as a linguist to structuralism, becoming the vital link between Trubetzkoy (then in Vienna) and the Prague Circle? Not much. Of course, Jakobson

[3] Shklovsky, 'Art as technique', in L. T. Lemon and M. J. Rice, *Russian Formalist Criticism: Four Essays*, Lincoln, Nebraska 1965, p. 12.

would prove adept at using the new linguistic perspective in the study of literature, as witnessed in the chief non-linguistic work from his Prague years (1920–39), a pathbreaking analysis of Czech verse. In the main, however, during these two decades Jakobson the critic stuck to his youthful formalist concerns.

One of them was a typically formalist way of dealing with the history of style. While still in Russia, Jakobson had described artistic styles by means of figures of language (for example, analysing cubo-futurist painting in terms of the principle of metonymy). Once in Prague he went on classifying styles in literature, art and cinema in this fashion. Romanticism and symbolism were said to be essentially metaphorical styles; realism, by contrast, was metonymical (a cherished example given by Jakobson referred to Tolstoy's masterly focus on Anna Karenina's hand in the scene of her suicide). Again, in modern art, while surrealism was deemed metaphorical, cubism tended to metonymy.

The use of polar concepts in general art history had been an established practice since the triumph of Henrich Wölfflin's (1864–1945) *Formgeschichte*. Wölfflin, a Swiss pioneer of modern art history, tried to account for the whole development of Western visual arts in terms of a cyclical shift from classical to baroque. Each of these styles, seen as recurrent phases, was cogently defined by one side of a set of five basic, highly formal polarities: linear versus painterly, closed versus open form, and so on. (What was most cogent was the actual comparison between the *historical* classic and baroque styles, rather than the implausible idea of taking them as a yardstick by which to 'read' art history as a series of cycles.[4]) Early in this century some German scholars began to extend Wölfflin's formal polarities to the history of literary styles. A minor Russian formalist much in their debt, Victor Zhirmunsky, saw classicism as an art of metonymy and romanticism as a style of metaphor. In Jakobson's hands, as we saw, the split fell rather within the post-classical age: realism took the place of classicism as the main metonymic contrast to romantic or neo-romantic metaphorism. But the point is that, once again, all was done in the name of a concern with form, regardless of content.

[4] For a masterly recent discussion of Wölfflin, see M. Podro, *The Critical Historians of Art*, New Haven 1982, chapters 6 and 7.

In 1941, when, as an exile in Scandinavia, he undertook a linguistic study of child speech and aphasia, Jakobson 'translated' the metaphor/metonymy dichotomy into the conceptual idiom of Saussure. He distinguished between two kinds of speech disorder. In 'similarity disorder' the aphasic resorts to metonymy; in 'contiguity disorder', to metaphor. Patients suffering from the similarity disorder are often unable to make the right linguistic connections, such as naming correctly or using proper synonyms. Nevertheless, the same patients prove quite adept at employing metonymy: they would speak for instance of smoke for fire or of table for lamp. In 'contiguity' troubles, just the opposite occurs.

Metaphor and metonymy are in turn equated with Saussure's two axes of language. Metaphor operates by *selection*; hence it belongs to the *paradigmatic* axis, the stock whence all possible, that is meaningful, linguistic signs are chosen in order for actual messages to be uttered in any natural language. Metonymy, on the other hand, substitutes contiguous terms for one another, and therefore works on the *syntagmatic* axis, where everything hinges on the *combination* of linguistic units (at all levels) in the chain of a given verbal message.[5]

This 'axial' distinction was to prove terribly important for Jakobson's later literary theory, which we shall consider presently. But for the moment, let us just stress the impeccable formalist pedigree of these ideas. One can see that in his youth Jakobson's criticism and literary theory were in thrall to two formalisms: the formal tradition in art history and, of course, the Russian formalism of Shklovsky. The main difference seems to be that while Russian formalism was in love with radical avant-garde literature, and hence besotted with deviation, *Formgeschichte* reflected the aesthetic ideals of classical, pre-romantic art, and consequently gave pride of place to the observance, not the violation, of stylistic norms. But the Russian formalists themselves were very much aware that today's deviations are bound to become tomorrow's norms.

[5] R. Jakobson and M. Halle, *The Fundamentals of Language*, The Hague 1956, pp. 69–96.

Czech Structuralism: Beyond Formalism

All in all, then, Jakobson's criticism stood closer to formalism than to the spirit of structural linguistics. Significantly, the field of research most receptive to Saussurean ideas in his Prague years was not his own literary criticism but aesthetics—an area in which Czech scholars had made several worthy contributions. Aesthetics had a long and distinguished presence in Prague, where since the mid-nineteenth century the discipline had been taught and developed by followers of J. F. Herbart (1776–1841), the 'fourth evangelist' of post-Kantianism. Unlike Fichte, Schelling and Hegel, Herbart had no truck with the metaphysics of the subject. Instead, he gave a stark *objectivist* account of knowledge and experience. In aesthetics, he was himself a kind of proto-structuralist, stressing that beauty was not an intrinsic quality of anything in particular but of *relations* between images.[6]

One generation before Mukařovsky took over the traditionally Herbartian chair at the Charles university of Prague (1938), Herbart's legacy underwent a 'revisionist' spell. The rigid objectivism of the Herbartians, which had eventuated into a series of rather pedantic disquisitions on things like the golden section, the theory of colour dissonance or the discovery of ratios in poetical imagery, yielded to a more flexible 'psycho-formal' approach:[7] phenomenology was in the offing, with a stress on the work of art (or the literary text) as an *intentional* object, namely, an object that exists as such only to the extent that it is addressed by our consciousness. Nevertheless, because of its Herbartian roots, Czech aesthetics could become more richly psychological without falling into the trap of subjectivism or, for that matter, into the metaphysical speculations indulged in by Western neo-idealism. So, instead of a Croce or a Collingwood, there came Mukařovsky and his structuralist aesthetics.

Mukařovsky's achievement was precisely to combine the

[6] On Herbart's theory of 'aesthetic relations', see K. Gilbert and H. A. Kuhn, *A History of Aesthetics*, New York 1972, pp. 513–16; and M. Podro, *The Manifold in Perception: Theories of Art from Kant to Hildebrand*, Oxford 1972, pp. 72–79.

[7] On this evolution, see Oleg Sus, 'On the Genetic Preconditions of Czech Structuralism, Semiology and Semantics', *Poetics*, 4, 1972, pp. 28–55; and 'Le Formalisme et le Pre-structuralisme Tcheques', *Change*, 10, 1972, pp. 190–98.

phenomenological accent on the 'intentional' status of the aesthetic object with two things: first, the old Herbartian focus on form as relation; second, and still more important, the *semiological* perspective opened up by Saussure. Mukařovsky wanted to insert the 'cultural sciences', always on the brink of collapsing into idealistic chimeras, into an empirically-based theory of the sign—and he found in aesthetics the perfect field for carrying out this cognitive re-adjustment. He insisted that the aesthetic object (the artwork as sign) should be regarded as the 'signified' of its material 'signifier' (the artwork as thing). At the same time, his semiotic approach was emphatically *sociological*: he enjoined us to examine the *institutional* dimensions of aesthetic phenomena as well as to scrutinize the relations between aesthetic norms and social structure, since neither the bindingness nor the variability of the former can be explained and justified solely from the viewpoint of either the species or the individual—they require an understanding of *society* and its history (he gave more weight to human universals when it came to the analysis of aesthetic value).[8]

Mukařovsky is very illuminating on the circulation of norms: the coming and going of aesthetic rules, the variations in their enactment and enforcement. Knowing that aesthetic norms are generally less stable than linguistic or legal ones, he strove to keep theory alive to their changeability, its causes and its effects. Now this sociological perceptiveness was bound to induce him to seriously qualify the doctrine of Russian formalism.[9] A man of modernist tastes himself, Mukařovsky had no quarrel with Shklovsky on the right or duty of living art to be 'difficult'. However, he took issue with the Shklovskyan mystique of deviation and distortion. For deviation to be meaningful, he warned, it has to act against a background of regularity. Therefore one should never put all one's eggs in one aesthetic basket—a formalist and avant-garde dogma demolished neatly by Mukařovsky's robust common sense. No wonder he did not subscribe to the cult of 'literariness' either:[10] artistic value, in

[8] See his 1934 essay, 'Art as a Semiotic Fact', in J. Mukařovsky, *Aesthetic Function, Norm and Value as Social Facts*, translated by M. Suino, Ann Arbor 1970.

[9] For his careful discussion of formalism, see R. C. Holub, *Reception Theory—A Critical Introduction*, London 1984, pp. 30–35.

[10] As noted by V. Ehrlich, *Russian Formalism: History–Doctrine*, The Hague 1955.

his view, was ultimately a matter of art's displaying the utmost 'transparency' to other social values—but art was not a bit less autonomous for it.

There is today a near consensus to the effect that Mukařovský 'marks a decisive shift towards a sociological explanation of the literary system'.[11] He saw literature as a set of *social* signs, both in their use and their content. And since the gist of his departure from the fetishism of form was to recover a sense of the changing social contexts of literary functions and literary meaning, I propose to call it *socio-semiotics*. Now Mukařovský's mature supersession (in Victor Ehrlich's apt phrase) of formalism had no discernible influence on structuralist literary theory of the 1960s: yet it proves that structuralism was not bound to repeat the shortcomings of formalist thinking. Indeed, many paths lead to or come from the Rome of Saussure. This only makes it more unfortunate that, in its actual methods of literary analysis, structuralist criticism since the war has forgotten the fine balance between form and reality, style and culture, art and history that interwar structuralist aesthetics so sensibly drew. The balance was only to be kept, up to a point, under Juri Lotman and his school of Soviet semiotics, a partial descendant from Czech structuralism.[12] As for the later criticism of Jakobson and that of Roland Barthes, the lesson of Mukařovský seems to have been lost on them.

The Unrepentant Formalist

Jakobson's main (and most influential) contribution to struc-

[11] For this judgement, see R. Selden, *Criticism and Objectivity*, London 1984, 61–62.

[12] Lotman's main work, *Struktura chudozestvennogo teksta*, quickly translated into German and Italian (*La Struttura del Testo Poetico*, Milan 1972), has now also an English version. The ninth chapter discusses 'The relativity of the opposition between text and extratextual structures'. Lotman and his school are not unrelated to Russian formalism but seem closer to critics such as Juri Tynyanov and Mikhail Bakhtin—who never lost sight of culture and motivation in their focus on form—than to 'hard-line' formalists such as Shklovsky and Jakobson. For discrepancies between the latter two and Lotman (and his point of agreement with Mukařovský), see D. W. Fokkema and E. Kunne-Ibsch, *Theories of Literature in the Twentieth Century: Structuralism, Marxism, Aesthetics of Reception, Semiotics*, London 1977, pp. 38–49.

turalist critical theory during all his years in America stems directly from his use of the paradigmatic/syntagmatic distinction. It is no less than a conceptualization of the *poetic function of language*. Jakobson begins by distinguishing six components in any speech event: sender, receiver, message, code, contact and context. Linguistic communication and ultimately the core of the speech event itself—the verbal message—may stress any one of these elements. Consequently there are also six functions of language: expressive (stress on the sender), vocative (on the receiver), meta-lingual (stress on the code), phatic (on the contact between sender and receiver), referential (on the context common to both) and, last but not least, poetic (stress on the message itself).

Jackobson states that 'focus on the message for its own sake is the *poetic* function of language'.[13] Now Jakobson claims that such a dominant concern with the message implies a peculiar attitude towards the two axes of language according to dear old Saussure, the 'two basic modes of arrangement used in verbal behaviour'. For when attention concentrates on the message in itself, rather than on its referent (or the other components of the speech event), it is as though *equivalence*—the principle that governs *selection*, the basic mode of arrangement along the paradigmatic axis—is somehow transferred into the other axis: the syntagmatic one, where the law is not equivalence, but rules of *combination* based on contiguity. Thus 'the poetic function projects the principle of equivalence from the axis of selection into the axis of combination'.[14] This, argues Jakobson, provides an 'empirical linguistic criterion' for detecting the poetic functioning of any message. Not only words but even syllables and stresses, pauses and boundaries, become equivalent in the verbal sequence, be it verse or not. Thus Caesar's famous '*veni, vidi, vici*' gets an extra impact because the three past tenses are equalized in size (two syllables each) and shape (the alliteration effect of the three *v*'s). On the other hand, under the sway of the poetic function, not just the phonological sequence but 'any sequence of semantic units strives to build an equation'.[15] Equivalence reigns supreme in both axes: that of selection (its

[13] R. Jakobson, 'Linguistics and Poetics', in T. A. Sebeok, ed., *Style in Language*, Cambridge 1960, p. 356.
[14] Ibid., p. 358.
[15] Ibid., p. 370.

natural home) and that of succession. Or to put it differently: selection and succession overlap.

In 'Linguistics and Poetics' (1958), the epoch-making paper (originally a closing communication to a symposium on style in language summoned by Indiana University) from which we have been quoting, the 'poetic function' is ascribed indifferently to language or to 'verbal art'—to poetry as an artistic technique. At one point he warned that 'any attempt to reduce the sphere of poetic function to poetry *or to confine poetry to poetic function* would be a delusive oversimplification'.[16] Yet in the same breath he also says that while the poetic function is not the only one in verbal art, it is 'its dominant, determining function'.[17] Moreover the whole drift of 'Linguistics and Poetics' underscores the tendency to conflate *a* function of *language* with *the* essence of *poetry*, if not literature at large ('verbal art')—a tendency no doubt reinforced by the fact that Jakobson, true to his erstwhile formalist faith, hastens to add (again in the same paragraph) that the dominance of the poetic function of language in verbal art 'deepens the fundamental dichotomy of signs and objects'.

We are plainly invited to believe: (a) that the gist of poetry, or even of literature, is a play with language, and (b) that in such play literature is as little referential as possible. 'Objects', that is to say, contents, do not matter—just as in Shklovsky. Actually, it is not untrue to say that the dominance of a non-referential self-absorption in literary messages boils down to a linguistic reprise of the Shklovskyan theme of 'literariness'—an aesthetic quintessence thoroughly severed from all external 'motivations'. Life, thought, culture and society—what a nuisance to genuine literature. . . . As Mallarmé once told Degas, literature is made up of words, not ideas. Formalist structuralism endorsed this with a vengeance: for it looked at the verbal stuff of literature as though its meaning lay in a narcissistic self-reflection. The first commandment of criticism became: never treat literature as if it were about anything except language.

Need I recall that such a stance did *not* automatically follow from the structuralist outlook *an sich*? The sheer existence of a

---

[16] Ibid., p. 356. Emphasis added.
[17] Ibid., p. 356.

structuralist semiotics of literature should convince us that this was in fact so. Mukařovsky in the thirties and forties never tired of stressing that aesthetic value (and consequently literary value) is grounded in a complex but wide-ranging transparency of the work to the world; more recently, Lotman went as far as emphatically to assert the *iconic* character of literary signs, laden with a semantic charge normally unknown to practical, pragmatic speech. Why did Jakobson's own structuralism take the opposite path? Clearly, his strong grounding in formalism cast a long shadow on his whole career as a critic.

Equally important, Jakobson's main methodological contribution to structuralist criticism, outlined in the closing pages of 'Linguistics and Poetics', was in full agreement with this highly debatable formalist option. For it hinges on the notion that literary texts hide a 'grammar of poetry' ultimately reducible to 'the poetry of grammar', a gorgeous display of 'grammatical tropes and figures' constituting patterns that embody in sundry forms the inexhaustible resources of the 'poetic function of language'. Jakobson himself showed great mastery in pursuing this theme, memorably analyzing a rich array of grammatical tropes in Antony's funeral oration in *Julius Caesar*, in Baudelaire's 'Les Chats' (in a well-known four-handed interpretation written with Lévi-Strauss) and even in sonnets by Shakespeare.

Now whenever such analyses are conducted by such a keen observer of verbal textures as Jakobson, the results are bound to be rewarding, if only to a certain extent. Moreover, close reading governed by an alertness to revealing linguistic details has always been a very fruitful approach to the interpetation of poetry in particular and literature in general, as witnessed by the tradition of stylistic criticism (best represented by great Romanists from Erich Auerbach and Leo Spitzer to Hugo Friedrich). To deny *a priori* the new tools of structural linguistics the power to widen (and in several cases, deepen) this approach to verbal art would be very foolish indeed.

Nevertheless, the emphasis on the 'poetry of grammar' as a method has evinced an inbuilt disadvantage. It can of course locate grammatical aspects which are really effective from the literary viewpoint, like the ironical change of conjunctions at the beginning of the Brutus sentences in Antony's speech ('*For* Brutus is an honourable man; . . . *And* Brutus . . .' and so on). But the method offers no warrant as to the literary relevance, let alone significance, of what it reveals.

As Michael Riffaterre saw,[18] the interpretative model defined by Jakobson's principle assumes that any play with grammatical categories in a poem constitutes a poetic effect—which is patently not the case. A poem can indeed: (a) contain linguistic structures with no function on its effect as a work of art; and (b) contain other structures that do on the contrary have such a function but which structural linguistics may have no power to identify, not because there is anything basically wrong with structural linguistics but simply because it was not devised to cope with *every* social phenomenon, not even in spheres where language is central.

From the fact that literature is made of language it does not follow that literary meaning (let alone value) is something reducible to language. My car is made of metal, glass and rubber; but it would never cross my mind to say that it is in any sense 'about' rubber, glass or metal; it is 'about' transportation. Matthew Arnold might have been linguistically (though not philologically) illiterate—but he was surely closer to the point when he said that literature was a criticism of life. It is a matter of not mistaking the function of a product, or goal of an activity, for what one needs in order to produce the former or perform the latter.

Nothing could be more true, nor more trivial. But the trouble is that within the conventional wisdom of structuralist criticism these humble truths were forgotten if not challenged—and in both the oblivion and the challenge the holy name of Jakobson was often invoked, as the living proof that the science of language itself blessed and urged a reduction of criticism to a linguistic analysis of literary texts. This was structuralist scientism at its worst—resorting to a superstitutious name-dropping to cover a fallacious view of the nature of literature. Jakobson's outstanding achievement as a linguist is not at issue; but as a literary theorist, he was not equal to himself as a linguist. His genuine authority in one field was used to legitimize shaky tenets in another. By the mid-sixties, a true believer like Tzvetan Todorov was dutifully decreeing that 'it is obvious that all (*sic*) knowledge of literature will follow a path parallel to that of the knowledge of language: moreover the two paths will

---

[18] Riffaterre in J. Ehrmann, ed., *Structuralism*, New York 1970.

tend to merge (*sic*)'.[19] Amen.

The contrast between Mukařovskyan socio-semiotics and Jakobson's 'linguistic' formalism as divergent paths for structuralist literary theory was indeed a strategic one—but of course it was far from exhausting the variety of routes open to interwar Slav criticism. On the one hand, the Russian formalists themselves often dithered in their position regarding the relationship between text and social context. Whilst a critic like Eichenbaum represented formalism at its most impervious as a structural approach to socially motivated content, and to the social conditioning of form and technique, other theorists, most notably Tynyanov, were prepared to acknowledge the interaction between the literary system and its social and cultural environment.[20]

Tynyanov managed to avoid Shklovsky's too unilateral stress on the teleology of 'device', substituting for it a more flexible account of literariness in terms of 'dominant' and 'secondary' elements.[21] In his much praised programme-article, 'Problems in the Study of Literature and Language',[22] written with Jakobson, he recognised the need for correlating the 'literary series' with other historical series. Although, it might be argued, this amounts to juxtaposition rather than to any developed sense— as in Mukařovsky—of the *interpenetration* of literary text and social context, doubtless it marks real progress as compared to what Aguiar e Silva, in what is to date the most comprehensive and level-headed critical survey of literary theory,[23] found in Jakobson's analyses of poetic texts: a persistent unwillingness to correlate the poem with—in Jakobson's own phrasing—'the overall system of social values'.[24]

[19] Todorov in R. Macksey and E. Donato, eds., *The Structuralist Controversy: The Languages of Criticism and the Sciences of Man*, Baltimore 1970, p. 126.

[20] Compare B. Eichenbaum, *Il giovane Tolstoy. La Teoria del Metodo Formale*, Bari 1968, with Yuri Tynyanov 1973.

[21] On this point, see Fredric Jameson, *The Prison-House of Language: A Critical Account of Structuralism and Russian Formalism*, Princeton 1972, pp. 92–94.

[22] The programme is translated in L. Matejka and K. Pomorska, eds., *Readings in Russian Poetics: Formalist and Structuralist Views*, Cambridge 1971, pp. 79–81.

[23] V. M. Aguiar e Silva, *Teoria de Literatura*, fifth edition, Coimbra 1983, p. 7. This impeccably scholarly treatise is consistently and cogently critical of formalist shortcomings; see especially pp. 51, 277, 392.

[24] R. Jakobson, 'Signum and Signatum', in L. Matejka and I. R. Titunik, eds., *Semiotics in Art,* Cambridge 1976, p. 181.

Writing under the pseudonym of 'Medvedev', Mikhail Bakhtin published in 1928 a critique of formalism under the title *The Formal Method in Literary Scholarship*. As his recent intellectual biographers Katerina Clark and Michael Holquist show, Bakhtin put a shrewd finger on the shortcomings of the Shklovsky-to-Jakobson line. He saw that the status of literary language, equated by the formalists with the distortion of practical speech, was too parasitic and vastly insufficient, as though one could reduce the complexity of literary quality to a mere difference from something else; and he denounced the psychologism of the 'deautomatization' concept, whereby the formalists, for all their overpublicized concern with the text, stuck to a definition of literature built crudely on psychological assumptions that hinged upon a mystifying theory of perception.[25]

To focus even briefly on Bakhtin's career would certainly have been as rewarding as our sketch of the contrast between Jakobson and Mukařovsky. But the latter had the advantage of presenting us with useful methodological statements, and in any case their instructive divergence (all the more instructive for being largely tacit) may be taken as truly exemplary of what French structuralism was later to discard so conspicuously: a sociological approach to sign and structure.[26]

[25] Cf. K. Clark and M. Holquist, *Mikhail Bakhtin*, Cambridge 1984, pp. 190–96.

[26] One should welcome, in this connection, Todorov's conversion from his erstwhile 'linguisticism' to Bakhtinian dialogism. See Tzvetan Todorov, *Mikhail Bakhtine, le Principe Dialogique, suivi de Ecrits du cercle de Bakhtine*, Paris 1981. On the other hand, the present work was already at proof-reading stage when I came across the first book-length study of Czech structuralism in English, František Galan's *Historic Structures: The Prague School Project, 1928–1946* (London: Croom Helm, 1985). Focusing on the structuralist conceptualization of literary history, Galan devotes a whole careful chapter to Mukařovsky's views on the role of the individual in literary development. But he tends to see Mukařovsky *and* Jakobson in the 1930s as partners in the supersession of formalism. Here I would demur. Even Jakobson's by then qualified formalism ('What is Poetry?', 1933) never yields a truly socio-semiotic approach to literature—something quite alien, of course, to his own 'poetry of grammar' later period.

3

Claude Lévi-Strauss:
The Birth of Structuralism
in Social Science

*Les sciences de l'homme seront
structuralistes ou bien elles ne seront
pas.*

Claude Lévi-Strauss

Claude Lévi-Strauss, the founder of sociological structuralism,
was born in Brussels into a family of French painters. Though
his grandfather was the rabbi of Versailles, Lévi-Strauss's home
environment was that of the assimilated Jewish intelligentsia; as
in the case of the more grand bourgeois origins of Raymond
Aron (1905–83), there was no trace of commitment to the
ancestral faith or indeed to Jewish culture as such. After studying at elegant lycées like Janson de Sailly, Lévi-Strauss read law
and had passed an *agrégation de philosophie* when an academic
mentor, the Durkheimian Célestin Bouglé, included him in the
team of budding French professors who helped to launch the
University of São Paulo around 1935. Shortly before, reading a
modern classic of anthropology, *Primitive Society* (1920) by
Robert Lowie (1883–1957), he fell in love with the science of
man. Lévi-Strauss spent five years in Brazil. In 1938, having
resigned his rather dull teaching job at the University,
he undertook field work (though less thorough than the
Malinowskian kind adopted by English anthropology) notably
among the Nambikwaras, Bororos and Caduveos, in Mato
Grosso. Back in France, he served for a while on the Maginot
Line. After the fall of France, Lowie and Alfred Métraux
helped him to avoid the fate of Jews under Nazi rule by
escaping to America, where he spent most of the war. In New
York, lecturing at the New School for Social Research, he
contacted Roman Jakobson and other leading structural

linguists. After serving as a cultural attaché at the French embassy in Washington during the Liberation, he returned to Paris, became curator at the Musée de l'Homme in the same year as he published *The Elementary Structures of Kinship* (1949), entered the École des Hautes Etudes (but not the Sorbonne) and was eventually appointed professor of social anthropology at the Collège de France (1959). In 1973, his election to the Academy came as a token of the full legitimation of structuralism in Parisian high culture.

The Odd Rationalist

In his outstanding intellectual autobiography *Tristes Tropiques* (1955), the book that made him famous well before the structuralist vogue, Lévi-Strauss avows that he turned to anthropology out of disappointment with modern philosophy, especially in its phenomenologico-existentialist form. Existentialism seemed to him too 'indulgent toward the illusions of subjectivity'. He warned against the danger of promoting 'private preoccupations to the rank of philosophical problems', a tendency that might 'end in a kind of shop-girl's philosophy'. Then, defining the true task of the philosopher, he went on: '. . . That mission (he holds it only until science is strong enough to take over from philosophy) is to understand being in relation to itself, and not in relation to oneself.' A quarter of a century later he still contrasted his own interest in science and his open-mindedness as regards scientific progress with the 'defiant and hostile' attitude of Sartre, who 'strove all his life to make philosophy into a domain hermetically closed to science'.[1]

Two things are worth stressing here. The first is that Lévi-Strauss was actually turning the tables against Sartre, who was himself wont to criticize other cultural trends as mere navelgazing, a good example being his description of surrealism as a revolt of *fils-à-papa*, a self-centred dramatization lacking objectivity and moral depth. Thus Lévi-Strauss's strictures against existentialism as a subjectivist self-indulgence are

[1] For the quote from *Tristes Tropiques*, London 1976, p. 71. For the second quote (on Sartre and science), see Lévi-Strauss's interview with *Le Nouvel Observateur*, 28 June 1980 (my translation).

ironical poetical justice—and none the less accurate for it.

Secondly, we may notice the curious position of Lévi-Strauss toward science. There is nothing disingenuous in his determination to break with the humanist phobias of modern European philosophy. Many a scholar could only feel embarassment at Bergson's ridiculous attempt to 'refute' Einstein's theories, or at the phenomenologists' and Wittgensteinians' careful avoidance of empirical psychology, or again at Heidegger's pompous dictum that 'science thinks not'. Yet, as Lévi-Strauss is the first to point out, it still falls to *philosophy* to interpret reality in an objective way, until science steps in. Are we to understand that this is particularly the case in anthropology? Clearly there are grounds for thinking so, especially in view of the fact that Lévi-Strauss himself, trained as a philosopher, ascribed his own conversion to the science of man to a distaste for 'metaphysics' rather than philosophy per se; and then erected an intriguing anthropological system fraught with moments of full-fledged philosophizing.

Indeed, to the pure historian of ideas—the anatomist of thought who tries to follow the life of concepts and theories without passing judgement on their truth-value—Lévi-Strauss is an odd character. On the one hand, he is the true anti-Bergsonian among modern French theorists—the first of prime importance to assert the virtues of intellect and discontinuity in the face of the mystique of flux and intuition, that is, of all the Bergsonian pieties of the humanist creed. Yet, on the other hand, his whole *scientific* work (and not only the 'literary' *Tristes Tropiques*) bespeaks a long and intimate affinity with music and symbolism and more generally with all the realm of the 'romantic image' (to use Frank Kermode's apt term).[2] In other words: the same man who set out to challenge the sway of subjectivism and irrationalism in thought was never much of a positivist; instead, he was steeped, by vocation as well as upbringing, in the tradition of the 'aesthetic revolt', both 'decadent' and modern. An author fed on Baudelaire and Wagner, he would never be capable of treating them as Sartre saw Baudelaire and Flaubert: as alien spirits, quintessential paroxysms of bourgeois alienation.

[2] The symbolist connection has been emphasised by J. Boon, *From Symbolism to Structuralism: Lévi-Strauss in a Literary Tradition*, New York 1972.

Standing Durkheim on his Head

Let us now broach his momentous grafting of structuralism onto social science. We might well begin by regarding his entire anthropological outlook in terms of standing Emile Durkheim (1858–1917) on his head. Besides being the founder of the so-called French sociological school, Durkheim became the main theoretical source of British anthropology, via both Malinowski and Radcliffe-Brown. Durkheim's method always moved *from the mental to the social*: from belief to social structure, as is most conspicuous in his enduring classic (and scientific testament), *The Elementary Forms of Religious Life* (1912). Categories were traced back to their social underpinnings; mind mirrored society. With Lévi-Strauss it is the other way round. In structuralism, we move *from the social to the mental*; from social relations or cultural constructs, like kinship systems or myths, to intellectual structures. No sociologist has ever displayed a keener interest in mind (*l'esprit*, a word that in French has long lost the spiritualist overtones still haunting 'spirit' and *Geist*).

Saussurean linguistics, it will be recalled, declared the independence of the sign. Likewise, Lévi-Straussian anthropology has insisted from the outset that its structures do not mirror social reality: 'A kinship system does not consist in the objective ties of descent or consanguinity between individuals. It exists only in human consciousness; it is an arbitrary system of representations, not the spontaneous development of a real situation'.[3] And since structure is not a copy of social reality, it is not only Durkheim who needs correction—Marxism, too, must be amended. A famous and rather obscure sentence in *The Savage Mind* states that 'there is always a mediator between *praxis* and practices, namely the conceptual scheme by the operation of which matter and form, neither with any independent existence, are realized as structures, that is as entities both empirical and intelligible'.[4] This assertion occurs at the close of chapter 4, which, together with chapter 3, forms the core of Lévi-Strauss's views on permutation and transformation processes—full-blown structuralist theory at its most ambitious. The ambiguity

[3] Lévi-Strauss, *Structural Anthropology*, p. 271.
[4] Lévi-Strauss, *The Savage Mind*, Chicago 1966, p. 130.

of these words derives from the cloudy status of 'praxis', placed as it is as the grounding of both the actual social practices and the 'conceptual scheme' (the mind's doing) which Lévi-Strauss is so obviously concerned to proffer as the missing link in the Marxist theory of superstructures. Early in the same chapter Lévi-Strauss warns against mistaking structuralism for an idealism: he starkly denies every intention to suggest that ideological, conceptual transformations beget social transformations. Emphatically stating that the truth is just the opposite, he claims that his bracketting of the social basis and its causal primacy was an 'inevitable' move, dictated by nothing more than 'reasons of method'.

More often than not, such sound qualifications and disclaimers in Lévi-Strauss's work come as *obiter dicta*, which obviously is not much help in terms of a clear grasp of his epistemological options. For instance, it is only by harking back to the already mentioned disavowal of idealism, twenty pages earlier, that the reader is able to understand that the *Ur*praxis preceding both the 'conceptual scheme' and the more humdrum social practices that in turn imply the mind's work, turn out to be no different from social relations and their occasional alteration—no different, that is, from social structure in the plain, empirical sociological sense. However, to be fair, structural anthropology should not be judged without a perusal of the true intentions of its founder. Therefore, it is important to bear in mind that Lévi-Strauss does not regard himself as an idealist. Perhaps one might sum up his position by paraphrasing Leibniz: 'There is nothing in the mind that was not already in praxis—except mind itself.'

Nor does he conceive his from-the-social-to-the-mental approach as reductionism. Structure, a metaphor of language as a system, serves the anthropologist as a 'logical model' for understanding other forms, or spheres, of social communication; but this is by no means equivalent to treating the model as the 'origin' of social forms—a possibility discarded forcefully in *Structural Anthropology*.[5] •

The only valid reductionism, for Lévi-Strauss, is strictly *epistemological*. As he wrote in a strategic chapter of *Tristes Tropiques* ('How I became an anthropologist'): what Marxism,

---

[5] Lévi-Strauss, *Structural Anthropology*, p. 83.

psychoanalysis and geology—the 'three mistresses' of his youth—
share is the realization that 'understanding consists in the reduction of one type of reality to another', for 'true reality is never
the most obvious of realities'. All of which is in keeping with
one of the favourite sayings of Gaston Bachelard, the patron
saint of structuralist epistemology: *'il n'y a science que du
caché'.* So not only, then, does structure not breed social
reality, contenting itself rather with giving 'form' to the empirical social 'matter' (and thereby making it 'intelligible'), but it is
far from exhausting the social field. Lévi-Straussian structure is
a far cry from the all-embracing range of Parsons's social
system, for example, or from any other holistic theory. Yet here
again there is some shadow of ambiguity. Sometimes Lévi-
Strauss firmly denies that he seeks a 'total knowledge' of society
by means of his structural models. In *Structural Anthropology*
he blames the phenomenological sociologist, Georges Gurvitch,
for so misconstruing his programme.[6] Nevertheless, in his inaugural lecture at the Collège, translated as *The Scope of
Anthropology*, he boldly states that anthropology should be
acknowledged as the legitimate occupant of 'all the domains of
semiology not claimed by linguistics'—an imperial perspective
on society at large, envisaged as a sum of sundry spheres of
communication ultimately organized by the combinatorial
powers of mind.

One thing is sure: if structure does not encompass everything
in society, conversely it is also—from another point of view—
greater than it: for a special characteristic of structure is that it
circumscribes not a set of given, closed totalities but, on the
contrary, an *open* set of totalities, actual and potential. In fact,
as has often been remarked,[7] the more one thinks about the
logical possibilities of possible transformations of a structure,
the more insight one gets into its empirical instances.

In Search of Intellect

I hope these rather broad remarks are enough to provide a

[6] Ibid., chapter 5.
[7] Cf. Pouillon, 'L'Oeuvre de Claude Lévi-Strauss', Les Temps Modernes,
126, July 1966, pp. 150–72; and E. Leach, *Lévi-Strauss*, London 1970.

general idea of Lévi-Strauss's structural approach to social science. We must now turn to something more specific, namely, the actual aims of structural anthropology. What makes structural anthropology tick is human *universals*. In his Unesco paper on scientific criteria for the human sciences Lévi-Strauss shows that the latter may have as their subject matter either *realia*, empirical beings, or *generalia*: a much less concrete stuff, in empirical terms. In this sense, linguistics deals with *realia* (the natural languages), whereas psychology deals with *generalia* (the mind's functions). But the distinction does not stop here. Within the human sciences dealing with *realia*, some tackle, and others do not, *tota*, namely objects that constitute discernible totalities fully located in time and space. In this further sense, the normal concern of both history and anthropology is with *tota*, for they study whole societies. By contrast linguistics studies *realia*, but not *tota*, since its object, language, is less than a social whole. Yet this same partial object is emphatically *universal*: language inheres in all societies; it is a human, not merely social, predicate. Only the object of demography—social number—is as universal as language—but language alone is both human and universal, and as such normally pervades all other social practices.[8]

Insofar as structural anthropology aims at unravelling 'conceptual schemes' active in social life, and embodied in institutions such as kinship or cultural products such as myths, it may be said that its final goal is to extract human universals from *realia* which are in themselves less than universal, and are generally studied in the perspective of *tota*, that is to say, of the social wholes to which they belong. For when Lévi-Strauss analyses kinship, totemism or caste (as in his two main works of the early 1960s, *Totemism* and *The Savage Mind*) or again, myth, his chief concern is never with a given society—rather, it is with classification as a peculiar propensity of the human mind, past or present, 'primitive' or modern. Even as he delves into a huge regional corpus, such as the eight hundred Amerindian myths scrutinized in the four stout volumes of *Mythologiques* (1964–71)—a structuralist *Golden Bough*, the lengthiest sustained effort of structural analysis to date—it is easy to see that his goal is to demonstrate the boundless application of some

[8] Lévi-Strauss, *Structural Anthropology II*, chapter 16.

fundamental universals of culture, the first of which is none other than the nature/culture antithesis itself—the theme of 'the raw and the cooked'. 'Starting from ethnographic experience', he writes in the book of that title, 'I have always aimed at drawing up an inventory of mental patterns'.[9] Therefore, he has studied symbolism not in order to grasp a particular cultural area but a universal kind of thought. No wonder he feels so much at home in the intellectual company of comparativists like Dumézil (whom he warmly received at the Académie Française).

So much for the aim of structural anthropology. Still, as we saw in discussing Dumézil, comparison and the search for invariants are not enough. *Structural* comparison requires something more. As every sophisticated anthropologist commenting on structuralism has stressed, from Sir Edmund Leach to Luc de Heusch, what distinguishes Lévi-Strauss from Frazer (as it did Dumézil from Eliade) is that the meaning of myths is reached through the comparison of structural *relations*, and not mere contents. For structuralism, true universals cannot be isolated cultural traits. Lévi-Strauss has benefited from the systematic comparison of cultures undertaken by G. P. Murdock and his team at the Human Relation Area Files—a Herculean perusal of five hundred and sixty five cultures focussing on the form of family, residence regime, marriage rules and type of economy;[10] but his own project was altogether different.

The key to the difference lies precisely in the quest for form beyond the commonalities of content. But mark: in structuralist doctrine, structuralism is not to be confused with *formalism*. Lévi-Strauss's methodological critique of the Russian folklorist Vladimir Propp states it baldly: 'Form is defined by its opposition to *external* content; but structure has no distinct content—it is itself content, grasped in a logical organization conceived as a property of reality.'[11] Thus while form hovers above content, structure, by contrast, sticks fast to content, without however being swallowed by it. Indeed, if structure were something adhering to a particular content, reality would be atom-like, not structured. But if, on the other hand, structure were a form so

[9] Lévi-Strauss 1969, p. 10.
[10] Murdock, *Social Structure*, New York, 1949.
[11] Lévi-Strauss, *Structural Anthropology II*, chapter 8.

detachable from content that it would be foreign to all social matter, then the very diversity of the social world would vanish into one big Form, printing on each bit of reality the mark of its monotone, monstrous perfection. Therefore structure is neither formless content nor a form external to content.

Ultimately, in Lévi-Strauss's own analyses, structure always denotes cultural products that exemplify logical principles by using natural matter to feed the mind's operations. Structural analysis focusses on relations, not terms, as well as on their permutations;[12] but, in the Lévi-Straussian oeuvre, structures always correspond to one taxonomy or another, *into* another, as though the main job of the mind were to cover reality with several grids of classification, mostly using natural categories for such a purpose.

Basically, then, sociological structuralism is very much *psycho*logical: it revolves emphatically around the mind and its properties. As Lévi-Strauss puts it, 'ethnology is primarily a psychology',[13] a theory of 'conceptual schemes'. Psychology, however, can deal with either the conative or the cognitive: it can be a theory of mind which concerns itself with drives or with cognitive powers, with emotion and motivation or with intellect and logic. Clearly, the psychology underlying structural anthropology belongs to the cognitive, not the conative, area. All that Lévi-Strauss picks up from Freud is the idea of the unconscious as the seat of structural mechanisms whose job is to make sense of reality. That the (social) unconscious can also be highly *expressive* does not in the least appeal to him. If he were interested in learning and in the individual, he would look at Piaget more than at Freud: for like Piaget, he has no truck with sentiment, only with the logical side of mind. This is most conspicuous in the structural study of symbolism. A generation before Lévi-Strauss, symbol theory in anthropology was saddled by Edward Sapir (1881–1939) with the task of discovering strong feelings under ritual symbolism: dread and hope, appetite and anguish became the target of many ethnographic

---

[12] Lévi-Strauss, *Totemism*, Boston 1963, Introduction.

[13] Lévi-Strauss, *The Savage Mind*, chapter 4. In his Collège de France inaugural lecture, he notes that Durkheim, in the foreword to the second edition of the *Rules of Sociological Method* (1901), invited the social scientist to think of a 'formal psychology' as common ground for individual psychology *and* sociology. Cf. Lévi-Strauss, *Structural Anthropology II*, chapter 1.

researches.[14] Lévi-Strauss is the anti-Sapir: the theorist for whom myth and symbol speak of intellect, not of emotion. And the same goes for everything else in the Lévi-Straussian world.

Words and Women, or Structure as Unconscious Exchange

Lévi-Strauss borrowed from modern linguistics, above all other things, two basic beliefs: the primacy of structure, and the idea that the hub of structure consists in a finite number of minimal components. As we learn from the very last page of *The Raw and the Cooked*, since 'matter', alias nature, alias the world, is only the instrument or raw material, *not the object*, of structural meaning, for the world to yield meaning one must first 'impoverish' it, retaining just a few elements suitable for expressing contrasts and forming oppositional pairs. This last aspect indicates Lévi-Strauss's major debt to the phonological method of Trubetzkoy and Jakobson, dominated by the functional role of *binary oppositions*. Thanks to these two props—the primacy of structure and the minimalism of antitheses—sociological structuralism was complete, methodologically speaking, after what is now considered the commanding chapter of *Structural Anthropology*: 'Structural analysis in linguistics and anthropology', originally published in *Word* in 1945. What better place for the opening salvo of the 'linguistics of culture' (Leach's phrase) than an authoritative journal of linguistics?

Nevertheless, in the conceptual framework of *The Elementary Structures of Kinship* (1949), in which structuralism in social science was established as an analytical strategy, these two *linguistic* weapons, the structural view in a formal (though not formalist) sense, and binary opposition, were forcefully linked to a third concept of impeccable *anthropological* pedigree. This was the notion of *exchange*. Exchange theory was the jewel in the crown of the French sociological school, the legacy of Durkheim's nephew and most original successor, Marcel Mauss (1872–1950). Mauss's seminal essay *The Gift* (1925) emphasised the role of exchange and reciprocity in primitive and archaic society. By highlighting the anti-economic, non-

---

[14] On Sapir's place in the history of symbol theory, see Merquior, *The Veil and the Mask*, pp. 92–99.

utilitarian meaning of rituals like the Kula ring in Melanesia or the potlatch, the tribal feast given by aspirants to high social status among certain North American tribes, Mauss tacitly joined in the criticism of the disruptive, anomic atomism of modern society—a traditional concern of Durkheimians.

Lévi-Strauss's reading of Mauss's *The Gift* aroused in him, in his own words, the same deep-felt emotion that Malebranche experienced on discovering Descartes. In 1950 he published a highly perceptive essay on Mauss.[15] The year before he extended the concepts of exchange and reciprocity into the area of kinship. *Elementary Structures* is a study of marriage as exchange. As explained in chapter two of *Structural Anthropology*, the marriage rules at the core of primitive kinship systems form 'a set of processes permitting the establishment, between individuals and groups, of a certain kind of communication. That the mediating factor in this case should be the women of the group, who are circulated between clans, lineages or families, in place of the words of the group . . . does not at all change the fact that the essential aspect of the phenomenon is identical in both cases.' Thus women in prescriptive marriage systems are likened to verbal 'messages' sent from each social clan to another; and Lévi-Strauss cannot resist making this surprising rapprochement by adding a typical masculine quip: yet unlike women, he says, words do not talk. . . .

A basic assumption in *Elementary Structures*, also much insisted upon in the first part of *Structural Anthropology* (a further theoretical comment on his own analysis of kinship systems), is that kinship is something very different from consanguinity. In this, Lévi-Strauss was following Durkheim, who sharply criticized late-nineteenth-century German anthropology for naturalistically suggesting that kinship nomenclatures mirrored blood ties.[16] But Lévi-Strauss resumed his anti-naturalist line of kinship theory with a vengeance: he claimed to have chosen kinship as a subject matter out of a wish to draw an 'inventory of mental constraints'. Kinship was quite a challenge because it seems at first sight a contingent, incoherent domain—and therefore, one all the more suitable for somebody interested

[15] See M. Mauss, *Sociologie et Anthropologie*, Paris 1950, pp. VIII-LII.
[16] Cf. Francis Korn, *Elementary Structures Reconsidered: Lévi-Strauss on Kinship,* London 1973, p. 2.

46

in eliciting order, the mark of the intellect, from apparently disconnected phenomena.

Elementary structures of kinship obtain in societies where men are forbidden to marry their own women (societies with multiple incest prohibitions) so that other men can marry them. These latter men belong to other clans or lineages in the same society, yet are kinsmen of the former because the marrying couple is often composed of cross-cousins, that is to say, of children of parents who are siblings of a different gender (a *cross*-cousin is one's mother's brother's child or alternatively, one's father's sister's child; a *parallel* cousin, by contrast, is one's mother's sister's, or father's brother's, child).

Lévi-Strauss's book is a comprehensive survey of such systems of prescriptive marriage. It examines forms of restricted exchange (a give-and-take-women game between two exogamous clans) and, more interestingly, systems of *generalized* exchange where one-to-one reciprocity is replaced by more complex patterns of social communication. Characteristically, Lévi-Strauss contends that one must think of incest not in its literal, negative sense but rather as a positive injunction. Without the incest-taboo, society would be torn into disparate biological units; therefore incest is forbidden *so that the exchange of women can take place at an adequate level*. What matters is not the taboo per se, but taboo as a function in a structural process. That is the point of women acting as 'messages'—like 'silent' words, they ensure widespread communication, a vital need of the social system.

Lévi-Strauss's approach (which had been to an extent adumbrated by some Dutch anthropologists) came to be known as the 'alliance theory' of kinship and marriage. Robin Fox, in his *Kinship and Marriage* (1967), draws an interesting parallel between the traditional and the structuralist study of kinship on the one hand and the approaches used by historians of princely dynasties on the other. 'One historian', says Fox, 'is primarily interested in the ways in which royal houses perpetuated themselves, arranged their rules of succession, and ensured that the succession did not fail. Marriages were means to this end. The other historian, however, sees the royal houses as units in a series of complex alliances binding together various countries, and these alliances are cemented or "expressed" by royal marriages. One sees marriage as useful in providing royal heirs: the other sees royal heirs as useful in that they can be used in dynastic marriages.' It is a clever simile, grasping the point of Lévi-Strauss's *Elementary Structures*.

In Lévi-Strauss's hands, kinship analysis tends to minimize empirical factors. For instance, it has been claimed that in patrilineal societies a man's desire to marry his matrilateral cross-cousin could well be a projection of the young man's comradeship with his easy-going maternal uncle, whose behaviour strongly contrasts with the stern attitude of his father. Lévi-Strauss shrugs off *observed* traits of this kind, because his point is to show that beneath the rule rationalized in such emotional terms there lies a structural meaning—the need for fulfilling communication between different clans. That the society is not consciously aware of this meaning is irrelevant. Better still: it can only bolster the theory. Any more than the principles ruling the combination of phonemes in a natural language, the underlying patterns of marriage as exchange need not to be (and normally aren't) present to those who employ them. We see how fully assimilated the lesson of linguistics has been: there is structure in the formal sense rather than the organic sense; structure breaks up into a finite number of minimal elements; and finally, the whole thing is said to work in society at an unconscious level—just like the basic rules of language itself.

Homo Distinguens

We know that Lévi-Strauss regards the human fondness for classification as conspicuous evidence of the central role of intellectual strategies in society. In *Totemism*, a slim book of 1962, he explored a field strikingly adequate to illustrate his thesis. Totemic institutions were a phenomenon much theorized by armchair anthropologists towards the end of the last century, who saw in it the source of religion or a low step on the ladder of civilization. The subject was subsequently neglected because of this long association with discredited evolutionist ideas.

When functionalism dislodged evolutionary theory as a paradigm of anthropological explanation, totemism became the subject of a particularistic analysis in monographs assuming that totemic systems served to give emotional value to animals and plants of great economic importance in a given society, thereby protecting such species from predatory action.

Lévi-Strauss condemns both the evolutionist and the functionalist accounts of totemism. Yet evolutionist theories had never properly recovered from their cogent demolition by Alexander Goldenweiser half a century before, a critical tour-de-force much admired by Lowie.[17] Therefore the brunt of the structuralist bite fell on the functionalist 'economistic' interpretation. Lévi-Strauss stresses that it is not so much totems as totemic categories that are valuable to society: before being good to eat, totemic species are 'goods to think with'—actually, excellent tools for the mind's classifying play.

To grasp the social meaning of totemism, it is not enough to ask questions about implausible one-to-one relations of resemblance between each social group on the one hand, and a given non-human species on the other. Instead, we must look for a relation between sets of classes or differences. 'On the one hand', Lévi-Strauss writes, 'there are animals that differ from each other . . ., and on the other hand there are men . . . who also differ from each other (in that they are distributed among different segments of the society, each occupying a particular position in the social structure). The resemblance presupposed by so-called totemic representations is *between these two systems of differences*.'

That what is being compared is not man and animal may be inferred from the fact that in any event the differences between natural species as a whole are far larger than the differences between human clans; social groups differ much less than animal kinds among themselves. 'But the point', says an able commentator, 'is that human groups are trying through "totemic" institutions not to match two pre-existing systems of differences, but rather to build one system with the help of the other.'[18] There we are again: structure results from the attempt to build human order in the mind's play with the stuff of nature.

La grille: no image (it is of course his own) better conveys

[17] On Lowie and Goldenweiser, see M. Harris, *The Rise of Anthropological Theory*, New York 1968, p. 346.

[18] Sperber, in J. Sturrock, ed., *Structuralism and Science: From Lévi-Strauss to Derrida*, Oxford 1979, p. 32.

the essence of Lévi-Straussian structuralism. Structural anthropology may be defined as a relentless pursuit of the manifold instances of the principle of the grid. Lévi-Strauss revels in devising unexpected classifications. He is the epitome of *homo distinguens et discernens*. No wonder he thinks highly of Mauss's essay on primitive forms of classification, authored with 'tonton' Durkheim (1901–02). Charting the world, casting a logical network over nature and society alike, building compartments for each big department of culture: such is the structuralist programme in social science. In principle, there is no limit to its range: everything in culture may fall under the gaze of structural analysis.

This breadth of scope is the real subject of Lévi-Strauss's most idiosyncratic book, which is also his full-fledged personal philosophy: *The Savage Mind* (1962). From totemism to castes and from painting to proper nouns, nothing escapes the reach of the structuralist net. The object of the savage mind is 'to grasp the world as . . . a totality, and the knowledge that it draws therefrom is like that afforded of a room by mirrors viced on opposite walls, which reflect each other. . . . The savage mind deepens its knowledge with the help of *imagines mundi*. It builds mental structures that facilitate an understanding of the world in as much as they resemble it. In this sense savage thought can be defined as analogical thought.'[19]

Giving free rein to his taste for binary antitheses, Lévi-Strauss displays in *The Savage Mind* a whole array of dialectical oppositions. For instance, resuming the analysis of *Totemism*, he contrasts the castes of Brahminic India with totemic systems, stressing that castes are endogamous while totemic clans are exogamous. Then, in a typical move, he reverses the opposition by noting that whilst castes keep their women but exchange goods and services with each other, totemic clans exchange women but generally consume their own products. Thus the contrast becomes dialectical by means of an unexpected negation of the negation: the difference concerning women is at once paralleled *and inverted* by that concerning goods.

In one of the quaintest passages of the book, birds' and pet dogs' names are also said to be in dialectical opposition. More often than not (says Lévi-Strauss) when we give human nick-

[19] Lévi-Strauss, *The Savage Mind*, p. 263.

names to birds, they are normal human names, like Pierrot and Robin for the sparrow or Margot and Meg for the magpie. On the other hand, when pet dogs are named (at least in Latin countries), 'special' proper nouns are used: Augustus, Pluto, Diana. Moreover while we employ such birds' names to denote the whole species, we use human names for individual pet dogs.

Now Lévi-Strauss contends that the basis for this discrepancy might well lie in the difference in these animals' relation to humans. *Birds* can be allowed onomastically to resemble us precisely because they are very different from us, being non-mammals and living in the air. Paradoxically, since they are so dissimilar from us, we like to see them as forming another society: we say they love freedom, build their homes, nourish their children, 'talk' with each other by singing . . . Pet dogs, by contrast, are mammals living in domestic proximity to us. The more metaphorical the relation between us and the animals concerned (as in the case of birds), the more metonymical are their given names, borrowed from our daily environment. Conversely, the more metonymical the beasts' relation to us (as with pet dogs), the more metaphorical, or 'symbolic' the nicknames will be, like dogs baptized after deities or historical celebrities. The pattern is therefore one of symmetrical inversion: what most *resembles* is exactly what *differs* most.[20]

Systematic inversion soon became a true *forma mentis* of Lévi-Straussian thought. Antithesis and *chiasmus*, or symmetrical inversion, are indeed, as Dan Sperber noted, a trademark of his analysis of cultural data.[21] And nowhere are they more wilfully indulged than in *The Savage Mind*, his manifesto-book, strategically published between his seminal and controversial revolution in kinship studies and his no less innovative refounding of mythology.

The 'savage mind' is by no means 'primitive thought' in any derogatory sense. As Lévi-Strauss warns, it is not the mind of savages but mind *in the savage state*. He wants no truck with the Lévy-Bruhl thesis and its attribution of 'prelogical' thinking to tribal cultures. In fact, if there is anything structuralism shares with functionalism, it is the anti-evolutionist rage of mainstream modern anthropology. The young Bertrand Russell could still

[20] Ibid., chapter 7.
[21] Sturrock, *Structuralism and Since*, p. 22.

write in his dairy that 'Shakespeare and Herbert Spencer differ as much from a Papuan as a Papuan from a monkey'. Lévi-Strauss takes just the opposite view: he is wary not to overstate the gap between the human and the animal realm; and he relishes stressing that Papuans, Bororos and their like are just as capable of complex logic as any 'civilized' man.

Do not savages often use a lot of abstractions in their way of speaking? Among the Chinook of North America, for instance, a statement such as 'the bad man killed the poor girl' is expressed like this: 'the man's badness killed the girl's poverty'. After all, Lévi-Strauss insists, none of the invaluable conquests of the neolithic revolution, from agriculture to pottery and from animal husbandry to weaving, could have possibly been achieved by a silly primitive mind, unable to connect logically many complex relations in the natural environment of prehistoric man. Therefore the difference between us and the so-called primitive lies not in mental power but in the areas of application of the mind's cognitive energy. 'Wild' thought, the savage mind, prefers to concentrate on multiple instances of the 'logic of the concrete': a vivid, sensuous way to exercise the intellect— but not a bit less logical for it. It is all a matter of 'modes' of knowledge: one eminently perceptual and imaginative; the other—that of modern science—distant from our aesthetico-fantastic faculties. 'It is as if the objects of science . . . could be arrived at by two different routes, one very close to, and the other more remote from, sensible intuition.'

Time into Space: the Realm of Myth

Lévi-Strauss's structural analysis of Amerindian myth provides us with an opulent domain of the 'logic of the concrete' working on a large scale. His tetralogy, the *Mythologies*, is a colossal attempt at showing how 'concrete' categories—countless natural classes of sundry sorts—work as abstract relationships, ordering the world, physical and social, in various complex ways. Furthermore, the structural analysis of myth has also proved to be the best exemplification of that close link between the concept of structure and the idea, both linguistic and mathematical, of *transformation*—a link duly underscored (in *The Scope of Anthropology*) at the very outset of Lévi-Strauss's teaching at the Collège de France, as well as of his minute dissection of hundreds of myths collected by Americanist ethnographers. To speak of a myth's structure recalls the discipline of topology, the study of constant spatial relations under conditions of continuous change of shape or size of figure. Lévi-Strauss willingly refers to the British naturalist D'Arcy Wentworth Thompson's notion of 'transformation groups'—a fair description of the backbone of his four-volume summa of myth analysis. D'Arcy Thompson (*On Growth and Form*, 1952) deduced the outlines of living forms with the help of algebraic functions. Lévi-Strauss quotes his endeavours in the Finale of *Mythologies*, only too happy to show that natural evolution itself can obey the same logic as myths.[22]

Myth brought Lévi-Strauss's restless mind from Oceania to the Americas. Whilst most of the kinship and totemic systems he studied until the early 1960s are or were in Australia, the numerous myths he examined afterwards are Amerindian (the first two volumes of the *Mythologiques* cover the myths of South American tribes; in the third, jocularly entitled *The Origin of Table Manners*, North America tribes also come under scrutiny, their myths regarded as transformations of their Southern counterparts.

But the most significant difference between Lévi-Strauss's previous work and his labours as a mythographer lies elsewhere. We saw how he likes to account for his choice of kinship as the first social field of structural analysis: kinship *seemed* the very land of contingency, and for this very reason represented a worthy challenge to the structuralist. Myth is a different matter. According to *The Raw and the Cooked*, it constitutes a far more suitable domain for structuralist exertions. For whereas nothing guarantees that marriage rules derive 'from within', instead of reflecting in the mind 'certain social demands objectified in institutions', the realm of myth emanates straight from the mental operations so cherished by the structuralist. In myth the play of mind with world seems unimpeded. Not even language

---

[22] *Mythologiques* IV, pp. 604–06. On the other hand, structural myth analysis is forcefully declared a prize domain of wild thought and its 'logic of the concrete'; actually, Lévi-Strauss from the outset places *Mythologiques* under the obligation to 'demonstrate its operations and reveal its laws'. See Lévi-Strauss, *The Raw and the Cooked*, New York 1969, p. 1.

foils analysis: for, unlike poetry, myths almost never suffer in translations.[23]

In an often more suggestive than assertive way, Lévi-Strauss sees myth as fulfilling at least three functions. First, myths act as knowledge, though not in the paltry sense of those childish attempts at explanation (of natural events) once ascribed to them, in their patronizing evolutionism, by the armchair classics of anthropology. As prize examples of the savage thought, myths reflect 'methods of observation and reflection' best adapted to discoveries 'that nature authorized from the starting point of a speculative organization and exploitation of the sensible world in sensible terms'.[24] The univese of myth is neither a Malinowskian charter of social relations nor a clumsy attempt at proto-science—but it does provide a knowledge of our habitat. Moreover, sometimes myth also imparts *fundamental* knowledge, that is to say, insight about man's place in the cosmos. For instance, the 'key myth' that triggers off the analysis in *The Raw and the Cooked* is a true piece of Bororo philosophical anthropology. It tells that man, before he mastered the use of fire, used to warm his meat by leaving it on stones under the sun. Thus heaven and earth, the sky and mankind, were brought together. Thereupon the discovery of cooking severed the gods from the daily life of man. At the same time, it also isolated mankind from the rest of the animal world, where food is eaten raw. In short, nature and culture were separated.

Besides procuring knowledge, myth often distils patterns of order required by society. Pygmies, for example, tell many myths about elephants and mice. Now it so happens that pygmies live in the forest, but so do villagers who are taller than they are and cut the jungle in order to make room for agriculture. Pygmies, needing the forest for their hunting, are deeply annoyed by this. Therefore their legends often speak of elephants as awkward braggarts who destroy the jungle but are invariably trapped by smaller animals defending themselves and their habitat. Natural categories (elephants and mice) are tools for the conceptualization of a situational logic. The logical order of myth bespeaks the strenuous social effort to ensure physical order as a matter of survival. Talcott Parsons's

---

[23] Lévi-Strauss, *Structural Anthropology*, p. 210.
[24] Lévi-Strauss, *The Savage Mind*, p. 16.

definition of order comes to mind: 'peaceful coexistence in conditions of scarcity'. The symbolic logic of myth fosters or reinforces—rather than expresses—this kind of basic social arrangement.[25]

Finally, myth deals with contradiction. 'The purpose of myth is to provide a logical model capable of overcoming a contradiction (an impossible achievement if, as it happens, the contradiction is real).'[26] Life and death, collapse and survival, male and female, nature and culture, and a host of further contrasts and paradoxes are both admitted and redeemed by mythical thought. While myth does not exactly offer any pax dialectica at the end of a long war of contraries, at least it shows mind constantly responsive to the hard core of insoluble contradiction in several human and social predicaments.

Yet when all is said and done, Lévi-Straussian myth possesses no Ur-meaning whatsoever. Here is the startling conclusion of *The Raw and the Cooked*: 'Each matrix of meanings refers to another matrix, each myth to other myths. And if it is now asked to what final meaning these mutually significative meanings are referring—since in the last resort and in their totality they must refer to something—the only reply to emerge from this study is that myths signify the mind that evolves them by making use of the world of which it is itself a part.'

The ultimate referent of mythological symbolism is the intellect, which secretes myth by using elements of this world. The intellect, in turn, is but a humble part of the same world. In myth, adds Lévi-Strauss, mind 'is reduced to imitating itself as object'. Saussure insisted on the independence of the sign; Lévi-Strauss does not balk at proclaiming the autarchy of the symbol. The true function of myth is to display the narcissism of the mind.

In myth, pre-eminently, time turns into space. Lévi-Strauss's recent *The View From Afar* (1983), claims that a verse from Wagner's *Parsifal*:

> *zum Raum wird hier die Zeit*
> here time becomes space

---

[25] On this point (and the pygmies illustration) see Colin Turnbull's essay in E. N. and T. Hayes, eds., *Claude Lévi-Strauss: The Anthropologist as Hero*, Cambridge 1970.

[26] Lévi-Strauss, *Structural Anthropology*, p. 229.

is 'doubtless the profoundest definition ever given of myth'.[27] The structuralist infatuation with spatial modes of thought starts with the first theorist to have led it beyond the pale of linguistics. We shall presently look into the ideological roots of Lévi-Straussian spatialism.

To an extent, however, the spatial approach was a precondition of analysis. The structuralist programme for myth analysis was laid down in a 1955 paper, 'The structural study of myth' (now the second chapter of *Structural Anthropology*). It is a 'pilot' text, giving the study of symbolism what the essay in *Word* gave kinship systems ten years earlier: a canon of research and interpretation. What are its main ideas? First, one has to realize that, in the complex symbolism of myth, *each symbolic unit* (called 'mytheme', on the obvious analogy of 'phonene' and 'morpheme') *never carries meaning by itself*. Mythemes only signify by dint of their opposition to at least one other unit. Second, these oppositions themselves—the soul of mythical meaning—may belong to several domains of reality: the natural world, social relations, culinary and sexual customs, and so on. Unlike psychoanalysis, structural anthropology does not grant any domain an ontological privilege. Third, oppositions may also split into further antitheses, as well as be *inverted* among themselves (symmetrical oppositions and chiasmus being, as we saw, staple manoeuvres in the play of mind). Finally, *each myth should be seen as a variation upon a theme*. No myth is, in this sense, an original: all are versions of themes and their transformations; no version is 'truer'. At most, a set of myths is detected whenever one can tackle, say, a Bororo tale as a transformation of certain Gê legends, the latter themselves functioning as echoes of Tupi myths, which in turn feature as variations on the Bororo story which served as a starting point. Such da capo loops are rife throughout the Lévi-Straussian oeuvre.

Lévi-Strauss has exemplified the actual technique of analysis by chopping the Theban myth of Oedipus into segments referring to relations between the main characters. He then assembles these narrative segments into four columns: (a) the first gathers elements like the Oedipus-Iokaste incestuous wedlock or the love of Antigone for her brother Polynices; (b) the

[27] Lévi-Strauss, *The View From Afar*, New York 1985, chapter 17.

second column links the relation between Oedipus and his father Laios to the struggle between the brothers Eteocles and Polynices; (c) the third one includes the slaying of the Dragon by Cadmus, founder of Thebes, as well as Oedipus's own triumph over the Sphinx; (d) lastly, a fourth column records anecdotal details such as the left-sidedness of Laios's and Oedipus's lameness.

Next, interpreting his four columns, Lévi-Strauss points out that the first of them is the very opposite of the second, in that the common denominator of (a) may be said to lie in an over-valuation of blood ties, whereas the common denominator of (b) is precisely an offence against them (Oedipus's parricide, Eteocles's fratricide). Similarly, he claims, (c) reversed (d). How? Because while (c) refers to monsters (the Dragon, the Sphinx) killed by men (d) is occupied by men who are themselves—by virtue of their physical handicaps—somewhat monstrous.

This latter opposition may seem too far-fetched. But Lévi-Strauss tries to strengthen it. When Cadmus killed the dragon he sowed the monster's teeth, thereby giving birth to the Spartoi (the sown), the ancestral warriors who helped Cadmus to build Thebes. In Greek mythology, beings born of the ground were termed 'chtonian'. In this sense, the Spartoi were chtonians turned into humans. Oedipus, by contrast, was a human staked to the earth (this is how he got his lame foot): though born of woman, he became 'chtonian'. Thus, we reach a double equation: (a) is to (b) what (c) is to (d). Conversely, however, the opposite columns are shown to be also identical, since—as most conspicuous in (c) and (d)—each of them is itself contradictory (how can chtonian be human, or humans chtonian?).

According to Lévi-Strauss, the riddle underlying the Oedipus story is that Greek religion claimed the 'autochtony' of man, and consequently had to square such a belief with the empirical truth that humans are born of woman, not of the earth. The conceptual role of the Oedipus myth would then consist in serving as a 'logical tool' that relates this problem to a derivative issue: is the same born *from the same* or from the different?[28] The sameness-in-opposition obtaining between the

---

[28]Lévi-Strauss, *Structural Anthropology*, chapter 11. I had to use the French original (p. 239), since the English translation is faulty at the crucial sentence: 'le même naît-il du même, ou de l'autre?' becomes 'born from different or born from the same'. The omission of the subject—même—is quite misleading.

columns that classify mythemes in the Oedipus story is a way of using symbolism to 'surmount' or at least 'replace' (Lévi-Strauss's words) acute contradictions in the social psyche.

Besides offering this programmatic analysis of the Oedipus legend, 'The structural study of myth' sketches another contradiction-bridging interpretation, that of the Trickster character in North American Indian mythology. The Trickster is a highly ambivalent fellow, both good and evil, a creator and a destroyer. Lévi-Strauss asks why is it that he is so often personified as a coyote or as a raven, throughout the tribes of North America. He suggests that the solution may be found if we bear in mind that 'mythical thought always progresses from the awareness of opposites towards their resolution'. Moreover, whenever two opposite terms have no intermediary, they 'tend to be replaced by two equivalent terms, which admit of a third one as a mediator'; then one of the polar terms and the mediator can be replaced by a 'new triad', and so on.

In our particular case, the Trickster myth among the Pueblo and other tribes, Lévi-Strauss starts from the life/death polarity. Life, in their myths, correlates with the agricultural; death, with war. Now between war and agriculture there is a mediation: hunting. For hunting is a means of getting food (as in agriculture) by using weapons, the very tools of war. Hence we have a triad: agriculture-hunting-war. How does it link up with our original unmediated polarity of life and death? Let's glance at our Indian myths again. In them, agriculture is often personified as a herbivorous animal; hunting, as a beast of prey. The natural mediators between herbivorous animals and predatory beasts are scavengers, who eat carrion yet do not kill other animals in order to eat. By being carnivorous, argues Lévi-Strauss, scavengers are like beasts of prey, and therefore like hunting; but they also are like food producers (hence like agriculture) in that they do not kill what they eat. Ravens and coyotes are notorious scavengers. Therefore, they mediate, through their bridging of the polarity agriculture/warfare, the initial antithesis of life and death, creation and destruction, inscribed in the character of the Trickster—et voilà!

The whole analysis is typical of Lévi-Strauss's personal technique, not least in the bold way he picks up unexpected similitudes, such as the surprising (some would say nonplussing) likening of scavengers to food producers. Many readers are flabbergasted by such cleverness—and are tempted to think of skullduggery. Could it be that a very learned trickster is interpreting at will the Trickster myths? But let us not leap to conclusions. For the moment, suffice to say that the bulk of *Mythologiques*, in each of the four volumes, swarms with dazzling, vertiginous analogies of this kind.

'Replacing' rather than surmounting the contradictions of man and world, myth cannot offer us any ultimate wisdom. No Jungian sage, Lévi-Strauss does not think of myths as arcana. In his *Mythologiques*, we embark upon long journeys of interpretation, witnessing endless permutations between chains of oppositions—but we end up none the wiser for it, nor is there any reason to think it went differently with the primitive mind, other than at a rather superficial level. Like music, to which it is so akin, Lévi-Straussian myth is 'both intelligible and untranslatable'.[29] The wonders of the intellect are by no means a way to Truth.

Towards a Balance Sheet

Assessing the value of Lévi-Strauss's work is a formidable task. His is probably the largest output among first rate anthropologists since Frazer—to whom he may indeed be compared in the tremendous scope of his erudition and the brilliance of his prose. Unlike Frazer, however, Lévi-Strauss is a pathbreaking theorist, a conqueror of new conceptual provinces in social sciences. Where Frazer was contented with collecting and classifying, he also analyses and theorizes, with a speculative boldness reminiscent of the great pioneers in the study of social existence: Marx, Durkheim, Weber. In what follows I shall not attempt to give more than a hint of the current estimation of his ideas among his fellow experts. In this, as in the preceding pages, I shall avoid all technicalities. Then, after something roughly corresponding to a balance sheet is drawn, I shall conclude our discussion of Lévi-Strauss's ideas by indicating the place he occupies in contemporary thought.

Lévi-Strauss has warned more than once about the danger of

[29] Lévi-Strauss, *The Raw and the Cooked*, Overture.

stretching structuralism into an ideological passepartout. He did so most explicitly in his speech accepting the gold medal of the CNRS, the French National Council of Scientific Research (1968)—a token of the Fifth Republic's gratitude for the prestige structuralism brought to France. Washing his hands of loose, far-fetched extensions of structuralist views and procedures, he cautioned that it should be kept as rigorous and technical as possible. Yet a classical issue in the Lévi-Strauss literature is: to what extent has he himself obeyed his own wise warnings? How faithful has he been to his own empirical data?

At first sight, Lévi-Strauss's aloofness from the mess of the empirical can be deemed a useful discipline, a praiseworthy intellectual asceticism. Sticking to the barest minimum in its assumptions about social needs and functions, structural anthropology seems to fare much better than functionalism, which at least under Malinowski was not above jumping to many a question-begging conclusion in explaining culture and society. By and large, structuralism managed to avoid most of the fallacies of biologism, psychologism and holism in the scientific account of social processes.

On closer inspection, however, things were not, alas, so neat and tidy. For all his professed materialism, the Master was the first to indulge, or verge on indulging, in another sin: logicism or conceptualism, the temptation to describe social realities as though they were pre-eminently, if not exclusively, concepts writ large. A good instance of this is the treatment of castes in *The Savage Mind*. Is it not true that a hierarchy as complex as the Indian caste system, full of religious and socio-economic determinations, is presented in chapter 4 of that book as if it were essentially a structural transformation of certain totemic systems? Here if anywhere, Lévi-Strauss appears to fall victim to the hubris of conceptualism.

Still, *The Savage Mind* is, precisely, too general a text—a manifesto, as it were, with just some samples (however dazzling) of analysis. What are we to think of more specific works, like *Elementary Structures* or the imposing *Mythologiques*? The study of kinship is a highly specialized field of anthropological research—and insofar as it is so, I hold no brief for pronouncing on structuralist results, and therefore restrict myself to just a passing reference to the critical fortune of Lévi-Strauss's contribution. Two points, one particular, the other general, should suffice to alert the reader to what is at stake. The particular issue refers to the nature of the terms linked by the rules of prescriptive alliance—in marriage, that is, as regular social exchange. We saw that Lévi-Strauss broke altogether with interpretations reducing kinship networks to relations of consanguinity. Nevertheless, he went on attaching a great deal of importance to *genealogical* concepts, as shown in the pivotal role he ascribes to cross-cousins in prescriptive marriage. However, not everyone agrees. Some experts think that genealogical ties, even of a purely conventional nature, are *not* the decisive criteria in systems of prescriptive alliance. Other criteria, such as group affiliation, may well provide the real stuff of the rules involved—but if so, the actual fabric of the Lévi-Straussian analysis is seriously damaged.[30]

In a more general vein, some anthropologists are simply disgruntled with Lévi-Strauss's haughty contempt for the empirical level. In a sustained critique of *Elementary Structures*, Francis Korn (a former student of Rodney Needham at Oxford) insists that one should be able to point out *whose* unconscious categories are being postulated in the course of such structural analyses, and that concentration on 'models' should not exempt the researcher from specifying *what* they are models of.[31].

If these strictures are accurate, the net result would reduce the claims of structuralism in this field to something far more modest. All that Lévi-Strauss would have achieved in this connection would consist in what Harold Scheffler (the author of the particular criticism just summarized) deems an unparalleled 'degree of integration of ethnographic data'. Overall, specialists reckon the *Elementary Structures of Kinship* at the very least a genuine turning point in the debate over the meaning of kinship in primitive society. Above all, Lévi-Strauss's theory, built as it is on well circumscribed objects (the closed system of marriage exchange) turns out to be *falsifiable*[32]—it qualifies as a fruitful scientific hypothesis. The detail of the theory may be proved wrong, but its cognitive potential seems

[30] For this criticism, see Harold Scheffler, 'Structuralism in Anthropology' *Yale French Studies*, 36–37, 1966, pp. 81ff; J. Ehrmann, ed., *Structuralism*, New York 1970.

[31] Korn, *Elementary Structures*, especially pp. 143ff.

[32] See R. Boudon, *A Quoi sert la Notion de 'Structure'?*, Paris 1971, chapter 4. For a divergent view, see P. Pettit, 1976, pp. 88ff.

well established.

A methodological, as opposed to substantive detail much questioned in Lévi-Strauss's brand of structural analysis, both in relation to kinship and elsewhere, is his inveterate *binarism*. We saw (p. 44 above) how heavily the founder of sociological structuralism relies on eliciting pairs of oppositions as the basic prop of structure. Antithesis reigns supreme, and underpins the trademark of Levi-Straussian analysis: the dynamics of inversion. Unfortunately, however, binarism may also act as a fetter, for although the human brain does tend to employ dualist devices abundantly, it can also do otherwise. As Leach has pointed out, a satisfactory computer-like model of the mind in keeping with structuralist hypotheses should contain *analog* features that do not occur in digital computers.[33] No wonder, then, if from time to time the relentless binary framework of structural anthropology seems to strain its own subject matter.

There remains the richest territory of the hunt for structure: the luxuriant symbolism of myth. Here again criticisms tend to split along two slopes: some are empirically based, others are purely conceptual. Let us look at the empirical weaknesses of *Mythologiques*. At the outset of his tetralogy Lévi-Strauss, anticipating criticism, calls his interpretative enterprise 'a nebula' that reality will guide, or so he trusts, as it moves on. At the end of the same section (the famous overture of *The Raw and the Cooked*) he disarmingly disposes of the issue of the validity of his bold interpretations by claiming that '. . . if the final goal of anthropology is to contribute to a better knowledge of objective thought and its mechanisms, it comes to the same thing in the end if, in this book, the thought of South American Indians takes shape under the action of mine, or mine under the action of theirs.'

But an Americanist like David Maybury-Lewis is not amused. He insists that we should be able to ascertain whether the meaning Lévi-Strauss elicits from the myths of Amerindian tribes does really correspond to Indian thought, at whatever conscious or unconscious level. Again, he is worried by Lévi-Strauss's Olympian neglect of the conventional niceties of mythography: rules of presentation of myths, proper research into the manner of their collection, the need for distinguishing

[33] Leach, *Lévi-Strauss*, London 1970, pp. 87–8.

62

anomalous elements of plot from standard ones, and so on.
Again, Lévi-Strauss often disregards the normal methods of
validating the interpretation of myth: he sets little store by
ritual, a classical source of evidence for symbolic meaning.[34]
Yet, as noted by Mary Douglas,[35] he goes as far as to depict a
myth (*The Story of Asdiwal*, 1958, reprinted as chapter ix of
Structural Anthropology II) with no echo in the ritual of its tribe
as an 'inversion' of rites of *another* tribe. No wonder Maybury-
Lewis protested that, for all the dialectical ingenuity displayed
by Lévi-Strauss, 'we still do not know who is supposed to be
saying what in what language to whom.'

We know the answer to such a query: it is just 'mind'. Mind
speaking of itself with the lexicon of the world. Still, if one
happens to think that the social incarnations of the mind are
context-bound, that is, motivated by their social environments,
instead of being free transformations, gratuitous avatars of a
self-sufficient intellect hovering over its social basis, then indeed one must cope with such qualms as the one voiced by
Maybury-Lewis. The mind-postulate is fascinating—but it can
turn out to be too question-begging an answer.

What about the *conceptual* criticisms? They are at their most
sophisticated in the contention, put forward by Dan Sperber,
that Lévi-Strauss's pet idea of applying Saussurean semiology
to symbolic thinking as embodied in myth is a sort of category
mistake. According to Sperber, symbolism, in structural myth
analysis, fails to qualify as an *encoding* process. Information
is surely organized by myth—but not truly encoded. In which
case we are left without any real *semiotic* meaning, meaning
based on coded pairs of signifiers and signifieds. Therefore, the
structural meaning of myths does not constitute a *language* at
all. There is no doubt that Lévi-Strauss launched a highly
rewarding heuristics—a new, broad path for exploring the
wealthy stuff of myths; but it is a heuristics, not (as he likes to
think) an underlying grammar of symbolism.[36]

In his foreword to Roman Jakobson's *Six leçons sur le son et*

---

[34] Maybury-Lewis, in Hayes, *Claude Lévi-Strauss*, chapter 11.
[35] In E. Leach, ed., *The Structural Study of Myth and Totemism*, London
1967, p. 60.
[36] D. Sperber, *Rethinking Symbolism*, Cambridge 1975, chapter 3.

le sens (1976) Lévi-Strauss outlined an indirect answer to such a criticism. Unlike linguistic statements, he says, myth never offers its receivers a determinate meaning. At most, it provides a grid that assigns meaning, not to myth itself, but to all 'the images of the world, society and its history' of which those who belong to a given cultural community are aware. Myth provides a matrix of intelligibility for all this; as for its structure, it is composed of elements perfectly meaningless in themselves. In this sense, mythemes are like phonemes, not like words or sentences.[37]

Up to a certain point, Lévi-Strauss's reply tacitly agrees with Sperber: for it grants that mythical meaning, a grid ordering connotations in a given cultural space, is *not in fact coded*; consequently, there can be no 'language of myth' in any rigorous sense of the word. However, even his sternest critics acknowledge that Lévi-Strauss revolutionized the analysis of myth; they make no bones about admitting that structural anthropology 'demonstrated that there are recurrent themes in myth, not merely in the traditional folklorist sense of textual motifs, but structural messages that may be expressed by varying symbols.'[38] Needless to say, the symbolism of primitive society is by no means the only one to benefit from the novelty and insightfulness of such an approach. When Lévi-Strauss began his work on myth, a certain Christian humanism expressed concern for the allegedly irreducible character of higher meanings. Ethico-religious significance would always remain beyond the clutches of structural analysis and its sacrilegious ironing out of vital meanings. How could the *kerygma* of Christ break up into paltry mythemes? Yet by the time this taboo was being pronounced (by the phenomenologist Paul Ricoeur in a famous roundtable at the progressive Christian journal *Esprit*) Edmund Leach had already started to apply structural interpretation to nothing less than the Bible itself[39]—and not less successfully than Lévi-Strauss.

---

[37] Lévi-Strauss, *Structural Anthropology II*, p. 16.

[38] Maybury-Lewis in Hayes, *Claude Lévi-Strauss*, p. 162.

[39] Paul Ricoeur, 'La structure, le mot, l'événement', *Esprit* (new series), 5, May 1967, pp. 801–21; E. Leach, *Rethinking Anthropology*, London 1961, and *Culture and Communication*, Cambridge 1976.

64

Right at the beginning of his short cogent study of Lévi-Strauss, Leach reminds us that there are basically two kinds of anthropologists. Some, like Frazer (1854–1941) do anthropology in the hope of discovering fundamental truths about humankind. Others, like Malinowski (1884–1942), are ultimately more interested in differences than in similarities between cultures. Now while some oscillation between universalism and relativism is probably endemic to anthropological thought, there is no gainsaying that once functionalism was past its prime, Malinowskian or otherwise, the need was increasingly felt for *a revival of the universalist viewpoint.*

Indeed, burdened with so many monographic descriptions devoid of theoretical moment, the science of humanity verged on dwindling into a mere particularistic knowledge of men and women. The rise of 'cognitive' or interpretive anthropology was an attempt to reverse this process of trivialization by excessive particularism, which the gallant but misguided forays of neo-evolutionism were unable to stop.

French structuralism was but one element in this cognitive reorientation of anthropology. The work of Edmund Leach, Victor Turner and Clifford Geertz also comes readily to mind as a source of different but equally thought-provoking performances in the interpretation of culture. Yet Lévi-Strauss was by far the most responsible for linking the new cognitive focus to a powerful re-statement of the problem of human universals. If I may borrow a few lines from an earlier discussion (inspired by Sperber) of this point: 'we may assert that Lévi-Strauss succeeded in rethinking the problem of anthropology as the study *of man* (and not only of cultures) because he refused to answer an intractable poser: Where are the universals in culture to be located? In the endless cultural variations of common traits or in the common denominators themselves? Pursuing the universal in the variations of cultural traits, one invariably runs the risk of losing sight of universality. On the other hand, sticking to a handful of "common denominators", one gets nothing more than vapid generalities, and, worse still, "fake universals" (Kroeber). The great merit of Lévi-Strauss lies in his understanding that cultural variations are but the raw material of anthropology, its real object being the systematic character underneath *their very variability*. Instead of listing flat, uninteresting common traits, structural anthropology set out to look for the fascinating mechanisms of their transformations. A quest for identity through the discovery of differences—such is the path opened by structuralism.'[40]

Now the main anthropological school associated with the ditching (or trivialization) of human universals had of course been functionalism. Fittingly, Lévi-Strauss's neo-universalism tends to scorn the concept of function. Whilst functionalism liked to equate custom with function, structural anthropology locates function at the most generic level. It acknowledges kinship as a social necessity, since patterns of marriage are vital to the reproduction of society; and it justifies other social taxonomies as a means of fulfilling the need to order the chaos of experience; but it regards each particular form assumed by these norms and devices as something vastly arbitrary—as *unmotivated* as words in relation to their referents. Nevertheless, the concept of function is, in phonology (Lévi-Strauss's methodological model), a fundamental one: in the structural analysis of phonemes, without functions, one gets no structure at all. But the paradox is not so hard to explain: it is all due to the embarassing ghost of functionalism as a target theory in anthropology.[41] Thus structural anthropology descended from structural linguistics, yet rejected the part of its heritage where structure and function went hand in hand.

Durkheim, in his famous *Rules of Sociological Method* (1895), warned that 'to show how a fact is useful is not to explain how it originated or why it is what it is.' Lévi-Strauss is neither keen on origins nor interested in usefulness. Overall, none of the two most scientifically interesting classical concepts of cause—final and efficient—appealed to his mind, ever fond of classification but seldom of causality. When his main rival in contemporary exchange theory, the sociologist George Homans, characterized Lévi-Strauss's thought as a mixture of final-cause and efficient-cause explanations (the chief efficient cause being human intelligence), Rodney Needham showed easily that the founder of structural anthropology actually cared for neither.[42]

In 1945, while he was absorbing the lesson of linguistics,

---

[40] Merquior, *The Veil and the Mask*, p. 51.
[41] G. Mounin, *Introduction à la Sémiologie*, Paris 1970, p. 203.
[42] Needham, *Structure and Sentiment: A Test Case in Social Anthropology*, Chicago 1962, Chapters 1 and 2.

poised to embark on writing the *Elementary Structures of Kinship*, Lévi-Strauss was invited to contribute a chapter on the French sociological school to an American reader on modern social theory.[43] The story he told helps us to understand how he sees his own place in social science. It runs in three stages. Act One: Durkheim clears the way to scientific sociology by getting rid of the historicist speculations of Comte and Spencer. Act Two: Mauss manages to avoid Durkheim's cumbersome 'collective unconscious' by stressing that social forces act as *structures*, as 'total' social facts which are more than visible institutions, because they imprint themselves in the minds of socii as internalized rules (like the 'oughts' in the gift rituals) operating at an unconscious level. Act Three (barely suggested in the 1945 paper): unconscious structure, intuited by Mauss, and subsequently spelt out by both psychoanalysis and modern linguistics, is enthroned as the master concept of social science thanks to the foundation of structural anthropology, a methodological scion of Saussurean phonology. Thus, as the main architect of sociological structuralism, the very completion of the science envisaged by Durkheim, Lévi-Strauss felt entitled to pay homage to the founder of the French sociological school: *Elementary Structures of Kinship* could be read as a rightful echo of Durkheim's *Elementary Forms of Religious Life*. Loyalty lay in advancement through learning the lesson of modern linguistics.

Six years later, with *Elementary Structures* already behind him, Lévi-Strauss wrote that the linguistic model could free social science from its old feelings of inferiority before the science of nature. In a momentous book, *Cybernetics* (1948), Norbert Wiener had denied the social sciences precision and objectivity because social phenomena do not yield statistics extensive enough to allow for mathematical induction and also because in social science the observer is too mixed up with its subject matter. Lévi-Strauss made a point of refuting Wiener on both accounts. He claimed that *language* was so widespread a phenomenon that it doubtless qualified as a sufficiently large stock of data. Besides, the linguist is able to study his subject without any significant interference, because language is struc-

[43] Lévi-Strauss, 'French sociology', in G. Gurvitch and W. Moore, eds., *Sociology in the Twentieth Century*, New York 1945, pp. 503–37.

tured by unconscious rules unaffected by observation.[44]

Any assessment of structural anthropology as *science* is bound to begin and end with a careful examination of this *linguistic premiss*. In the next chapters we shall discuss more than one central instance of the linguistic methodological metaphor in several structuralisms, literary, philosophical or psychoanalytic. Yet in structural anthropology itself linguistics was not intended as a model at a remove, a vague metaphor; rather, structural anthropology conceived of itself as a legitimate *extension* of linguistics—the lawful occupant, as we saw, of all the sundry spheres of social communication beyond the pale of the science of language, as far as the latter's object—*but not its method*—is concerned. Therefore no critical appraisal of sociological structuralism can avoid gauging the validity of a 'linguistics of culture'. Is the purported extension licit or not? If so, the 'structuralist revolution' delivers the goods and brings new, sounder scientific standards to bear on the knowledge of things social. If not, structuralism boils down to an ambitious, yet ultimately misguided, violation of Saussure's own warning (reproduced as an epigraph to our first chapter): if analogies are unwarranted in the study of language, just imagine how misleading they can be when drawn between the facts of language and other, non-linguistic phenomena!

We have seen that the idea of structure is no magic wand: its invocation does not automatically confer validity on hypotheses concerning the working of kinship systems or the correct interpretation of myth symbolism. On the other hand, mistakes or loose ends attendant on such hypotheses do not invalidate the probing value of structural perspectives on materials previously dealt with in more atomistic ways, or even in inadequate structuralist ways (as in the many blunders of the biological approach to society).

In any event, to acknowledge the overall fruitfulness (as opposed to the full validity) of the Lévi-Straussian theories, it is not necessary to invoke the conspicuous and far more problematic structuralisms of Barthes and Lacan, Foucault or Althusser, much indebted as they all are, in different measures, to their anthropological forerunner. Far from it. Arguably, it is in less well-publicised enterprises that we find worthwhile structuralist

---

[44] Lévi-Strauss, *Structural Anthropology*, chapter 3 (originally a 1951 paper).

results. To mention just a few: the work of Louis Dumont on India's caste system (*Homo Hierarchicus*, 1967); the essays of classicists like Jean-Pierre Vernant, Pierre Vidal-Naquet or Marcel Detienne; the renewal of Marxist anthropology with Maurice Godelier; or the free inspiration found in Lévi-Strauss by British anthropologists (Leach and Needham, to be sure, but also the works on ritual and symbolism by Victor Turner and Mary Douglas). While experts continue to disagree a great deal about the merit of each of these contributions, none of them is refused the status of thought-provoking scholarship, truly novel in their respective fields. It is much to be regretted that we cannot, for reasons of space, give a page or two to discussing each of them. But their importance within the humanities and social sciences today does suggest that structural anthropology is not found altogether wanting in intellectual stamina.

A Thermic View of History

So much for structural anthropology, then. Yet Lévi-Strauss is by no means reducible to it. The social scientist, in his case, seldom overshadows the writer and moralist, surely one of the most original of our time. And since our brief survey is not at all confined to the description and assessment of structuralism as science, but also as an ideology, we had better conclude by placing him in the context of modern thought.

The social scientist as sage: this is not at all a role easily accepted by Lévi-Strauss. In 1980, the year Sartre died, he told *Le Nouvel Observateur* that the age of the *maîtres-à-penser* was over. Shortly before the publication of *Structural Anthropology*, he became incensed by the fact that Jean-François Revel included him among philosophers in his sharp debunking pamphlet, *Pourquoi des philosophes?* (1957). He certainly does not see himself as a prophet, a guru, least of all an intellectual leader dabbling in politics, as Sartre, Malraux, Camus or Merleau-Ponty all did in their day. He does not sign manifestoes, only petitions entreating governments to protect threatened tribes. Nevertheless, he is not above commenting on the course of civilization, which he finds appalling, or occasionally even sketching his own Utopia. In *The Scope of Anthropology*, having once more deplored, Rousseau-like, 'the age-old course that forced it to enslave men in order to make progress possible', he went on to dream of a '. . . society (which), placed outside and above history, would once again be able to assume that regular and quasi-crystalline structure which, the best-preserved primitive societies teach us, is not contradictory to humanity. It is in this admittedly Utopian view that social anthropology would find its highest justification, since the forms of life and thought that it studies would no longer be of mere historic and comparative interest. They would correspond to a permanent possibility of man.'

History, says Lévi-Strauss, has given us two basic kinds of culture: 'cold' and 'hot' societies.[45] The former are the few surviving small primitive communities, adept at three forms of self-restraint: they preserve their environment by sticking to a humble standard of living, they manage to keep a very low rate of population growth, and they see to it that power rests on the broadest range of consent. Together, these customs, by reducing tensions to a minimum, maintain such societies at a degree of 'historical temperature' close to zero. 'Hot' societies, by contrast, plunder nature, exploit man and swarm with people. As a result, they normally undergo tensions and conflict—and they *internalize change.*

Lévi-Strauss compares 'cold' societies with mechanical machines, say, clocks. They have a fixed amount of energy and work the same way until friction slowly puts them out of order and in need of re-adjustment. 'Hot' societies, on the other hand, resemble thermodynamic machines, like steam engines. They work a lot more; but they soon run out of energy and must be constantly re-fuelled. Furthermore, just like a thermodynamic apparatus, a hot society draws energy from differences within its own system: it uses gaps in wealth and power to extract as much work as possible. A cold society, it goes without saying, does just the opposite. Cold communities are egalitarian; hot social structures are class societies. Hot cultures, being energy-spending, produce a great deal of social order, but they also suffer a large amount of *entropy.* Cold, energy-saving societies produce little order, yet know little entropy. The

---

[45] Lévi-Strauss, *Structural Anthropology II*, chapter 1, 'The Scope of Anthropology'. See also *The Raw and the Cooked*, pp. 39–45.

former feed on change, the latter resist it: '. . . every human society has a history. . . . But whereas so-called primitive societies are surrounded by the substance of history and try to remain impervious to it, modern societies interiorize history, as it were, and turn it into the motive power of their development.'

In *The Scope of Anthropology*, this *thermic* view of history ends up by unfolding a Utopian landscape at once primitivist and futuristic. On the one hand, Lévi-Strauss credits the industrial revolution with the opening up of a new path to progress. From the neolithic revolution until the rise of the machine, the root dynamic making for progress was social exploitation; now, in the electronic age, it finally becomes possible to glimpse a future where progress will come from new machines without human toil and bondage. Lévi-Strauss nods to Saint-Simon (1760–1825) and his technological paradise, where men rule over things but no longer over their fellow humans. He might well have mentioned Lewis Mumford and all those who, like him, pin their hopes on the replacement of crass industrial palaeo-technics by the cleaner, subtler neo-technics of post-industrialism.

But the point is, he would have us look to both Saint-Simon and Rousseau—the Rousseau of the *Discourse of Inequality*, who blamed progress for entailing misery and oppression. That is why the closing sentences of *The Scope of Anthropology* are full of praise for the primitive as people who 'obstinately resisted history'. If the future beckons us to salvation, it can only be as long as our predatory, exploitative and over-crowded societies will be able to put new technologies at the service of their economic, political and demographic wisdom.

Thus a radiant future is (fleetingly) contemplated—but the march of history, and especially of modern history, is condemned outright. It is not hard to see where the appeal of this vision lies: it is in keeping with the anti-progressivist mood of so many contemporary intellectuals. It encapsulates the current ecological Angst with a fair amount of Malthusian pathos to boot—the same Malthusian stance that filled the visitor to India and Pakistan (as he tells us in *Tristes Tropiques*) with sheer horror and disgust before the endless sprawl of their creeping crowds. And on top of it all, there is the kernel of latter-day humanism: a rhetoric of resolute *anti-anthropocentrism*, sometimes verging on *anthropoclasm*, a general demotion of man from his king-of-

Creation throne, a defence of 'nature rather than culture'. Gone is the day when humanism (as in the Renaissance) extolled the dignity of man, alone of all creatures, as God's image, master of the universe. Far from subscribing to this time-honoured anthropolatry, Lévi-Strauss preaches closeness to nature. In an intriguing allegory towards the end of *Tristes Tropiques* (chapter 37), 'The apotheosis of Augustus', he suggests that divinity is tantamount to a state of full contact with nature—contact, not command. Lévi-Strauss's anti-historicism is a *naturism*.

Naturisms do not necessarily go with naturalism: one can worship nature without regarding the study of man as a natural discipline, and while still claiming that his sui generis status requires a special form of knowledge, different from the objectifying gaze of natural science. But Lévi-Strauss is both a naturist and a naturalist. He loves nature yet refuses to exempt man from the intrinsic naturalism of science, however social. Those who, like Jean-Marie Benoist,[46] choose to interpret the 'structuralist revolution' as a neo-idealism, the baroque substitution of Leibniz for Descartes, cannot help chiding Lévi-Strauss for his 'Spinozianism'. Benoist's argument deserves a hearing. The theory of structure is a hyperhumanism in that it asserts, as we saw, that culture systems are as arbitrary as the sounds of words. Therefore structuralism is as threatened by the ghost of Spinoza as it is by the spectre of Descartes, conjured up by Noam Chomsky, with his stress on innate linguistic competence. The trouble is that Chomsky's competence has nothing to do with the metaphysics of the cogito, for the good reason that the cogito belongs quintessentially to the realm of *consciousness*, not to the unconscious abode of structure. As for Lévi-Strauss's Spinozism, it is real; but this only proves that, at least originally, structuralism—unlike most neo-Marxisms, for instance—did not conceive of itself as a culturalism, but as an unabashed (albeit sophisticated) naturalism.

Naturalism was tinged with the more ideological overtones of anthropoclasm in one of Lévi-Strauss's most provocative moments, the notorious passage on the 'dissolution of man' in *The Savage Mind* (chapter 9). Here it is: '. . . the ultimate goal of the human sciences (is) not to constitute, but to dissolve man.

[46] Benoist, *La Révolution Structurale*, pp. 104–07.

The preeminent nature of anthropology is that it represents the first step in a procedure that involves others. Ethnographic analysis tries to arrive at invariants beyond the empirical diversity of human societies . . . However, it would not be enough to reabsorb particular humanities into a general one. This first enterprise opens the way for others . . . that are incumbent upon the exact natural sciences: the reintegration of culture in nature and finally of life within the whole of its physico-chemical conditions.'

How very shocking to standard humanists, wholeheartedly sympathetic as they are to the anti-Promethean outlook of the anthropological moralist! Here is an anti-progressivist who does not pour contempt on science. Worse: adding insult to injury, he commits *human* science to the base naturalism of scientific reason! However, this is just one among several paradoxes in the 'countercultural' message of Lévi-Strauss.

Take, for instance, his views on power. First, the power *of society*. Few successors of Rousseau have done better in the indictment of civilization as an oppressive fate. Every reader of *Tristes Tropiques* must be impressed by the story of the Nambikwara chief who tried to have Lévi-Strauss teach him how to write so as to enhance his own rule over the other Indians. Still more striking, though, is what Lévi-Strauss inferred from such episodes: '. . . one must admit that the primary function of written communication is to facilitate subjugation. The use of writing for disinterested purposes, for intellectual or aesthetic gratification, is a secondary consequence, and even this very often serves to reinforce, justify, and conceal the other uses of writing.'

The least one can say is that this is an exceedingly one-sided account of the historical role of writing. Why decide a priori that the invaluable boost given by writing to knowledge is of less importance? Or again, why ignore the effect of literacy on the self-assertion of hundreds of thousands of underprivileged people throughout modern history? A powerful rhetoric, using the glamour of ethnographic exotica, beclouds these issues— and explains them away in a mist of countercultural prejudices.

Let us now turn to power-holders as such. Again, the Nambikwara provide the ground for the anthropology-as-anarchism theme. Although Lévi-Strauss is the first to say that he only stayed a short while in their midst, when their tribe was dwindling into near extinction owing to the spread of Western diseases, so that their customs were no longer genuine and traditional, he does not refrain from contending (as he had done in his first book, a monograph on the Nambikwara) that among those Indians, rulership is just a social service based wholly on consent—actually, leadership required in times of food collecting. As soon as the leader loses the trust of the tribe, its members simply quit, ready to join other groups in the jungle. Faced with widespread exodus (or exit, as Albert Hirschman would say) the chief surrenders power or re-adjusts it to real social needs. Had he lived to read *Tristes Tropiques*, Kropotkin would have been overjoyed: what a perfect illustration of cooperative anarchy!

One should expect anarchism to kindle democratic feelings. But no: Lévi-Strauss is not keen on democratic politics. Significantly, his fondness for Rousseau does not extend to the *Social Contract*. He shares with Jean-Jacques the distrust of progress, the love of nature and the craving for solitude and independence—but not the politics of modern individualism expressed in that great gospel of republican democracy. In his early seventies, Lévi-Strauss even confessed to being closer to Chateaubriand than to Rousseau, whose politics smack too much of the *esprit de système* (a typical conservative criticism, echoing Tocqueville and Taine).[47] The implication is obvious: between the two stands the revolutionary impact of the republican ideal that Rousseau helped so much to forge and Chateaubriand strove so hard to contain.

Short of a democratic commitment, is he at least a liberal? Nobody would ever accuse him of writing anything against the idea of liberty. Still, to judge from his latest pieces, he displays a highly conservative view of civil freedoms. In 1976 Lévi-Strauss was requested by the chairman of the French National Assembly, Edgar Faure, to speak his mind before a committee for freedoms. The development of his ideas on this subject became the last chapter of *The View From Afar*. He draws on Montesquieu and Renan to stress that freedom is a context-bound concept, modern liberty in the Anglo-Saxon sense being the fruit of a long, highly peculiar historical experience. Two cheers for

[47] Interview in *Le Nouvel Observateur*, 28 June 1980; interview in *Encounter*, July 1979.

historism—a traditional weapon of conservative thought.

Lévi-Strauss goes as far as to say that the votaries of a totalitarian ideology can feel free enough as they obey the harsh laws of their countries. Above all, he warns against making liberty a fake absolute. Quoting Sir Henry Maine's strictures on 'juridical superstitions' as the fetishism of human rights, he claims that a rationalist, universalist definition of freedom clashes with social pluralism. One right alone commands true universality: not the freedom of man 'as a moral being', but his freedom 'as a *living* being'. It follows that the sole human right finishes where the right to live of other species begins. We started with Rousseau and anarchism, we end up in the spirit of Burke. Beneath the passionate plea of the conservationist there speaks the voice of a conservative.

One might say that such is the second paradox in Lévi-Strauss the thinker: to the anti-progressivist devotee of science add the conservative anarchist. A third paradox would be that the same man who lashes out at modern, Western civilization as a 'monstrous cataclysm' theatening to engulf the whole planet is not—against all normal expectations—a fan of the Orient. Although he eulogizes Buddhism, he is appalled, as we saw, by the swollen demography of India. As for Islam, it is just 'the West of the East' (*Tristes Tropiques*, chapter 40). Countercultural intellectuals traditionally respond with far more sympathy to the charms of Brahma and/or the Word of the Prophet.

Lévi-Strauss on Art and Music

A fourth and final paradox refers to *art*. Quite often, pundits of anti-modernity are in favour of modern art—an ideological instance fraught with unmistakably 'countercultural' motives. Not so Lévi-Strauss. But before casting a glance at his animadversions on modern art, let us look, if only for an instant, at his general views on art.

The penultimate section of chapter 1 in *The Savage Mind* constitutes a kind of *parva aesthetica*—and a very pithy one to boot. For Lévi-Strauss, art comes midway between science and myth. Mythical thought, working with signs, aims at the elaboration of structures out of the debris of events. Science, on the contrary, employs intellectual structures as a tool for the mak-

pithy i boot

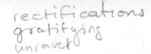

ing of events. Whereas myth performs a constant protest against meaninglessness, feeding always on the Utopian dream of escaping history, science, which is bound to operate through endless rectifications, aspires to knowledge, not meaning.

Like the mythmaker, the artist is a *bricoleur*, a craftsman creating structures out of three kinds of contingency: that of his material; that of his model; and that of the future use of his work. But unlike the mythmaker, and similarly to the scientist, the artist produces an object functioning as *knowledge*.

In *Entretiens avec Georges Charbonnier* Lévi-Strauss underlined the cognitive function of art. Far from merely gratifying the senses, art, thanks to its ability to unravel objective structures that are not immediately offered to our perception, is also 'a guide, a means of instruction and, I dare say, almost of learning the environment'.

There is nevertheless an important difference between scientific and aesthetic knowledge. The artistic object partakes very often of the nature of a miniature: it is a *modèle réduit*. This is nowhere more conspicuous than in the field of plastic art, where each art must of necessity, for the sake of representation, give up at least some dimensions of the model (thus painting dispenses with volume, and both painting and sculpture ignore the temporal dimension of their subjects).

In *The Savage Mind*, Lévi-Strauss replaced this emphasis on aesthetic cognition by a somewhat more balanced picture. He came to think of art as a form of knowing through signs instead of concepts. In a truly structural way, art is not defined per se; rather, it is defined by its 'insertion' into a set of resemblances and oppositions, formed by the partly common, partly mutually exclusive properties of several human practices, such as myth and science. Thus science produces knowledge by means of concepts: myth produces meaning (although, as we saw, also some knowledge) by means of signs; and finally, art produces a mix of meaning and knowledge by means of signs.[48]

Mark that meaning, in the Lévi-Straussian world, is doomed to be forever incommensurable with knowledge. The locus classicus of structural anthropology remains in this connection his introduction to Mauss, where Lévi-Strauss postulates the

[48] The last four—and next five—paragraphs rely heavily on J. G. Merquior, *L'Esthétique de Lévi-Strauss*, Paris 1977, pp. 130–36.

existence of a 'floating signifier': 'Since his origins man possesses an integral stock of signifiers that he is at a loss to allocate to a signified which is given as such without however being known.'[49]

To elaborate: language, hence meaning, cannot have appeared, in human evolution, otherwise than suddenly. All of a sudden, mankind has passed from a stage where nothing signified to another where everything has a sense. Still, this dawn of the meaningful did not, of course, warrant any further *knowledge* of the components of the universe. Meaningfulness was a sudden fiat (however lengthy its incubation); knowledge, an infinite step-by-step progress. The order of meaning has been since its very inception the realm of discontinuity; the order of knowing is by definition—pace Thomas Kuhn—ruled by continuity.

Therefore, in our attempt to understand the world, we always dispose of a 'surplus of meaning' periodically re-allotted by the mythopoetical imagination, so that the wholeness of meaning becomes precisely the main task of religion, myth and art.

As one of the main bridges to the wholeness of meaning, art operates imaginary syntheses, mediations of the deficiencies in our (that is, human) symbolic system. But when Lévi-Strauss, long before *La Pensée Sauvage*, set out to analyse concrete works of art, discussing the principle of 'split representation' in human and animal figures—a bold comparative study in primitive and archaic art, ranging from Guaycuru facial painting and his beloved Northwest Coast Indian masks to Maori and ancient Chinese cultures—he pointed out some very interesting instances of mediation between the symbolic *and the social*.[50]

In the short chapter on Caduveo tattoos in *Tristes Tropiques*, these intimations of social content lurking behind symbolic syntheses finally developed into an illuminating, if too brief, elaboration. The disruptive effects of the Caduveo caste system, untempered by any moiety system similar to those adopted by their neighbours, found an 'imaginary solution' on the aesthetic plane: '. . . the gratuitous complication of Caduveo art may well be a phantasm created by a society whose object was to give symbolic form to the institutions which it might have had in

---

[49] Lévi-Strauss in Mauss, *Sociologie et Anthropologie*, p. XLIX.
[50] Lévi-Strauss, *Structural Anthropology*, chapter 13.

reality, had interest and superstitution not stood in the way. Great indeed is the fascination of this culture, whose dream life was pictured on the faces of its queens, as if, in making themselves up, they figured a Golden Age that they would never know in reality.'

It is as though the Caduveo, deprived of a mediation between their caste system triad and what should mitigate it—the binary moiety partition—had decided to *dream* the missing synthesis, turning its graphic form into the axis of their facial ornamentation. Thus split representation, which acted among the Guaycuru as an *instrument* of culture, aimed at reinforcing the sense of persona and the awareness of status, became in *Tristes Tropiques* not so much the emblem of institutional social structure as its faithful *negative*. From a symbol of conscious social order, art turned into the embodiment of society's own repressed fantasies.

In this perspective (merely adumbrated in a non-scientific book, and somehow repressed in *The Savage Mind*'s *parva aesthetica*) 'meaning' tends to prevail over 'knowledge'. At the same time, however, it acquires a cathartic flavour, a Freudian depth, largely surpassing the rather limited scope of conscious cognition through artistic objects.

What happens to the meaning/knowledge balance when it comes to *historical* art? In Lévi-Strauss's informal aesthetics,[51] the trouble begins with *early* modern art, that is to say, the art tradition evolved since the Renaissance. Unlike primitive art, which was deeply collective, the artworld of the modern put a premium on individual style and elite connoisseurship. It was also geared from the outset to *representational* forms and self-conscious technique—a kind of academicism. Its deadly sin is figurativism à outrance, something that Lévi-Strauss regards as the result of 'a loss or weakening of the signifying function of the work of art'. Again, it is a matter of balancing meaning and knowledge—but this time, art exhausts meaning by virtue of too strong a commitment to representation.

However, it would be wrong to think that Lévi-Strauss is disparaging the referent, the mimetic pole, of the work of art. On the contrary, he makes a point of stressing that primitive art avoids hyperfigurativism not because it is objectless, but rather

[51] G. Charbonnier, *Conversations with Claude Lévi-Strauss*, London 1969.

because of a *surplus* of object—an awesome respect before being, before the holiness of the world. Post-medieval art, by contrast, bristles with possessiveness towards reality; and, in its figurative rage, ends by seriously harming the potential structural strength of artworks.

The same lack of structural virtue prevails in arts other than the visual ones. In verbal art, as we pass from myth to fable[52] and from fable to literature, narrative undergoes 'a degradation of structure into seriality'. This sentence appears in a section of *Mythologiques III* entitled 'From myth to novel' ending with a wistful page on the decline of plot in modern fiction. Lévi-Strauss entrusts the novel of Proustian ancestry with the noble task of desperately pursuing structure through the shambles of symbolic experiences. Through memories and dreams the novelist builds a narrative whose chief function, as an art form, is to forestall the vanishing of order and meaning from both life and literature.

We seem to be dealing with two ideas. Sometimes, meaning is equated with structure and opposed to figurativeness. In his brilliant book on Indian masks of Northwest America, *The Way of the Masks* (1975), Lévi-Strauss warns that 'a mask is chiefly not what it represents but what it transforms, that is, what it chooses *not* to represent.' When he turns to western art, he occasionally uses a similar argument, at least in the already mentioned *Conversations with Georges Charbonnier* (1961), a broadcast series that contains much of his informal aesthetics (alongside interesting elaborations on the theme of the cold/hot society). Thus the merit he sees in Cubism is that by breaking with centuries of figurativism, it tried to rescue the lost significance of structure.

But more often than not what worries Lévi-Strauss is not representation as such, but that its perversion as figurativeness is in league with a wilful appropriation of nature—the hubris of 'hot' societies. The world shrinks under humanity's continuous assault upon its physical environment. Impressionist painting, for example, is often praised for its ability to conquer new domains—like suburban settings and scenes of daily life—until then largely neglected by the fine arts tradition. Lévi-Strauss does not reject this valuation, which incidentally chimes

---

[52] Cf. Lévi-Strauss, *Structural Anthropology II*, chapter 8.

with his own praise of Cubism for turning to an artifical world of cultural objects in the fact of a shrinking nature. But he attaches far more importance to another consideration. The decisive factor in Impressionist landscape, he told Charbonnier, was that the noble and serene Arcadian countryside that inspired Poussin had become less and less accessible or significant to the average human experience in the course of the nineteenth century. In a similar vein, he treasures the now forgotten views of French seaports by the eighteenth-century painter Joseph Vernet because in them one can sense a human settlement still in harmony with, rather than encroaching upon, a natural environment.

What about the other great art form—music? Lévi-Strauss has crowned Wagner 'the father of structural myth analysis'. His *Mythologiques* are a *Ring*-like tetralogy whose 'Overture' and 'Finale' (his own titles) contain extensive and highly suggestive reflections on music and its experience. In the early seventies he wrote an essay on *Parsifal* at the behest of the Bayreuth festival (and did not miss the opportunity to show that the Grail myth can be construed as an inversion of the Oedipus story).

From the Lévi-Straussian standpoint, while literature lives under a permanent threat of destructuration, music is by its very nature endowed with hyperstructural powers. Among the four main objects of structural analysis—mathematical entities, natural languages, musical works and myths—music occupies, beside myth, a curious midway position. Mathematical entities are wholly disincarnate structures; language facts exist only when fully embodied as sound and sense. Between these two extremes come myth and music—but from opposite sides. For whereas myth is structure adhering to sense, and stripped of sound, music is structure stripped of sense, thoroughly grounded in sound.

Let us recapitulate our little structuralist exercise. Disembodied mathematics, which moreover are pure forms with no substantive meaning attached to them, are structures neither 'somatic' nor 'semantic'. By contrast, language, fully embodied in both sound and sense, is a structure at once somatic and semantic. Between them lie myth—a purely semantic structure—and music: a strictly 'somatic' structure. Therefore, myth and music oppose each other because they occupy antithetical positions in the middle ground between total disembodiment (mathematics) and total embodiment (language). Yet, from another viewpoint, semantic myth and somatic music do converge. For, as it happens, the listener of both myths and musical pieces becomes a sort of *signified* for the mythical or musical signifier he listens to. Is it not true that whatever meaning we discover in a mythical or a musical message seems to lie in an uncanny silent dialogue between our personal experience and the sequences—the temporal structures— of either the mythical tale or the musical piece told or performed?

The Overture of *The Raw and the Cooked* includes a fine description of this subtle interplay between two sources of our response to music: on the one hand, the personal, bodily rhythms of breathing; on the other hand, the expectations we normally develop (when listening to music) out of our cultural background, or (to be more specific) out of our immersion in a given musical culture: 'Musical emotion springs precisely from the fact that at each moment the composer withholds or adds more than the listener anticipates on the basis of a pattern that he thinks he can guess, but that he is incapable of wholly divining because of his subjection to a dual periodicity: that of his respiratory system, which is determined by his individual nature, and that of the scale, which is determined by his training. If the composer withholds more than we anticipate, we experience a delicious falling sensation; we feel we have been torn from a stable point on the musical ladder and thrust into the void, but only because the support that is waiting for us was not in the expected place. When the composer withholds less, the opposite occurs: he forces us to perform gymnastic exercises more skilful than our own. Sometimes he moves us, sometimes he forces us to make the movement ourselves, but it always exceeds what we would have thought ourselves capable of achieving alone. Aesthetic enjoyment is made up of this multiplicity of excitements and moments of respite, of expectations disappointed or fulfilled beyond anticipation.'[53]

In his book *The Sense of Order* (1979), a treatise on the psychology of non-representational art, Sir Ernst Gombrich rightfully compares this passage with the descriptions given by composers, like Paul Hindemith (1895–1963), of the experience

[53] Lévi-Strauss, *The Raw and the Cooked*, p. 17.

of 'following' music.[54] Hindemith also emphasises the joint work of brain and breath, mental guess and heartbeat, in our enjoyment of music. Paul Valéry, in his beautiful dialogue on music, *Eupalinos*, had already called musical experience 'a changing plenitude', flame-like, brightening and warming up our being by 'a ceaseless burning of memories, forebodings, regrets and omens, as well as of endless emotions without cause . . .' 'Dances without dancers, statues with neither face nor body, yet outlined with the utmost delicacy'—all this surrounds and seduces (says Valéry) as soon as we become a prey to the bewitching 'general presence of Music'.

Susanne Langer made contemporary aesthetics familiar with the notion that music is our myth of the inner life. While Lévi-Strauss's analysis certainly lends new weight to such a view, it also draws attention to the mingling of intellectual and bodily activities—delectable activities—involved in it. The Finale of the *Mythologiques* points out that in following the sinuous flow of first rate music we are often gently led from anguish to bliss, through many hopes and disappointments, expectations and achievements. Experiencing music provides, in this sense, a kind of miniature of life itself—and in this fashion, music, too, belongs to that principle of *reduction* we saw at work in other arts. The point is, however, that this psychological journey from stress to joy thrives on an exquisite link between the most intellectual of senses—hearing—and the obscurest hidden accents of organic life—our very visceral, cardiac and respiratory rhythms. As Lévi-Strauss puts it in his Finale: the gift of music is a truly 'sensuous metamorphosis of the understanding'.

Dr Johnson famously called music 'the only sensual pleasure without vice'. Maybe so: but Lévi-Strauss made a point of adding at least some sex to it. In the Finale, noticing that music, like myth, 'invites the listener to a concrete union', in which it is the listener who confers meaning on the sounds or on the parts of a tale, he states that music induces 'an intellectual and affective mating between listener and composer. Neither is more important than the other, for each holds one of the two "sexes" of music, whose performance allows and celebrates the carnal union.'[55] Thus *melos* marries *eros*—music is an

[54] E. H. Gombrich, *The Sense of Order*, Oxford 1979, pp. 303–05.
[55] Lévi-Strauss, *L'Homme Nu*, Paris 1971, p. 585.

eroticism of the mind.

However, the wonderful exploits of *melos* turned into *eros* could never come about without hyperdialectic, all-mediating structure. Music employs in its performances both a natural and a cultural grid. It makes itself 'nature' by addressing our inner sense of time. Yet it is also an eminently 'cultural' phenomenon, since it works with scales of sounds whose number and whose intervals vary widely from one society to another.

Now music strengthens and enhances both these grids. It reinforces the natural pole by appealing to the 'visceral', bodily rhythms; and it plays also with a strengthened cultural grid, because the sounds which compose the scales are already cultural data, quite distinct, as such, from noises, the only genuinely natural sounds.

Music, therefore, may be reckoned a super bridge between nature and culture. No wonder Lévi-Strauss the aesthetician is so keen on 'chromatic' minds like Rousseau and Wagner—a musicologist and a musician literally obsessed by the painfulness of the necessary interval severing culture from nature.

In the Finale of *Mythologiques*, the theme of the affinities between myth and music, introduced by the Overture, is given a curious diachronic twist. With a near-Hegelian move, Lévi-Strauss contends that the fugue-like structure of myth, appropriated by Western polyphony just when, in the age of Galileo and Newton, 'the forms of mythical thought loosened their control for the benefit of newly-born science', is now about to be inherited by . . . structural myth analysis itself! From mythos to melos, and from melos to logos: 'The orders of culture replace on another and, just before its vanishing, each of them hands over to the next one what was its essence and its function.' Thus, with the exhaustion of tonal music, *structura structurans* takes refuge in anthropological semiotics.

We can see that Wagner is indeed the father of structuralism—in a strictly 'genealogical' sense! There is a confession by Wagner that used to haunt Baudelaire: 'I left once and for all the field of history and settle in that of legend.' It seems to have lingered also in Lévi-Strauss's mind. Not only does he view the Master of Bayreuth as the father of structural mythography but he pronounces him to be a composer of 'myth' par excellence, as compared with Bach, a 'code' composer, or Beethoven, a 'message' composer (at this point, I am reminded of Thomas

Mann's saying that in Wagner, what is literary is *the music*).

An Attack on Modernism

Nietzsche claimed that ancient tragedy was born 'out of the spirit of music'. To Lévi-Strauss, it is the very science of man—insofar as it espouses the savage mind's 'logic of the concrete'—that is a last efflorescence of the spirit of music, itself an heir to the highly structured world of mythical thought. All this, for all its resemblance to the art/religion/philosophy sequence in Hegel's system, is made easier by the fact that Lévi-Strauss holds modern music in cordial detestation.

After Wagner, he likes Debussy and Ravel (and goes so far as to analyse the famous *Boléro* in *Mythologiques IV*); pays a passing reference to Stravinsky—but that is all. Serial composers are compared to the 'rhapsodic' structure of the novel, but the latter is itself a degradation, as we know, of myth and fable. Post-Stravinskyan music concentrates too much on the reinforcement of the cultural grid; in consequence it foregoes the no less vital part of our bodily rhythms. Since Schoenberg, music overlooks the 'natural anchor' of its own charm and glory: by being literally too artificial, it destroys that subtle interplay between nature and culture, body and intellect, where lay the strength and delight of tonal music.

Modern literature fares no better. *L'Homme Nu* (*Mythologiques IV*) sneers at 'the unbearable boredom' of contemporary texts (maybe Lévi-Strauss was thinking of most *nouveau romans*). And the same antipathy is expressed, this time at length, towards modern painting. First, in the early sixties, in the *Conversations with Charbonnier*, and again towards the end of chapter 1 of *The Savage Mind*; then, in later pieces, especially in *Structural Anthropology II* (chapter 15, sections 3 and 4) and its sequel, *The View From Afar*. The latter book includes (chapter 19), disguised as a *pièce de circonstance* (the foreword for a watercolour album by the German painter Anita Albus), Lévi-Strauss's shrewdest and least casual remarks on the evolution of painting since the Impressionists.

To tell the truth, the situation he describes harks back even earlier than that—to the Renaissance itself. Resuming his critical analysis of post-medieval art, Lévi-Strauss quotes approvingly a dictum of Alois Riegl (1858–1905), one of the great pioneers of art history, according to which the golden age of plastic art was over after the beginning of modern times. A few pages later he lays the blame on Leonardo da Vinci. Leonardo's decision to commit painting's faithfulness to nature to *sfumato* and *chiaroscuro*, instead of upholding the neatness of outlines, is said to have been a fateful move. This is harsh on the finest mind of the High Renaissance—but it makes a lot of sense when Lévi-Strauss's reasoning is considered in its entirety.

What he means is that painting went wrong by taking either of two paths: the first amounted to remaining *on the hither side of nature*; the second, to trying to go *beyond nature*. The this-side-of-nature error was inaugurated when Impressionism substituted its subjective approach for the objectivity of traditional painting. Where the older painters had shown deference to the boundless wealth of the world, the Impressionists yielded to the self-indulgence of sensation, neglecting a whole universe of objective details: 'In one case, one sticks to the changing appearances of the self-same things; in the other case, to the objective reality of different things.'[56]

Before Lévi-Strauss, more than one outstanding pen had questioned the stylistic ancestry of impressionism—but without putting the blame on the Renaissance. Thus Burckhardt, the first great interpreter of Renaissance art, despised in Rembrandt a plebeian, Protestant art of subjective impression, working—unlike the Catholic painting of Rubens—by dint of light at the expense of objects; and by the same token he also disapproved of the main course of French painting after the last Rubéniste, Delacroix.

As impressionism declined, the victim of a double loss—of object and of structure—Cubism attempted to redress the balance. Unfortunately, however, it went too far in the opposite direction. Its aim was to bypass nature; the nemesis of such a sin was a quick fall into mere decorative values. Lévi-Strauss became increasingly derogatory about Cubism. We saw how, in his talks with Charbonnier, he at least justified Cubism historically, by pointing out that Picasso and his friends turned their backs on nature simply because the latter was no longer 'there': in the average social consciousness, it had vanished still

[56] Lévi-Strauss, *Le Regard Éloigné*, Paris 1985, p. 334.

further since the days when the impressionists could no longer enjoy the landscapes that Poussin did enjoy. By the mid-sixties, however, Lévi-Strauss confessed to bearing a grudge against Cubism because the art of Picasso, which promised so much in the 1920s, seemed nothing more than a period piece by then.[57]

Impressionism harmed painting by trying to stand on this side of nature; Cubism did equal damage by trying to go beyond it. Today, their symmetrical mistakes are repeated with a vengeance. Abstract expressionism, the dominant pictorial trend between the war and the sixties, trod the same subjective path as Impressionism, only replacing the quivers of visual sensation by the thrills of personal emotion. Then, reacting against the insubstantiality of these lyrical abstractions, there came Pop art and 'hyper-realism', the painting fashions during the prime of structuralism. And what did they do? They exchanged the still 'poetic' objects of Cubist canvasses for the waste of industrial culture, to no avail (or so Lévi-Strauss believes) in terms of wealth of meaning and vigour of structure. Thus each misleading solution—this side of nature, beyond nature—ended in its own stale caricature. For a century now, painting has been weakened over and again, because over and again it has missed its proper object.

The overall outcome of the two blind-alleys was a general *decline in craftsmanship*. Without all the artistry linked to their former love for the natural world, the visual arts will go on starving, deprived of genuine aesthetic vitamins and devoid of any permanent value. Picasso becomes a period piece; Mantegna doesn't. The road to regeneration, claims Lévi-Strauss, lies wide open before us. It consists in the laborious, painful reinvention of many lost skills. Art must recover the wisdom of the craftsmanship behind medieval illuminations, the Italian primitives, the Flemish masters, the Japanese printers, the 'Gothic' Ingres and the surrealist Max Ernst, for whom abstract art is but an escapist device of modern alienation. Such are the models invoked by the anthropologist turned critic.

A short text in *Structural Anthropology II*, occasioned by the big Picasso retrospective of 1966 (a masterpiece of Malrauxian showing-off), puts a finger on the wound: what ails modernist art, says Lévi-Strauss, is its 'profoundly rhetorical character'.

[57] See Lévi-Strauss, *Structural Anthropology II*, chapter 15, p. 3.

Ironically, if we remember its anti-academic origins, modern art seems bent on, indeed almost obsessed with, applying recipes. Picasso was a rhetorician with a paintbrush. In any case, when it came to criticizing him, Lévi-Strauss was not alone. If I remember well, Giulio Carlo Argan in Rome, Roger Caillois in Paris, John Berger in London were not exactly kind to the grand old man of modern art. There was at the time more than one harbinger of the present dissatisfaction—not widespread, to be sure, but increasingly articulate—with the 'tyranny of imagination' and all the modernist prejudices we flatter ourselves to call open-mindedness.[58]

While modern art is profoundly rhetorical, true art, says Lévi-Strauss, is the realm of the *unpredictable*—hence something by definition out of the reach of any rhetorical premeditation.[59] And because it is so ingrained a rhetoric of creation, modern art is just the empty '*form* of an art, capable only of procuring the illusion that there is still one.'

But *why* is it so? Why is it that modern art stumbles from style into style, 'experiment' into 'experiment', almost never attaining the rich meaningfulness and the lasting power of its predecessors? Lévi-Strauss's answer to this riddle was given when the journal *Arts*, in 1965, asked him to foretell what art would be like twenty years hence. The art of the past, he writes, fed on that delicate balance between man and nature that concerns him so much. Moreover, it tended to express, in a wholly natural way, many pervasive collective beliefs. Old civilizations were, in this sense, 'carnal' cultures, thriving on these two crucial elements: balance and belief. With modern

[58] For the general issue of subjectivism in modern 'experimental' art—the 'tyranny of imagination' problem—see Merquior, *As Idéias e as Formas*, Rio de Janeiro 1981, pp. 107–17. The feelings of the best European art criticism towards Picasso in the mid- and late 1960s can be gauged by Argan's dictum 'il suo è stato il coraggio dei gesti e non delle scelte'. G. C. Argan, *Salvezza e Caduta Nell 'Arte Moderna*, Milano 1960, p. 24.

[59] Jon Elster, *Sour Grapes: Studies in the Subversion of Rationality*, Cambridge 1983, p. 77–85), discussing choice and intention in art, also stresses that bravura—the concern with 'making an impression'—can be self-defeating, especially if (as is the case in conceptual art) no room is left for the assessment of degrees of achievement. The notion of a 'better than', claims Elster, is crucial for artistic intention and aesthetic judgement—and this is what lenient views of conceptual art and minimal art, like Richard Wollheim's (*On Art and the Mind*, London 1973) tend to overlook.

civilization, a sea-change came about: '. . . we know since Descartes that the originality (of our civilization) consists essentially in a method whose intellectual nature makes it improper to breed other civilizations of flesh and blood, but which can impose its formula on them and compel them to become similar to it.'[60]

Modern civilization cannot beget carnal cultures, and therefore does not know how to generate a proper art. Its nature is virus-like: it represents a form of life that needs other living beings in order to survive. A viral organism injects its formula into other beings, forcing their cells to betray their own genetic code and obey that of the invading virus. In a word: modern civilization is a parasite, living off the body of previous, richer cultures. It is not even a vampire, for vampires drink blood, and blood is organic. The parasitism of modern history is something less fiendish and yet more heinous in its sheer destructiveness. Here, at the bottom of a powerful unconventional diagnosis of the predicament of modern art, we find a familiar face: the face of Claude Lévi-Strauss, an enemy of our time.

We shall presently conclude our discussion of his ideas by delving into this principled revulsion against modernity. But it should be emphasized that his criticism of *modernism* in art does *not* stand or fall with his critique of *modernity*. It can and must be judged in its own right. I have expatiated on Lévi-Strauss's aesthetics (and implied art history) because—besides being less well-known a province of his more philosophical work—it has the obvious advantage of at least addressing problems—such as the state and prospects of avant-garde art— that are evaded by most (though by no means all) aesthetic discourses in the tradition of analytical philosophy. A reflection which, for all its idiosyncrasies, short-cuts and omissions, bluntly pushes aside the cant of modernism to raise crucial questions about the role and value of contemporary art deserves a good hearing.[61] The late Harold Rosenberg, who baptized action

[60] Lévi-Strauss, *Structural Anthropology II*, pp. 282–83. Translation modified.

[61] For a critique of avant-garde ideology which owes a great deal to Lévi-Strauss's strictures, see Jean Clair, *Considérations sur l'Etat des Beaux-Arts: Critique de la Modernité*, Paris 1983. Lévi-Strauss's remarks on the 'lost craft' of painting aroused an interesting polemic in *Le Débat*, 10, March 1981; 14, July–August 1981 and 15, Sept.–October 1981. The painter Soulages, the critic Pierre Daix, the political philosopher Jacques Ellul and the art historians Pierre Vaisse

88

painting and blessed the 'aesthetics of impermanence' wrote of minimal art: 'the less there is to see, the more there is to say'. Should we not try and do more than echo the usual avant-gardese about the end of a whole visual world, the skills that made it and the trained sensibility that responded to it? The modernist establishment shouts 'Philistine and reactionary!' at any such question. We should be grateful to Lévi-Strauss for his courage in re-opening the debate. Maybe today the truest lovers of art are, like him, 'philistines'.

The Archaeology of Space

'I view myself', says Lévi-Strauss in *Tristes Tropiques*, as 'a traveller, an archaeologist of space, trying in vain to restore the exotic with the help of fragments and debris.' In vain indeed: for who could hold the sea of history with their bare hands? As for the 'fragments and debris', they are a staple article in Lévi-Straussian imagery, belonging as they do to the world of *bricolage*, one of the main themes of *The Savage Mind* (chapter 1). The bricoleur is a handyman, pottering about from one odd job to another with the self-same 'tools', quite often made up of bits and remnants of what once were proper instruments. Unlike the engineer, the bricoleur always *adapts* to each new job and situation, drawing upon his or her own resources, trying to cope with just *les moyens du bord*. By this quiet tenacity, the brico-leur strives to elicit order from ruins, saying no to the ever-scattering action of time. Mythical thought is an 'intellectual bricolage', since its repertoire and 'language' are, like the bricoleur's, both limited and heterogeneous. But anthropo-logists are still another sort of bricoleur, because their passion is to rescue, intellectually if not physically, whatever fragments of doomed societies they can manage, and restore them to some order and meaningfulness.

One wonders whether the vogue enjoyed by the Lévi-Strauss-ian paean to bricolage (a pet subject among reviewers of *The*

and Bruno Foucart took part in it. Vaisse's article (*Débat*, 10) is a penetrating critical demolition of the Manichaean avant-garde concepts of 'academic', 'official' or 'bourgeois' art, as derogatory labels applied to almost everything outside the 'tradition of the new' since Impressionism.

Savage Mind) was not suited to the traditional French love for individualist crafts as opposed to the impersonal technologies of the industrial age. In any event, as the philosophy of bricolage became fashionable, the Fifth Republic mustered its economic forces and engineering capabilities to land France once and for all in full industrialism. Perhaps anthropological ideology was the swan song of *vieille France*, or even a help in easing the transition to modernity that began in earnest soon after the Liberation. Still, one thing is certain: in Lévi-Strauss's work, the bricolage motif went hand in hand with a gut feeling of *revulsion against history*.

Lévi-Strauss's remarks on history fall into two categories: epistemological and substantive. Let us start by briefly recalling his strictures on history *as knowledge*. To begin with, he questions the wisdom of taking an historicizing approach as the starting point of social science. As he writes in *The Scope of Anthropology*: 'In all forms of human thought and activity, one cannot ask questions regarding nature or origin before having identified and analysed phenomena and discovered to what extent their interrelations suffice to explain them. It is impossible to discuss an object, to reconstruct the process of its coming into being without knowing first what it is; in other words, without having exhausted the inventory of its internal determinants.'

As that no-nonsense Victorian, Leslie Stephen, used to say, you can admire a girl without having to find out first whether or not she got her looks from her grandmother. Or, in the classical functionalist analogy: just as, in order to grasp the anatomy and physiology of a horse, one does not need to know anything about its ancestry, one can understand the structure of a society and the working of its institutions without knowing its history. Ergo, synchronic description takes precedence over diachronic enquiries.

Precedence, however, does not mean exclusion. And in this functionalist oracle, little store is set by the fact that, in Evans-Pritchard's pithy comment, with remarkable constancy, horses tend to remain horses throughout the ages, whereas societies do tend to change in a deep, often radical way.[62]

---

[62] E. E. Evans-Pritchard, 'Anthropology and History', in *Essays in Social Anthropology*, London 1962.

It is only fair to note that structuralism took pains to approach this thorny question on a far more sophisticated basis, trying to avoid the functionalist tone of benign neglect whenever it came to history. In principle, Lévi-Strauss grants that the synchronic and diachronic viewpoints are in fact complementary, 'since the historian strives to reconstruct the picture of vanished societies as they were . . ., while the ethnographer does his best to reconstruct the historical stages that temporally preceded their existing form.'[63] But in reality he has never brought structural analysis to bear on diachronic phenomena. And of course dealing with pre-historic material, that is, more or less undocumented by recorded history, has always been an excellent alibi for those who choose to ignore history. In Sir Edmund Leach's perceptive remark, ultimately all historical knowledge is to Lévi-Strauss vitiated by its present-mindedness. Time remembered is time recovered in the interests of the present, as suggested by the Proustian title of *The Savage Mind*'s last chapter: *Le Temps retrouvé*.

In 'History and Anthropology', a 1949 essay later reprinted as chapter 1 of *Structural Anthropology*, Lévi-Strauss framed the question in terms of a constitutive difference of approach between these two disciplines. History and anthropology, he argued, differ less by their subject matter than by their ways of looking at it. Historical interpretation focusses on conscious motives of the actors (with which the historian identifies himself); anthropological (and linguistic analysis), on 'the unconscious conditions of social life'.

Yet in the polemical closing chapter of *The Savage Mind* he goes beyond this. He blames historical knowledge for being of necessity riveted on a past chosen by contemporary concerns. Thus, we are 'in focus' with the French Revolution, but no longer with the Fronde—and that is why the Revolution provides us (as it did Sartre) with a model of both interpretation and conduct. Briefly, historical intelligibility is a function of today's praxis. Thus we begin by sympathising with the historical actors' conscious motives, only to realize that our very choice and classification of the past is basically a *projection* of our own present situation (a most Sartrean term). Far from ensuring more objectivity through distance, history fastens our

---

[63] Lévi-Strauss, *The Savage Mind*, p. 256.

knowledge to the narrow circle of our life and time. Not surprisingly, the end result of Lévi-Strauss's position in this regard seemed, even to a sympathizer like Maurice Godelier, a denial that 'historical processes are analytical objects'.[64]

The notion of historical knowledge as irredeemably time-bound was in fact a reply to Sartre's Marxist *Critique of Dialectical Reason* (1960). Sartre had claimed that primitive thought was a form of analytical reason, the main difference between the latter and dialectics being that dialectics knew, and analytical reason knew not, how to transcend a historically given social context. *The Savage Mind* returned the compliment: now it was *history*, the very pith and marrow of dialectical reason, that was shown to be the slave of time. Furthermore, as though it were not enough, Sartre committed his *Critique* to laying the foundations of a 'philosophical anthropology': historicizing philosophy trying to set rules for the theory of humankind . . . It was really too much for an anthropology convinced that its first duty was to redefine the concept of 'man'.

Quite apart from this 'battle of the arts' between philosophy and anthropology, Sartre actually made things worse by his thesis that every society only joined history when willy-nilly incorporated into modern civilization, historically led by Western expansion. This sounded like the umpteenth remake of Hegel's scorn for 'historyless nations', and, as we know, Marx himself thought not a jot differently, as proved (among others) by his remarks on the establishment of the British Raj. Yet Lévi-Strauss concentrated on Sartre, the self-appointed leader of Western Marxism, to roundly call this wretched idea a piece of 'intellectual cannibalism'.

Actually Sartre's notion of historyless societies concerned classless, stateless tribal societies. As such, it was quite distinct from the Hegelian concept of *historical* nations that nevertheless did not qualify for the race of world history—a concept borrowed by Engels in 1848 to 'explain' why Slovaks, Croats

---

[64] M. Godelier, *Horizon, Trajets Marxistes en Anthropologie*, Paris 1977, p. 7. Significantly, in informal texts contemporary with the speculative 'pause' (his own word) of *The Savage Mind*, Lévi-Strauss was insisting on the *absolute* precedence of synchrony. Explaining why societies transform themselves over time, he pointed to 'external factors', yet only to add at once that in any case 'there would have been no Darwin had there not previously been a Linnaeus'.

and so on failed to achieve the status of independent nation-states.

Moreover, the Sartrean antithesis, static versus dynamic societies, was at bottom—ironically enough—*accepted* by Lévi-Strauss. The real conflict was in the open disparagement of historical dynamism, instead of the usual Marxo-existentialist praise of historical 'totalizations', hence of historical change. But for both thinkers primitive societies are not, or very little, historical in the western sense. However, in the simplifying ideological effect generated by their polemic, such fine distinctions and subtle convergences were not much noticed. For a moment, the brunt of the structuralist critique claimed that whatever was shared by Sartre and Lévi-Strauss was more apparent than real. To say that primitive cultures try to withstand history instead of giving their souls to change was one thing; to suggest that they have no history worth the name, quite another. Obviously, the naive and indefensible ethnocentrism implied by the Hegel-Marx-Sartre view meant that, in the polemic over the status of historical knowledge, first blood went to the structuralist camp.

On the other hand, there is no gainsaying that Lévi-Strauss's skepticism about the objectivity of historical science went too far. Put in a nutshell, his critique of history as knowledge amounts to two main statements: (a) that our idea of historical facts boils down to mere conceptual conventions, starting, of course, with more or less arbitrary chronological codes, so that historical facts are in the end just cultural artefacts and 'myths of our culture' without correspondence in the reality of the past; and (b) that 'irreducible intrahistorical discontinuities (for example discontinuities between different historical domains and consequently between the chronological codes thereof) rule out any possibility of achieving *integrated* historical cognition. Now (b) denotes a genuine problem in historical research. Actual history seems indeed made up of *histories* rather than of a readily perceptible unified process—and this in turn renders highly implausible Sartre's ambition in the *Critique*, aimed as it is at a reflective totalization of historical experience grasped by a comprehensive theory as historicist (though far less deterministic) than that of Marx. *Scientific* history cannot deliver on such a tall order.

But criticism (a), on reflection, does not fare so well. For example, Herminio Martins has raised some as yet unanswered queries.[65] Among them, two seem particularly cogent. First, Lévi-Strauss's case for a strongly conventionalist view of historical knowledge rests heavily on the ultimate arbitrariness of chronological codes; yet historians themselves would be the first to grant that the more purely chronological an historical account, the more trivial, less instructive it tends to be. Furthermore, and most decisive, it would appear that what is most conventional in historical science is not the temporal element *as such*, since after all our way of selecting *places* in order to do geography is in principle not a bit less 'arbitrary' than our way of choosing dates and date-classes. If topographic codes are just as conventional as chronological ones, then what we have to face, from the viewpoint of critical knowledge, is a general problem of description and not something specifically 'wrong' about temporal phenomena.

Admittedly, the *découpage* of human facts normally presents greater difficulties, since in this case one has to disentangle several levels of meaning in order to reach a less subjective account of phenomena. This much was fully recognised in what passed for the most sustained French effort at the epistemology of social science during the rise of structuralism, Gilles-Gaston Granger's *Formal Thought and the Sciences of Man* (1960). However, difficulties in *découpage* for analytical purposes do not bar an objective treatment of temporal phenomena; problems of description and interpretation do not amount to any exorcism of time for the sake of science. But such was the direction the structuralist debunking of history dangerously verged on taking.

When all is said and done, one can see that the last chapter of *The Savage Mind* does succeed in preventing us from subscribing to blind assumptions of automatic objectivity in historical science; but what it does *not* do is to demonstrate that time is an intrinsically and hopelessly elusive object of knowledge, so as to undermine beyond retrieval the legitimacy of history as a scientific enterprise.

There remains the anthropological ace in the debate with Sartre: Lévi-Strauss's rejection of ethnocentricity. But here the

---

[65] Martins in Rex 1974, pp. 264–67; cf also the criticisms by J. A. Barnes in *Man* 6 (1971).

first salvoes well antedate the clash with Marxo-existentialism. Even before the passionate plea of *Tristes Tropiques*, the anti-ethnocentric stance was the focal point of a 1952 study commissioned by UNESCO, *Race and History*: 'We cannot . . . claim to have formulated a convincing denial of the inequality of the human *races*, so long as we fail to consider the problem of the inequality—or diversity—of human cultures.' Lévi-Strauss proceeded to show that cultural differences should be respected not only because of a moral right to survival but also because they are a precondition of progress. For progress is a result of the interaction of cultures. Civilization advances through 'coalitions' of cultures. The best evidence for it is the Old World, where cultural interchange soon became the rule, and the 'pool' of decisive inventions grew accordingly.

In the New World before the Discoveries, on the other hand, although the cultural level was by no means inferior to Europe's (think of the zero, the base of arithmetics, used by the Mayas half a millenium before scholars in India), there were many gaps in inventional breakthroughs. Why? In pre-Columbian America the cultural 'coalition' was formed by partners *less different between themselves* (being as they were far more recent settlers with less time to diverge from each other). Difference was relatively underdeveloped, and progress thrives on difference. Such is the truth that the callousness of historicism fails to understand.

However, one suspects Lévi-Strauss's ultimate concern is not progress, but difference: 'The true contribution of cultures consists, not in the list of their particular inventions, but in the differential distance existing between them.'[66] This is a telling detail because it shows that in the last analysis progress is valued only insofar as it derives from the play of difference. What is really being upheld is difference, for which the chapters on progress seem to provide little more than a palatable United Nations framework. At the outset of *Race and History*, mind

[66] My translation. Where I say 'differential distance' the French original says (throughout several editions) 'écart différentiel'. Moreover, the phrase comes underlined by the author. But the Unesco edition, in English, *Race and History*, Paris 1952, chose to translate it as 'differences from others' and the translator of *Structural Anthropology II* (which reprints *Race and History* as its last chapter) decided to render it by 'contrastive features', as though differences were necessarily contrasts.

you, Lévi-Strauss even has the cheek to say a kind word on Gobineau (1816–86), widely if inaccurately reckoned one of the sources of racialist ideology. For Gobineau, he says, racial purity should be preserved not because he believed any particular race to be superior, but because he attached enormous importance to their *diversity*. As he was in thrall to the concept— nowadays rightly discredited by science—of race, Gobineau erroneously equated cultural diversity with ethnic differences. But he saw the light: he realized the terrible importance of difference in culture.

So diversity is the thing. It does not mean isolation. Far from it: 'human societies are never alone'; even when they seem to be so, they actually come in bundles. No culture is an island. So 'diversity is less a function of the isolation of groups than of the relationships that unite them.' Difference means structure, a set of relations (it remains to Derrida, the high priest of post-structuralism, to put it the other way round: structure means difference).

Now if difference, not progress, is what really matters, then cultural relativism must be in the offing—and so it is. Therefore Lévi-Strauss makes a point of respecting the views of alien cultures. The anthropologist, says *Tristes Tropiques*, is a critic at home but a conformist elsewhere. Anthropology, after all, is a technique of detachment; *une technique de dépaysement* (*Structural Anthropology*). Ernest Gellner has criticised the anthropologists' tendency to play liberals in their own society and tories on behalf of the society they study: they 'understand' the tribesman yet condemn the missionary. To Lévi-Strauss this is not a problem but a solution. To touch on a primitive culture, he warns, would be to wipe it out. What one ought to do is *learn* from it in order to change *our own* society. At any rate, such is the moral he places at the end of *Tristes Tropiques*.

The trouble, as Gellner has seen, is that an over-charitable attitude of the anthropologist towards the concepts ruling a given culture may 'blind us to what is best and what is worst in the life of societies. It blinds us to the possibility that social change may occur through the replacement of an inconsistent doctrine or ethic by a better one, or through a more consistent application of either. It equally blinds us to the possibility of, for instance, social control through the employment of absurd, ambiguous, inconsistent or unintelligible doctrines.[67]

Gellner is not for a moment suggesting that the anthropologist relinquish the *sense of context* he needs to understand and explain. All he means is that it should not be abused, for the sake of understanding itself; for, if the anthropologist respects too much the ruling concepts of the society he studies, he may, ironically, miss several possible changes inscribed, in a state of latency, in the very ideology of the society under scrutiny (as when efforts are made to bring social practices closer to religious beliefs or again, when *different* concepts vie with each other to hold a grip on social behaviour). Even in primitive, as distinct from historical but traditional, societies room must be allowed for the possibility of these gaps. Consequently, the thorough, empathetic identification of the anthropologist with his object becomes both unwise and, at bottom, problematic. Moreover, the social scientist should never rule out a priori the possibility of concepts being used to foster social control and manipulation, in the fashion of what since Marx we call ideology—something that *may* also occur outside the space of class society.

Significantly, the essay where Gellner issues these caveats, 'Concepts and Society' (1962), refers to *Race and History* and its vehement rejection of ethnocentrism. Lévi-Strauss brilliantly dismisses ethnocentrism by showing that every 'barbarian' is ethnocentric. So when *we* despise other peoples as savages, we are doing exactly what savages do. Thereupon Gellner points to the vicious circle involved: 'A barbarian is he who believes that some others are barbarians. Notoriously, there are such people. They, therefore, are barbarians . . . Hence, we believe they are barbarians. Ergo, we too are barbarian (by reapplication of the initial definition).'[68]

But the thrust of Lévi-Strauss's onslaught on ethnocentrism does not bother about such quandaries, perhaps because the egalitarian logic of cultural relativism is not his final destination: very quickly, he passes from the defence of difference to a straightforward condemnation of *one* particular culture—ours.

---

[67] Gellner, *Cause and Meaning in the Social Sciences*, London 1973, p. 39.

[68] Ibid., p. 28. In his contribution to the *Festschrift* published to honour Lévi-Strauss's sixtieth year, Raymond Aron made exactly the same remark (J. Pouillon and P. Maranda, eds., *Echanges et Communications*, The Hague 1970, pp. 943–52). Aron added that by this inescapable logic, one ends up by losing any right logically to condemn racism.

All cultures may well be ethnocentric, but modern civilization does it with a vengeance: it is geared to the destruction of all other cultures. And let no one tell you (as Roger Caillois told Lévi-Strauss in their 1955 polemic) that at the very least, the West has the saving grace of being the only culture up to now to produce the corrective of ethnocentrism, namely, anthropology itself. Lévi-Strauss will have none of it. Granted that the West alone questions ethnocentricity—but if it does, it is out of sheer *remorse* for its own destructiveness in regard to other cultures, to the past and the Other. Such is the unforgiving rejoinder towards the close of *Tristes Tropiques* (chapter 38). So when we sin (by being ethnocentric, as everybody else), we sin twice, for we add oppression to prejudice; and if we atone for our sins (by respecting, through social science, the cultural differences we threaten in historical practice), the atonement only proves how sinful we are. It's a heads-I-win-tails-you-lose situation. And insofar as the West embodies modern history, it takes the brunt of Lévi-Strauss's *substantive* (as distinct from his epistemological) critique of history.

In *Race and History*, as we saw, progress was still acknowledged as something positive. Hence we might ask: Does this not mean that modern culture cannot be all bad, since it obviously represents the zenith of progress (if only as a last recipient, by virtue of the cumulative effects of cultural interaction over millenia)? If progress derives from diversity and modern culture is progress at its peak, then perhaps modern culture is not so inimical to diversity? Not at all, says Lévi-Strauss. It just means that modern culture achieved diversity (in order to generate progress) by wicked means—notably by creating *inequality*. It bred inequality at home through class exploitation; and it created forced 'coalitions' of culture abroad by colonialism and imperialism. So progress was attained, but the mischievous nature of modern civilization is not denied; quite the contrary . . .

Almost a decade later, Lévi-Strauss repeated his indictment. In *The Scope of Anthropology*, despite the half-hearted Utopianism of the conclusion, the stronger accents were placed, as we saw (see above p. 69), on the Rousseauian protest against the 'curse' of progress; and in the talks with Charbonnier, the idea that hot society achieves progress at the expense of harmony and justice returns in full force.

Tristes Tropiques metes out its most scathing sentences to the Western-made prospect of a *monoculture* encompassing the world—and in the process, any positive assessment of progress goes overboard: '. . . 20,000 years of history have been gambled away. . . . Mankind has established itself in a monoculture; it is preparing to produce civilization en masse, as if it were a sugar beet. Its meals will henceforth consist of only this dish!' The book's very last sentences include a gloomy forecast: 'When the rainbow of human cultures will have finally collapsed into the void created by our frenzy . . .' A 'monstrous cataclysm', to be sure; and one which is already, to Lévi-Strauss, less a prospect than a process, an ongoing catastrophe.

Lévi-Strauss likes to tell the story of Curt Nimuendaju, an ethnographer who managed to be adopted by a poor tribe of Eastern Brazil. Whenever Nimuendaju came back to the Indians after a spell in civilization, the natives wept with pity at the thought of the sufferings he must have gone through when away from their village, obviously the only place in the world worth living in . . .[69] The whole spirit, if not the letter, of Lévi-Strauss's musings over history and civilization seems to give reason to Nimuendaju's natives. Of course, he knows very well that no society is either fundamentally good or absolutely bad.[70] But the recurrent pathos of his thought gives the lie to this sober appraisal, by mounting an embittered attack on modern civilization and indeed on the main course of recorded history.

For Lévi-Strauss, 1955–56 was the year of controversy. Besides the rift with Caillois (who later gave him a grudgeless reception at the Académie) and a fierce argument with Georges Gurvitch, he replied to a Marxist critic, the noted Islamist Maxime Rodinson.[71] Rodinson's strictures against structural anthropology in *La Nouvelle Critique* can be read as a Marxist pendant to Caillois's objections in the conservative *La Nouvelle Revue Française*. In his view, structuralism, like mainstream American anthropology, was unable to grasp the unity of social formations and the springs of social change. Compared to historical materialism, anthropology, from Boas to Lévi-Strauss,

[69] Lévi-Strauss, *Structural Anthropology II*, p. 346.

[70] Lévi-Strauss, *Tristes Tropiques*, chapter 38.

[71] The rejoinders to both Gurvitch and Rodinson were published as chapter 16 of *Structural Anthropology*.

remained 'agnostic' as concerns progress and evolution. Lévi-Strauss's reply had no difficulty in spotting elements of vulgar Marxism in Rodinson's brand of evolutionism. But the latter touched a real problem: how was structuralism to make sense (if at all) of history, other than by uttering a rueful lament on the 'gambling away' of the last two hundred centuries in the life of mankind?

There are basically two ways of explaining the rise of modern civilization and its underpinnings: industrialism, science and the general evolution towards democracy. One (the answer of Marx and Spencer) claims that modernity is the outcome of an evolutionary potential shared by all human societies, regardless of the diversity of their cultures. This is the *evolutionist* account, whose trademark, as Gellner noticed,[72] is a vegetal model, an acorn-to-oak tree view, where all societies, however primitive and backward, are held to contain in their womb the *seed* of modernization.

The second way of explaining modernity (the Max Weber answer) prefers to stress the peculiarity of historical individualities. The focus falls no longer on the species as a whole, or society in general, but on the West as the bearer of the first, now largely imitated, modernization. It is the *historist* account, which replaces the acorn-to-oak image by the 'gate-keeper' model, with an emphasis on a *unique* combination of factors at one given point in history, within one cultural area. While the evolutionist view regards progress as a *necessary* development, the historist view sees it as a highly *contingent* outcome of a rare constellation of assets and opportunities.

The superiority of the historist account lies precisely in its ability to face the decisive point in historical terms: *why here*, instead of elsewhere, or everywhere? Why did it all come about in the modern West (Weber's life-long question) and not in other places and times? 'Gate-keeper' theories at least try to cope with this riddle; acorn-to-oak theories do not.

On the other hand, a core of truth in the evolutionist view seems to survive rather well. The widespread diffusion of modern forms of production and modern values would suggest that for all the local contingency of the *origin* of modernity, once it developed there occurs a fairly universal propensity to adapt to

[72] E. Gellner, ed., *Soviet and Western Anthropology*, New York 1980, p. xiv.

it—and even adopt it—almost everywhere. Consequently, although the 'seed' appears to require a lot of exogenous incentives to grow, *at least it is there*, as a potentiality—which of course was very much part of the evolutionist explanation.

The debate between these two historical accounts of modernization is one of the epic sagas of social theory, and we certainly need not go into it in this book. But some reference had to be made to this problem, for the question naturally arises as to whether the thesis of *Race and History*—that progress is a function of cultural interchange (Lévi-Strauss's only sketch of an account of progress)—does add up to a third position in such a crucial debate. Now by insisting that 'there is no cumulative society in itself and by itself', Lévi-Strauss *seems* to side with the evolutionist camp. Surely there is a non-historist streak in *Race and History*, which leads the author to play down the uniqueness of the West in generating modern culture and the industrial revolution. The book conspicuously pits the significance of the *neolithic* revolution against the making of industrialism. At the same time, however, the whole essay (as indeed all the work of Lévi-Strauss) breathes a remarkable antipathy to the evolutionist creed, both classical and modern (for example, the American neo-evolutionist theory of the 1950s). Furthermore, although progress may be, to the structuralist sage, an abominable curse, it is by no means a fate: evolution remains an error, not a necessity, no matter how feeble (at this late hour in history) our powers of resistance to it. Yet in the end *Race and History* sidesteps the historist account, since, by stressing that progress grows out of a 'pool' of cultural differences, questions of origins and turning-points ('why *here*, instead of elsewhere, or anywhere?') obviously cease to apply.

Moreover—and here we stop our brief discussion of the explanatory aspects of Lévi-Straussian philosophy of history—*Race and History* does not tackle another serious problem either: the problem of progress *in the present*. For from the fact that no society is cumulative by itself, that progress implies a pool of contributions from different cultures, it does not follow that there is not, at any given point in time, a cultural area that occupies a leading position in terms of the *overall* levels of know-how, comforts and inventions. So, in explaining progress, one has to focus on cultural *lead* as well as on cultural interchange—as the actual experience of modernization races, prompted as they are by the awareness of handicaps and dis-advantages, makes abundantly clear. (To suggest, as does *Race and History*, that progress is simply and brutally visited upon underdeveloped areas by an external expansion is at best only half the explanation—and in fact, it comes ironically too close to admitting something not very different from the smug histori-cist thesis of 'historyless nations'.)

Some would say: it is all very well, but in any event this is not the proper study of anthropology; the latter's object is the world of primitive or at most archaic culture, not the present competition between states. But to endorse this disclaimer is to take for granted a narrowing down of subject matter which the 'structuralist revolution' itself rendered far less easy to accept. For structuralism, and more generally the rise of cognitive anthropology, have brought home to social scientists that anthropologists, in Clifford Geertz's apt phrase, 'don't study villages—they study *in* villages'. In other words, their science is not primarily about men and women but about *man*. And if human universals are the stuff of anthropology, then one cannot legitimately narrow its scope and restrict anthropology to the consideration of tribal society or prehistoric culture.

In this sense *Race and History* was no digression from anthro-pological theory—which only undergirds our right to assess its contribution to our intelligence of progress. As that able histor-ian of modern anthropology, Adam Kuper once wrote (in *New Society*) Lévi-Strauss 'is probably the last social scientist with a complete view of human development'. There is therefore no reason to avoid asking him to account for history as a whole— past and present. Now while his stress on the relationship between cultural exchange and progress was doubtless a major gain (differing as it does from the simple tenets of the diffusion-ist school, the old opponent of evolutionary anthropology), the downplaying of *modern* progress reflected a Rousseauesque bias in his personal ideology—and as such, is much more emotional than illuminating.

It is indeed an outlook dominated by the belief in *entropy*. Social order, for Lévi-Strauss, is forever doomed to *disinte-gration*. In *Structural Anthropology* he goes as far as to suggest that the very existence of several spheres of order in culture, conceptual as well as practical, entails a degree of institutional tension and attrition fatefully conducive to disorganization.

One of the very last paragraphs of *Tristes Tropiques*, after calling man a machine working to undo a primeval order, an unwitting vehicle of the principle of inertia, invites us to conceive of anthropology as an *entropology*, 'a discipline devoted to studying this process of disintegration in its highest manifestations'. Even the wondrous works of the mind do not compensate for this, since they are only meaningful to man, in a cosmos itself bent on attaining the final peace of disorder.

Thus ultimately the 'archaeology of space'—the intellectual rescuing of cultural difference—means more than just the piety of social science towards dwindling societies and dying cultures. Beneath its mournful overtones, this metaphor of the anthropological mood harbours a still darker vision. Claude Lévi-Strauss is one of the most uncompromising pessimists in our post-classical culture, someone to be placed alongside Leopardi, Schopenhauer, Burckhardt and Beckett, melancholy preachers of renunciation and detachment. He placed *Tristes Tropiques*, a book largely written with the ink of sadness, under the motto of Lucretius, the classical pessimist among philosophical poets. Structuralism is a geology of the mind, a search for discontinuities as footprints of the intellect; but the moral its creator draws from it—and which may be regarded as quite independent from it—has the poignancy of a *Liebestod*, a craving for the nirvana, a deep desire for rest, dictated by disillusion and disenchantment. It is not 'the sense of an ending'; rather, it is a wish for the end. That same feeling of meaninglessness which, for Sartre and Camus, led to nausea leads now to a lust for extinction. For all its elegy on vanishing cultures, structuralist thought longs itself to give the quietus to culture *as such*.

Above all, this 'Buddhist' streak in structuralism[73] struck a forceful alliance between anthropology and *Kulturkritik*. Mark that this is quite different from a mere question of doing critical anthropology, that is to say, of making anthropology critical. Naturally, anthropology always implied some degree or another of critical distance in regard to our way of life. Even Frazer, in the golden days of armchair anthropology and its smug evolutionism, was sometimes read as though his tales of blood and superstition were innuendos *de nostra re*. But gaining

---

[73] Stressed by O. Paz, *Claude Lévi-Strauss: An Introduction*, Ithaca 1970, pp. 19–42 and 151–52.

critical distance from a given set of customs does not entail the
conversion of the anthropological consciousness into a war machine, directed against modern culture. The difference can be
fully appreciated if we compare the Lévi-Straussian cast of mind
with some towering figures of his craft in the 1920s and 1930s.
For instance, Lowie was a critical anthropologist (notably of
evolutionism) but not a *Kulturkritiker*. Similarly, Malinowski
challenged several Victorian taboos (notably on sex) but he did
not write in pitched battle against the grain of modern civilization. The plain truth is that half a century ago, the alliance
between anthropology and the countercultural spirit had not yet
been forged. In the thirties and forties, radical estrangement
from the culture of modernity was expressed neither by anthropology nor, for that matter, sociology but by certain (rival)
streams in continental philosophy: Heidegger's critique of *die
Technik* on the one hand, the so-called Frankfurt school and the
theme of 'reason's betrayal', with progress denying its own
promise of happiness, on the other.

Now I am not suggesting that the anti-modernity theme, so
conspicuous in the thought of Lévi-Strauss, has become the rule
in all contemporary anthropology. Perhaps the impression of an
epoch-making conversion to the antinomian values of modern
humanism stems from a sheer coincidence: the conjunction in
the same person of the most innovative theoretical mind in
contemporary anthropology with such a passionate revulsion
against the course of modern history. David Pace in his interesting book *Claude Lévi-Strauss: the Bearer of Ashes* calls him 'a
prophet of our decentred post-colonial age', certainly not to be
confused with those gurus of Leftist irrationalism such as Marcuse and Laing—but equally intent on devising a new ethic and
a new philosophy of history for a self-doubting West.[74]

In the history of ideas, the net result of the Lévi-Straussian
merger of anthropology and radical cultural criticism will probably count as a curious change in the tradition of *Kulturpessimismus*. The ideology of cultural pessimism had long been
associated, thanks to Oswald Spengler (1880–1936), with the
theme of western decline. For Lévi-Strauss, on the contrary,
the monoculture, a child of the West, is not bound to die but to

[74] D. Pace, *Claude Lévi-Strauss: The Bearer of Ashes*, London 1983,
pp. 17, 186.

win—to conquer the world by 'viral' contagion. To Spengler, the West was a corpse; to Lévi-Strauss, it is a cancer. To a certain extent, structuralist philosophy thus reverts to an older stance in *Kulturpessimismus*: the position of Jakob Burckhardt (1818–97), for whom Western, modern progress was firmly in the saddle, but was a tale of greed and violence, the triumph of inhumane *Machtsinn*.

Western pessimist thought has more than one temper. There is the Schopenhauerian brand that depicts pain and suffering as the gist of the cosmic process and concludes that total withdrawal is the last word of wisdom. But there is also a more embattled variety that prefers to challenge entropy or sclerosis by asserting the dignity of the will in the face of recurring or increasing decadence: such was the temper of Sorel, Weber and Gramsci, pessimists always on their mettle.

Which family of pessimists does Lévi-Strauss belong to? Susan Sontag, writing in the sixties, found in *Tristes Tropiques* a 'heroic, diligent, and complex modern pessimism'.[75] I agree that it is complex (not the least in its distance from mainstream countercultural ideology, which deprecates science as well as progress) and diligent (precisely as an active source of new approaches in social science); but I fail to see where lies the heroism of such an outlook. By that I do not mean, of course, that Professor Claude Lévi-Strauss, a gentleman-scholar of immense erudition and a model of hard work worthy of comparison with the Victorian giants of research and output, is defective in any moral dimension. All I am saying is that his worldview speaks of detachment and despondency, not of resistance and defiance. Like Schopenhauer, he is not a heroic thinker but a subtle master of renunciation.

In the sixties his structuralism was often construed as a new scientism, a positivism as naturalistic as the nineteenth-century one, but shorn of any belief in evolution.[76] Little by little the humanist elements in the thought of Lévi-Strauss became more apparent. In the main there is now more disagreement over his science than over his 'message'. Structural analysis, or at least

---

[75] S. Sontag, *Against Interpretation*, London 1966, p. 81.

[76] Such was the interpretation of Hegelians such as Eugène Fleischmann, 'L'Esprit humain selon Cl. Lévi-Strauss', *European Journal of Sociology*, 7, 1966.

his use of it on kinship and myths, tends to be questioned; but the tenor of his particular contribution to the critique of modernity gets a wide acceptance. The sage prevails over the scientist.

I think this kind of assessment is basically wrong. As far as I can see, Lévi-Strauss's gifts to social science are sounder than his vision. Structuralism may fall short of its own epistemological Utopia, an *instauratio magna* in social science as a whole; still, it did establish a new and fruitful way of looking at cultural phenomena. Most flaws in the analytical work of its founder can be reckoned as contingent, not as deriving from the structuralist perspective in itself.

Moreover, the insightfulness of structuralist research does not even depend on accepting the Lévi-Straussian frame of reference. For instance, as Kuper noticed,[77] Leach put the structuralist emphasis on exchange and communication as key social phenomena to a quite different use from Lévi-Strauss's own obsession with universals of mind. He claimed that social forms of exchange, especially the structure of marriage choices, should be seen as responses to political and material circumstances, so that if wife-givers enjoyed systematically higher status than wife-takers (or the other way round) this would reflect differences in power and wealth among the groups involved— but Leach did this out of a legitimate concern with particular social systems rather than with psychological universals. To put it bluntly: the method is by no means tied to the theories of its initiator—which is praise enough for any method.

The Lévi-Straussian 'message', however, is fraught with as much prejudice as insight. True, the moral it distils—a humanism knowing how 'to place the world before life, life before man, and the respect of others before self-interest'[78] is a wise and useful warning against mindless, ruthless forms of economic and technological drives, well in tune with the growing consciousness of our duties towards mother nature. 'The moral of myths', the epilogue to *The Origin of Table Manners*, extols the wisdom of the primitives' realisation that it is man who pollutes the environment, not the other way round. In their

---

[77] A. Kuper, *Anthropologists and Anthropology: The British School 1922–72*, Harmondsworth 1975, chapter 7.
[78] Lévi-Strauss, *Mythologiques III*, last page.

very etiquette the Indians behave on the assumption that man smears the world: whilst we use cutlery and canned food to protect our meals from infection, they think it is the world which needs protection against our activity. In one more jibe at Sartre, Lévi-Strauss remarked that 'hell is the others' is less a philosophical proposition than a token of our culture's folly. Much more modestly, savages just know that hell is in ourselves. Now etiquette literally means 'little ethics'. Structuralist wisdom is an attempt to have such an ethic writ large in our ageing industrial society. Lévi-Strauss the moralist rekindles in our hearts something we are in dire need of: a Goethean ethics of respect.

It would indeed be a pity if we minimized the significance of this plea for self-restraint. For all the contempt poured on processed food, this is obviously much more than a philosophical manifesto in favour of the *nouvelle cuisine*. The sociology of (the lack of) respect in our midst is something far more serious, and urgently called for. Yet ecological rationality and a more considerate ethic do not imply a comprehensive indictment of history and progress, nor such a sweeping diatribe against modern civilization. Sometimes, as when he ponders over the predicament of modern art, Lévi-Strauss's animus towards the century hits the nail on the head. But more often than not what we have boils down once again to the spectacle of a first-rate writer indulging in one of the favourite games of contemporary intellectuals: kick the West, bash modernity, down with progress. Of course the clock of history cannot be turned back. But then, is there really a case for thinking that progress is such a scourge, inflicted upon primitive and traditional societies against their will and better humanity? Let no rhetoric conceal this: the burden of proof belongs to the accusers. It is perfectly possible to find much of value in Lévi-Strauss's more philosophical reflections without subscribing to his dismal, yet largely unjustified view of our society and our age.

4

Literary Structuralism: Roland Barthes

Honneur des hommes, saint Langage.

Valéry

When we consider a book, we mustn't ask ourselves what it says but what it means.

William of Baskerville,
in Umberto Eco, *The Name of the Rose*

Between Orpheus and Medusa

As we have seen in Chapter Two, structuralist criticism, springing from the work of one of the founders of phonology—Roman Jakobson—evolved a theory of literature and an analytical methodology *before* the rise of Parisian structuralism as a whole. Moreover, both the literary theory and the methodology championed by Jakobson between the twenties and the sixties remained essentially akin to the doctrines put forward by Russian formalism during World War I. In this sense, Jakobson's ideas about the 'poetic function' and the 'poetry of grammar' may be reckoned a kind of linguistic 'translation' of formalist tenets; and as such became the paradigm of most French strucuralist criticism since the sixties. Now the end result of this afterlife of formalism as structuralism was a critical ideology: I mean, an ideology of criticism that was conspicuously scientistic. Two beliefs were widely shared by the various forms of *nouvelle critique*: (a) that criticism could and should be a scientific discipline, like the new social anthropology of Lévi-Strauss; and (b) that in order to be so, literary analysis had only to follow in the steps of structural anthropology and model itself on linguistics.

The man who first (if rather briefly) embodied the scientism of structuralist criticism and then did most to deflate it was Roland Barthes, today reckoned by many to have been the greatest French literary critic of our century. In 1967, writing in the *Times Literary Supplement*, he defined structuralism as a method of analysing cultural works *inspired by modern linguistics*. The 'structuralist activity,' as he put it in a famous essay, aimed 'at "reconstituting" an object so as to manifest the rules of its functioning.' We recognize the search for invariants, the lesson from linguistics and the Lévi-Straussian programme for anthropology. Yet in a 1971 interview for *Tel Quel* (no. 47) Barthes disparaged his own prior endeavours in structuralism and semiotics as a transient 'dream of scientificity'. By then, he had come to hail the 'pleasure of the text' and the rights of an unbounded subjectivity in responding to literary signs. Some of his most fervent admirers have not yet recovered from the shock of this unabashed volte-face.

Born in 1915 in Normandy into a Protestant family from the Languedoc, Barthes lost his father (a navy officer) in the war and remained passionately attached to his musically gifted mother, who as a widow had to work hard as a book-binder. Half of his often poverty-stricken childhood was spent in Bayonne, in the Pyrenees; then in Paris, on the Rive Gauche, with school holidays back in Bayonne, the provincial bourgeois home of his paternal grandparents, of which he left delightful memoirs in *Barthes by Barthes* (1975). A sickly youth, he studied classical literature at the Sorbonne, specializing in Greek tragedy, and taught at some lycées before the fall of France, but was in sanatoria for most of World War II, reading Gide, discovering Marxism and devouring everything by Sartre he could lay his hands on. He went to teach for a while in Bucharest and Alexandria (where A. J. Greimas introduced him to modern linguistics). Soon after, he was appointed researcher at the CNRS (1952). Barthes began publishing rather late in his uneventful life. He was nearly forty when he became enthralled by Brecht's 'epic theatre'. In the late 1950s, having joined the heretical Marxist journal *Arguments*, edited by a group of academic *défroqué* Communists, he championed the nouveau roman of Robbe-Grillet. He entered the Ecole Pratique des Hautes Etudes in 1960, ran a crowded seminar in the mid- and late sixties and was given a new chair—'literary semiology'—at the Collège de France (where he joined Lévi-Strauss and Michel

Foucault) in 1976. One fine day in 1980, as he left a luncheon with his friend, the future president François Mitterrand, in the Quartier Latin, a car ran him over. In a few hours he was dead.

By 1950, the canonic text of left French criticism was Sartre's *What is Literature?* (1947), an eloquent plea for political commitment among writers. Barthes described his first book, *Writing Degree Zero* (1953) as an attempt to 'Marxify Sartrean commitment'. Sartre is not named but he is the obvious main addressee of the pamphlet's argument. Writing, claims Barthes, is never a neutral instrument; far from being merely a means of denotation, language is the place of whatever commitment a writer chooses. Ideological choices in literature are evinced in the way a writer employs words. Sartre was right: literature is no innocent; willy-nilly, writers uphold values and take their stand in the ideological fray. But Barthes wants to give as materialist as possible an account of it—and therefore he looks for *engagement* not at the level of ideas but at the level where writers are at their most original and peculiar: their own language.

Barthes introduces a very interesting (if intriguing) distinction between language, style and writing. *Language* is to him a 'natural order' of meanings, unified by tradition. For the writer, it is just a 'frontier', overstepping which would entail a loss of meaning for every social purpose. Language is a 'horizon', a 'boundary', a 'possibility' of expression, but for this very reason something that writers do not elect in any serious sense: as a precondition of writing, it is there for them to use, 'a response involving no choice, the individual property of men, not of writers', and as such less a 'fund' to be drawn upon than a 'limit'.

Style, by contrast, is above all the mark of individuality: 'imagery, delivery, vocabulary spring from the body and the past of the writer and gradually become the very reflexes of his art.' The idiom of the unconscious self, style has 'its roots in the depths of the author's personal and secret mythology.' But by the same token, like its opposite, social language, it is 'in no way the product of a choice'—a 'thrust' rather than an intention. Style is an individual fate placed 'outside art, outside the pact which binds the writer to society'; a 'humoral' phenomenon with a 'biological origin'. For a moment, Barthes seems carried away by his determination to render the unconscious into 'carnal' metaphors. He notes that whilst poetry since Hugo and Rimbaud is 'saturated with style' some authors—such as Gide in his classicism—'prefer the security of art to the loneliness of style'.[1] Still, if style is a personal *fatum*, an individual destiny, one can hardly expect a writer to be style-less—though some styles may very well be less 'fleshly' than others.

In fact, were it not for this peculiar stress on the somatic, on the 'body-and-past' of each writer, Barthes's concept of style would not differ much from the 'critique thématique' of the Swiss school (G. Poulet, J. Rousset, J. Starobinski). Understandably, Barthes's second book, *Michelet* (1954), a brilliant study on style so defined, has often been compared to the works of thematic criticism. Within 'thematic' criticism and its largely 'phenomenological' orientation, however, Barthes was closer to the 'psychoanalysis of matter' of Gaston Bachelard (1884–1962; *L'Eau et les Rêves*, 1942; *Poétique de l'Espace*, 1958) and of Bachelard's avowed disciple, Jean-Pierre Richard, whose first book, *Littérature et Sensation*, was hailed by Barthes when it came out in 1954 (writing in the *Mercure de France*, Gaëtan Picon, a devotee of Malraux, actually linked Barthes's *Michelet* to Richard's work, as two fine examples of the new psychological criticism).

In *Michelet*, Barthes seizes on the fact that the sentences of the great historian of the Revolution display an unflagging attention to the moral significance of physical traits of each actor (individual or collective) in the political drama. Michelet's powerful theatrical imagination builds the nodal points of historical narrative around scenes fraught with carnal symbols and metaphors, as when the warm women of Thermidor hurl themselves upon the desiccated dying body of Robespierre, the prim, priggish dispenser of Terror for the sake of virtue (one wonders whether Wajda read Michelet before shooting his *Danton*). Barthes's comments ('then the Woman-Blood devours the Priest Cat', etcetera) underscore Michelet's compulsive ability to interpret character in bodily terms, to render unconscious drives as visible flesh. Barthes deems Michelet's 'petty-bourgeois' ideology beneath contempt, but visibly delights in browsing through the 'organized network' of his obsessions. Yet Michelet's keeness on the humoral variety of mankind is in turn governed by his own idiosyncrasies: blood,

[1] Barthes, *Barthes: Selected Writings*, London 1982, pp. 33–34.

heat, migraine, womanhood—hence by this unescapable *style*.

Between social language and personal style, claims Barthes, there is *writing* (*écriture*). And here, at last, we have choice: 'a general choice of tone, of ethos . . . where the writer shows himself clearly as an individual because this is where he commits himself. . . . A language and a style are blind forces; a mode of writing is an act of historical solidarity.' Writing is language endowed with a 'social finality', 'form considered as a human intention and thus linked to the great crises of History.'[2]

Thus writing is essentially 'the morality of form'. We seem to have landed without much ado in a concept of form as the vehicle of Sartre's disembodied commitment. However, things are not so simple. Barthes makes a point of stressing that all the writer can do, no matter how bold the project in hand, is to change the idea of literature, not its actual effects on the social landscape. The writer's moral choice, as reflected in writing, 'is a matter of conscience, not of efficacy'. Worse still: because the constraints limiting the consumption of literature cannot be changed, the writer 'voluntarily places the need for a free language at the sources of this language and not in its eventual consumption. So that writing is an ambiguous reality: on the one hand, it unquestionably arises from a confrontation of the writer with the society of his time; on the other hand, from this social finality, it refers the writer back, by a sort of tragic reversal, to the sources, that is to say, the instruments of creation.'[3]

As a result, writers, choosing their writing, fall back on the pressures of history and tradition, on previous modes of writing, including their own. Writing as Freedom is 'a mere moment'. Commitment becomes a narrow *situation*—a freedom, a choice, on the thin edge of many constraints. No wonder Barthes declares writing to be 'in no way an instrument for communication . . . as an open route through which there passes only the intention to speak.' This is a far cry from the Sartrean Utopia of prose as transparent speech.

Yet like Sartre, Barthes is keen on historicizing literature. He called *Writing Degree Zero* 'a free reflection on the historical

[2] All quotes from Barthes, *Selected Writings*, pp. 31–35.
[3] Ibid., p. 36.

condition of literary language'.[4] He ascribes a different kind of writing to each historical regime, dwelling on the classical age, the French Revolution and the language of Marxism. In an oft-quoted passage, he interprets the passé simple and the narrative in the third person as trademarks of the 'literary institution' under nineteenth-century bourgeois ideology. As for the 'zero degree' of writing, it is the very opposite of the spirit of the 'literary institution': it amounts to a verbal asceticism entrusted with the task of expiating the guilt long associated with the practice of literature as a means of legitimizing prejudice and oppression. Like the classical writer, the author of such 'white writing' seeks to use language as a docile instrument; but now the language tool is freed from the accretions of ideology and tradition, so that the degree zero writer manages to see the human problem in its naked truth. Unfortunately, as Barthes recognizes, this bare, unadorned writing, best exemplified by Camus's *Outsider*, tends to slip quickly into a new formal canon, undermining its very power to disrupt the 'literary myth' the socially controlled 'ritual' of literary art.

Despite its allegiance to the Sartrean demand for commitment, *Writing Degree Zero* often seems to fall under the spell of another, quite different philosopher-critic (and writer-critic): Maurice Blanchot (b. 1907). Blanchot began his theoretical work during the Occupation in a spirit akin to the dissident surrealism of Georges Bataille (1897–1962), a crucial fore-runner of several tenets in structuralism and post-structuralism. Bataille was as impressed as Lévi-Strauss by Mauss's *Gift* (above, pp. 44–45); but where Lévi-Strauss saw exchange and reciprocity, he saw only the glory of conspicuous waste. He titled his 'essay on general economics' (actually very general but with no economics) *La Part Maudite* (1949), and wrote it as a hymn to the holiness of the superfluous, the supreme virtue of utter prodigality, placed under the symbol of the sun, which gives heat without return. He employed the Dionysian message of Nietzsche to preach a full break with bourgeois rationality and morality, stressing both the libertarian and the communing dimensions of 'border experiences' such as evil and eroticism (most logically, he launched a revival of de Sade). Bataille authored a lot of high pornography and wrote in praise of Aztec

[4] Foreword to the 1964 reprint of *Le Degré Zéro de L'Ecriture*.

human sacrifices, much in keeping with the 'theatre of cruelty' of that other pontif of 'black' surrealism, Antonin Artaud (1896–1948). A quiet librarian dreaming of violence and violation, he was a prize instance of a typical figure among the French intelligentsia: the pyromaniac in slippers, the wild barbarian who actually does not hurt a fly. But this Sunday immoralist was to haunt the post-existentialist mind. His seminal intimations of a lay mystique based on the lust for *transgression* and the *withdrawal from communication for the sake of communion*, as outlined in *L'Expérience Intérieure* (1943), became a gospel of structuralist culture.

Blanchot's writings in literary theory (since *Faux Pas*, 1943) are very close to Bataille's anti-discursive aesthetic of darkness and the *extasis* of transgression. But Blanchot added significantly to Bataille. He built a weird metaphysics of literature by blending insights from such disparate sources as Hegel, Mallarmé and Heidegger. Blanchot concocted a negative ontology of writing in order to describe the paradoxical nature of modern literature (as instanced pre-eminently in Kafka's powerful mix of the absurd and the fantastic). From Mallarmé he took the ideal of a poetics of abstraction, forever bent on naming the flower 'absent from all bouquets'. From Hegel he borrowed the highly idealist thought that naming obliterates objects as existent to bestow upon them the worthier reality of the Idea. And from Heidegger he culled a bleak pathos of death-consciousness. More generally, Blanchot translates the Hegelian stress on the 'power of the negative' into the driving force of literature according to Mallarmé's poetics of silence and negation; and he further translates this power of negativity within literary language into a 'work of death' depicted in all the tragic hues of an existentialist Angst.

Weaving all these notions one into another in the solemn, oracular beauty of his prose, Blanchot dramatized a notion of literature as a stubborn helplessness, feeding on absence and abstraction, and exercising a tragic 'right to death'. Thus writing itself becomes a 'border experience' in Bataille's sense. Blanchot is deft at denunciations of the illusions of expression: they are bound to fail, since every writer, in trying to convey his or her experience, transmutes it into something impersonal and (as soon as it is interpreted by others) untrue to its living source. In literature language can only bring about suicide and destruction, eliminating the self as well as the world. The law of literature becomes the passion of Orpheus, who could not avoid looking at the dead because he knew that in art desire leads to annihilation, that Eurydice was lost beforehand and so prepared himself, unawares and from the outset, for 'an infinite sojourn' in the country of Death.[5] Only the darkest literature—the tales of Kafka—dwells allegorically at the heart of this predicament, the 'question of literature', as Blanchot dubs it.

Above all, literature so conceived is devoted to *de-realizing* the universe (Mallarmé again). Imagination, writes Blanchot, is not a region beyond reality but reality *as a whole*, cancelled out by the negating power of language. As for writers, sentenced as they are to this work of suppression, they can only find some solace in the *'materiality of language'*, in the thick, obscure density of the word-as-thing. But this exacts a high price: for 'language' is a cold mistress, an authorless art, a writing without writers, a haunting darkness at the furthest remove from any rational consciousness. Instead of permitting lucidity, it basks in utter ambiguity. A treacherous fate goads the writer into a ceaseless struggle with engrossing, inexhaustible riddles, much as the fight against evil spoken of by Kafka: a 'combat against evil ending in evil', 'just as quarrels with women end up in bed'.[6]

Barthes quotes Blanchot on Mallarmé and Kafka but in fact the influence of Blanchot seems broader than these topics suggest. Overall, Barthes keeps at arm's length something cherished by Sartre: denotation, the ideal of a crystal-clear referentiality in writing. The Blanchotian theme of literature as de-realization was given full rein in Barthes's subsequent works; and the same applies to the idea of a 'materiality of language' acting independently of the illusions of self. As he puts it in the foreword to his *Critical Essays* (1964), the raw material of literature is 'not the unnamable but the named', therefore writing consists of getting rid of all previous meanings: the task of art is to *'unexpress the expressible'*—a paradox that Barthes himself relates, in a clear nod to Blanchot, to the *'orphic situation'* of literature.

Now and again, Barthes even writes as a Blanchot in a

[5] M. Blanchot, *L'Espace Littéraire*, Paris 1955, pp. 179–84.
[6] Blanchot, 1943, pp. 303–45.

brighter mood. Listen to this: 'Literature is like phosphorus: it shines with its maximum brilliance at the moment when it attempts to die.' Nevertheless, the prevailing colours of *Le Degré Zéro de l'Ecriture* are far less sombre than the tragic pathos of Blanchot. Significantly, although Barthes also identifies a 'tragedy of *écriture*', he locates it in a framework that is more historical than anthropological: the struggle of the modern writer enmeshed in a plurality of modes of writing, striving to give a fresh account of new social realities yet riveted to an inherited instrument—a literary language—laden with outmoded class biases. Indeed, much if not all of his pamphlet reads as a sober prelude to an onslaught on bourgeois ideology.

The onslaught dominates Barthes's third book, *Mythologies* (1957), a collection of fifty-odd short articles first published (with only two exceptions) in the monthly *Lettres Nouvelles* since 1952. 'Debunking raised to the power of art' catches the gist of it all. Barthes pours scathing comments on the tritest trivia of the media: horoscopes, movie idols, wrestling and cycle races, stripteases and murder trials, tourist guides and holidays, toys and detergents; but he also pins down the hidden connotations of more spectacular topics such as UFOs, or again the folklore concerning Einstein's brain, the preaching of Billy Graham, the rightist populism of Pierre Poujade and the worship of royalty. The author of *Mythologies* is a literary critic turned spontaneous critical sociologist, a master of 'semioclasm' (Barthes's word). Take, for example, his text on abbé Pierre, the debonair monk who, in the grim winter of 1952 sets out to succour the homeless *clochards* of Paris: Barthes pokes fun at his beard and haircut as signs of reassuring bourgeois virtues. While the coarse short hair of abbé Pierre was conventionally unconventional, his flowing, shaggy beard, harking back to the heroics of monkish piety, connoted a Christianity truer to the spirit than the letter. The article closes by asking rhetorically whether this moving iconography is not an 'alibi' through which the signs of charity were substituted for real social justice.

Mythologies is a book against myths. What, then, does Barthes mean by myth? He answers in a long final essay in the book entitled 'Myth Today'. Barthes knows that myth is unlike language in at least three respects: (a) it has no individual sender of its messages—the sender is by definition a social group (in *Mythologies*, the bourgeoisie, often the petty-bourgeoisie); (b) for the same reason, there is no answering back: the receiver never becomes in turn a sender; and (c) myth specializes in *connotation*, using the linguistic code (which can be both denotative and connotative) as a signifier of the myth-ical signified. Thus, as these last words show, myth, albeit a semiosis (a sign process) different from language, is amenable to an analysis using linguistic categories. Indeed, 'Myth Today' marks the first appropriation by Barthes of Saussurean termino-logy; in the foreword to the paperback reprint of *Mythologies* (1970), he says he had read Saussure *before* writing his article—but in his 1971 interview for *Tel Quel* he states, much more plausibly, that he only read it afterwards.

Above all, myth is a process of signification 'constituted by the loss of the historical quality of things'. History into nature: such is the soul of myth, and that is why *ideology*, a cultural construct that lives by disguising itself as 'the very nature of things', uses and abuses myth. In his first months as a critic for *Lettres Nouvelles*, in an appreciative article on *Masters and Slaves*, the classic study by the Brazilian social historian Gil-berto Freyre, Barthes wrote that criticizing myths is 'the only effective way for an intellectual' to be politically militant. As an ideology, he claims in 'Myth Today', myth is an 'interpellation': it *addresses* citizens imperatively so that they may acknowledge the signifying intention that has shaped it (well before Althusser, Barthes equated ideology with interpellation). But the inter-pellating process works on an *unconscious* level. A good ex-ample from *Mythologies* is the article on the trial of Dominici, an old rural boor accused of the murder of an English tourist, Sir Jack Drummond, and his family. Dominici's guilt being doubtful, the prosecution conjured up a whole array of moral stereotypes inculcated by 'normal' literature, as typified in the novels of Giono and Genevoix, or the drama of Salacrou. Justice and literature in league, using myth to mystify, to 'sell' the shallowest social biases as though they were the very nature of a higher, permanent moral order—what a treat for the iconoclast!

But why is it that semiology must always act as semioclasm? The naive answer to that—because the intellectual in Barthes, true to the *Quartier Latin* spirit at the time, simply had to hate the bourgeois—is not far wide of the mark. The whole book breathes the air of the *bien-pensant* left, in its good causes (such as anti-colonialism) as well as in its prejudices (such as its relentless and indiscriminate anti-Americanism). Furthermore, Barthes presents himself as a blinkered believer in the most conventional revolutionary socialism. He roundly decrees that myth dwells 'statistically' and 'essentially' on the right, whereas if it happens to come about on the left, that can only be because the left has ceased to be truly revolutionary. Again, he does not even wince in asserting that the language of 'producers' *cannot* think in mythical terms, or again that 'Revolution excludes myth'. All of which sounds appallingly doctrinaire and dogmatic, suggesting that its author, in those Cold War years, kept his eyes closed to the cogent demolition of certain myths of the radical left undertaken by people such as Albert Camus (*The Rebel*, 1951), Merleau-Ponty (*Adventures of the Dialectic* 1955) or, last but not least, Raymond Aron (*The Opium of the Intellectuals*, 1955). Yet Barthes had written for Camus's *Combat*.

Furthermore, it is not only a question of failing to extend 'semioclasm' to leftwing ideology. Within his criticism of the bourgeois world, Barthes indulges in much biased question-begging. Let us return for a moment to his page on abbé Pierre. Is it not obvious that by focussing his criticism entirely on the symbolic meaning of the good monk's capillarity, Barthes bars outright every discussion of the actual results of his action? If we look at his text, we discover why this is so: it is because Christian charity does not live up to real social justice. Now this is just where the question-begging creeps in. For the abbé Pierre's organizational skill did help a lot of Parisian paupers. There was therefore no reason to dismiss it out of hand as utterly negligible, as our semioclast did for the sake of *his* ideological prejudices. Anyone acquainted with the unique blend of sociological realism and human sympathy, with the sober balance of acumen and poignancy, showed by Orwell in his pages on tramps and *clochards* in *Down and Out in Paris and London* should have no difficulty in understanding the moral quality and the practicality of the abbé's work. Nor is it any good to say that we shouldn't level such objections at Barthes because he was, after all, just a semiologist (a literary critic writ large) and so had the right to ignore substantive issues connected with social welfare. That would not do at all, for

118

Barthes himself made plain that he was writing social criticism—and if he was, there is no reason to exempt him from an obligation to take into account social realities beyond the signs he analyses. How else could he justify his demystifications, if not by pointing to the gap between ideology and social fact (as he did in unmasking Poujadism). The unreserved praise given to *Mythologies* by commentators delighted with the wit of Barthes's attacks on the bourgeoisie is rarely fazed by the fact that his 'semioclasm' often feeds on the unexamined assumptions of glib radical sociology.

A possible line of defence would be for Barthes to resort to one of his pet ideas in characterizing myth: the notion of *doxa*, which he tended to use more often as he quietly dropped, throughout the sixties, most of the vocabulary of revolutionary socialism. 'The doxa,' he writes in *Roland Barthes by Roland Barthes*, 'is the voice of the natural.' Once again, we have history concealed by a pseudo-nature. The doxa, Barthes adds, is what 'goes without saying'—'current opinion, repeated meaning'. It is also Medusa, because it petrifies those who stare at her into the conventional wisdom of ideology (in literature, it is the realm of verisimilitude, so dear to Aristotle). Yet in reality the doxa, though 'evident', is never properly seen. In order to escape the deadly, 'castrating' gaze of the Doxa-Medusa, the writer has to behave as a wily 'eavesdropper', trying to overhear truth behind the doors of myth, listening to something 'said' in a place whence he or she will always be 'excluded'.

Now this provides some defence against the charge of dogmatism in that, if we drop the romantic cliché—the writer as Outlaw—we are left with a view of myth as something less class-bound than the fairly Manichaean picture drawn in *Mythologies*. The critic goes on demystifying the social culture, but at least it is no longer seen as an ideological set-up ('conspiratorial' or not) on behalf of a ruling class. Not surprisingly, by 1970, we find Barthes granting that there may be 'minority doxas'; that since the working class can scarcely be expected to determine by itself the meaning of most cultural discourses, there are bound to be procurators of 'proletarian meaning' who are definitely not 'producers'; and even that the idea of 'revolutionary students' can be one of the 'finest myths' ever.[7]

[7] Barthes, *Selected Writings*, pp. 388, 398, 387.

Quite a progress. On the other hand, it is also true that Barthes, after he widened his original narrow class perspective never achieved the same witty acumen evinced in debunking the fetishes of the French bourgeoisie in the mid-fifties. But perhaps (as John Casey suggested in his review of *Mythologies* for the *Spectator*) in the end, for all his anti-bourgeois ferocity, the real function of Barthes's onslaught on the trivia of bourgeois society may have been simply to add glamour to trinkets— surely a paradoxical counter-effect, from his 'semioclastic' viewpoint.

To point out another paradox in the early work of Barthes: when he, by his own admission, set out to explore a Sartrean problematic, in *Writing Degree Zero*, the end result was less a vindication of *engagé* literature (Sartre's recipe) than an almost Blanchotian theory of literary language as a contradictory mix of fate and freedom, a *'tragique de l'écriture'* miles away from the straightforward denotative prose Sartre called for, to the greater glory of 'democratic revolutionary socialism'. Conversely, where, as in *Mythologies*, Barthes had escaped a Sartrean problematic he was at his most Sartrean, adopting the class Manichaeism and the shallow revolutionary rhetoric of Marxist existentialism.

Be that as it may, by 1960 he became apparently disillusioned by engagement. In that year, writing in *Arguments*, he drew his celebrated distinction between *authors* and *writers*. For the writer (*écrivant*), writing is a means, an eminently transitive activity, geared to ready communication. For the author (*écrivain*), on the contrary, writing is an end in itself, a self-suffucent 'gesture', a narcissistic function. Writers are 'clerical' intellectuals; authors, 'priestly' artists. Authors are as old as the literary institution; writers came much later, 'at the time of the Revolution'.

It has been said[8] that for Barthes all interesting users of writing are 'authors' in this special sense. Indeed he dwells on 'the man who radically absorbs the world's *why* in a *how to write*' and yet, through this self-same 'tautological' and narcissitic activity, 'provokes an interrogation of the world'. Moreover, by stressing that authors 'work up' their texts, Barthes suggests (as John Sturrock noted) a kinship between literature

[8] J. Culler, *Barthes*, London 1983, p. 27.

and labour certainly appealing to left-wing intellectuals ever guilty about the social gulf between themselves and the working classes they profess to defend.[9] Claiming that language is not an instrument but a structure, Barthes warns that authors are objectively denied two kinds of discourse. They cannot write doctrine, since every explanation is bound to become, in literature, a 'spectacle', unwittingly condemned to ambiguity (authors being 'inductors of ambiguity'). Nor can they write as witnesses, for, however sincere, no consciousness succeeds in writing a testimony without making it turn more around language than about the moral goal that prompted it: both of which make a mockery of the demand for commitment in literature. The only way for literature to be responsive to the world is to let authors be responsible to literature itself.

However, it should be emphasized that Barthes is fully aware of the ideal typical nature of his distinction. He warns that in our time the two roles, author and writer, 'coexist'. In fact, 'our age produces a bastard type: the author-writer.' To tell the truth, since the French Revolution authors themselves, from Chateaubriand to Zola, 'broadened the literary function' and put the literary institution at the service of 'a new action'. Modern society has strengthened this trend by integrating intellectual authors into institutional circuits such as the university. Although Barthes's short essay is not exactly a model of sociological clarity, it is easy to see what he is up to: he cannot bring himself to confess that antinomian intellectuals are fully accepted (in status if not in their beliefs) in our liberal industrial culture; but he comes close to implying it by recognizing that, for all the 'cat-and-mouse games' society may play with them, our culture assigns to its sworn enemies a place and a role—'a function of complementarity'.[10] As for pure authors, far from demanding—as did that arch-intellectual, Sartre—that they become 'writers' and trade on ideas, Barthes is quite happy to leave them to their priestly craft, their Blanchotian rites of oblique language and obscure meaning. Why should we compel Orpheus to face Medusa? Better to leave that to the reluctant Perseus—the critic as eavesdropper of mythical noise, the author-writer such as Roland Barthes.

[9] Sturrock in Sturrock, *Structuralism and Since*, p. 67.
[10] Barthes, *Selected Writings*, p. 192.

The Argonaut and the Semiocrat

'Literature,' Barthes writes in the foreword to his *Critical Essays*, 'resembles the ship *Argo*': throughout her long history, the *Argo* was never a unitary creation, only a thing of *combinations*: each one of her pieces was endlessly renewed, and yet she remained forever the self-same vessel. Similarly, the desire to write is the 'constellation of a few obstinate figures', combined and re-combined over and over again. The proper method of studying literature is therefore structuralism, a search for invariants alive to structural transformation. The critic is an Argonaut, ever on the look-out for the combinatorial play of signs. In addition, texts are 'links in a floating chain of meaning' whose signifiers come from outside—from the changing social world, that is.

The same year (1963) in which he wrote this foreword, Barthes published a book in which he invited the reader to 'try out on Racine, in virtue of his very silence, all the languages our century suggests'. The result was his first sustained structural analysis, *On Racine*. In the idiom of his *Critical Essays*: what are the 'rules of functioning' of Racinean tragedy? By means of an 'anthropology of Racinean man' couched in a 'mildly psychoanalytic language', Barthes highlights hidden patterns in the dozen tragedies by Racine. The general picture strongly recalls the central theme of Freud's *Totem and Taboo* (1912): it tells a grim tale of blood and power. Jealous, guilt-ridden rebellion meets (self-inflicted) punishment. There are those—the strong ones—who embody the law of paternal domination, even, or especially, when they are women (Aggripine in *Britannicus*, Roxane in *Bajazet*); and there are those—the weaker ones—who act (as the rebellious sons in *Totem and Taboo*) in an attempt to become in turn 'fathers' in their own right, like Pyrrhus in *Andromaque* or Néron in *Britannicus*.

But Barthes warns that this is not a general key, a mechanical sesame accounting in a uniform way for all the plays. Rather, he concerns himself with filling it in with a far more detailed analysis that owes much, as he is the first to acknowledge, to Charles Mauron's *L'Inconscient dans l'oeuvre et la vie de Racine* (1957). Building on Mauron's work, Barthes displays remarkable originality in sorting out several figures and functions in the stifling Racinean world.

He begins by distinguishing, in Racine's plays, three tragic locations: the royal chamber, silent seat of power and its secrets; the world outside the palace, which feeds the tragedy with events but where tragic characters only set foot to escape or die: and, between the two, the antechamber, the place of language, hence the very scene of tragedy, since the behaviour of Racine's heroes is essentially verbal. In this closed space the spring of conflict lies in Eros, especially in the disruptive power of troubling passion, expressed in the famous *récits* of Racine's most highly sexed characters: Bajazet, Phèdre, Néron (from *Britannicus*) Pyrrhus (in *Adromaque*). Love, however, just triggers off the more basic Racinean bind we mentioned: the power relation. Barthes captures the root of Racine's tragedies in a double equation: A holds absolute power over B; A loves B, who does not love A. Not passion, then, but passion within violence is the law of such theatre.

Now power, in Racine, is the authority of the past, embodied in loyalties (to the Father, to the Father-husband) preceding the irruption of (illicit) passion. The sway of the past in turn governs time, for in Racine what was, *is*: time is repetition and therefore action is ritual. Hence two main categories among the weaker characters: those who remain bound to the Father or his memory (for example, Iphigénie, Andromaque) and those— the true Racinean heroes—who dare 'to fully accede to the problem of infidelity' (Néron, Titus, Phèdre, Pyrrhus), thereby emancipating themselves (whatever the consequences) from the authority of the past. Thus while Andromaque wants to remain faithful to Hector's memory, Pyrrhus—whom Barthes regards as the main character of the play—eventually chooses, by loving her, a 'new life' for which he will pay with his own; and the same predicament distresses Néron, who tried in vain to escape the past by marrying Junie. Néron's despair, as she rejects him, condemning him to repeat the murderous pattern of his life and family, is not the gloom of a man who has lost his mistress; it is, Barthes writes, 'the despair of a man doomed to grow old without having ever been born'.

There is an unmistakable existentialist echo in this idea of birth as a metaphor of freedom. Yet tragedy, unlike Lévi-Straussian myth, 'freezes the contradictions', keeps conflict alive: 'tragedy is the myth of the failure of myth'—and Barthes's analysis, with its avowed openness to our contemporary 'languages', is remarkably perceptive about several general traits of the Racinean tragic formula. If here and there some interpretations are strained, especially as he sticks to narrow psychoanalytic keys, there is no gainsaying that by and large *On Racine* is a masterpiece of intelligent criticism, doubtless the fruit of Barthes's long familiarity (attested by seven of the *Critical Essays*) with drama and, more specifically, with classical tragedy. Barthes, who never wrote anything of note on verse, signalled a genuine breakthrough in our understanding of the underlying mechanisms in the plays of France's greatest poet.

In particular his felicitous scrutiny of the economy of Racine's drama is head and shoulders above the 'genetic-structuralist' reading of Lucien Goldmann (*The Hidden God*, 1956), which, having spotted a significant relation between Racine and the tragic vision of the Jansenist *noblesse de robe*, failed to demonstrate the correlation at a proper structural level, valid for most, if not all, the tragedies.[11] If there is a case of vintage structuralism in literary criticism, such an instance is *On Racine*. When the book appeared, an unpretentious critic (René Matignon in *Arts*) said that it did for Racine what Malraux's Ministry of Culture was doing for the historical monuments of Paris's architecture: a *'ravalement'*, the cleaning of surfaces that restore the beauty of the stone work in Notre Dame or the Louvre. And so it did.

The only real trouble, in my view, concerns not his critical performance but his own description of it. For with the best will in the world, *On Racine* fails to yield 'rules of functioning' of Racinean tragedy. In other words, as the equivalent of a generative grammar in playwriting, Barthes's analysis simply doesn't deliver the goods. Barthes is not the Chomsky of Racinean tragedy—and we are none the sadder for it. Instead of a deep structure in any stable transformative sense, what we get is a vital advance in the mapping out of the Racinean universe. Doubtless, recurrent themes and patterns of dramatic conflict can be taken as invariants—but they do not belong to any generative model, as promised by Barthes's talk of 'rules of functioning'. Ultimately, although it obviously concentrates on elements other than sheer imagery, the interpretive achievement

[11] This contrast is well drawn by R. E. Jones, *Panorama de la Nouvelle Critique en France: de Gaston Bachelard à Jean-Paul Weber*, Paris 1968, chapter 4.

of *On Racine* is not in essence a cognitive operation very different from the thematic probing of his *Michelet*. But then there's no harm in that—except in the opinion of structuralist zealots.

Anybody slightly acquainted with the history of modern criticism knows that Barthes's book on Racine, though some of its text had been published since 1960, raised quite a fuss in the mid-sixties—the so-called *nouvelle critique* controversy, which revealed structuralist criticism to the public at large. We shall discuss it in a moment. But before doing so we must say a word about Barthes's next step—the completion, in fact, of his own official transformation into a structuralist. Naturally enough, this came about by means of a resolute espousal of Saussurean categories, still in the early 1960s. But the espousal brought about a curious reversal of perspectives. Saussure conceived of semiology as a general science of signs, with linguistics as a special region of it. Not so Barthes. In his *Elements of Semiology* (1964), a kind of crib drawing freely on Saussure, Hjelmslev and the Prague Circle's linguistics, he took issue with the Master and stated that far from being just a part, albeit a privileged one, of the general science of signs, linguistics should be seen as encompassing semiology: 'it is semiology that is a part of linguistics.'

However, this more-royalist-than-the-king move failed to convince most knowledgeable people. Barthes's own use of linguistic categories remained too loose to be taken altogether seriously. As the semiologist, Georges Mounin, was quick to show, both in the articles of *Mythologies*, which Barthes subsequently rationalized as semiological texts, and in much of his later work the objects of his study were seldom signs in the Saussurean sense of arbitrary, coded representations but rather symbols, and, far more often, indices.

Symbols in Saussure mean units of meaning in which the relation between signifier and signified is natural rather than arbitrary. Thus when Barthes, in his legendary piece on wrestling, says that in this sport the very physique of the wrestlers establishes 'a basic *sign*', in the terminology of Saussure (which he adopts in his theoretical coda, 'Myth Today'), he should more properly speak of *symbol*, not just sign.

Indices, by contrast, are immediately perceptible facts indicating something not readily perceptible. Now whenever Barthes scrutinized, say, the popular press, the rituals of sport and entertainment, the face of Greta Garbo, the vocabulary of fashion (in *Système de la Mode*) or again, images of Michelet, plots of Racine or a short tale by Balzac (in *S/Z*), he was always *taking indices for signs*, because he always began by examining all these forms of communication—the photo or text in the newspaper, the rules of a given sport, the movie image, the classical play or the novel—in order to elicit from each of them a *further* meaning, a *hidden* content.

Mounin is right: the theoretical Barthes quite often seems to reason as though: (a) everything endowed with a meaning were a sign; (b) all collections of signs were a system of signs, and (c) every system of signs a language. Therefore (following these prior paralogisms) he inferred that the sets of data whose psycho-social meaning he strove to grasp were languages,[12] and that the modest formula of Saussure (with linguistics as a part, no matter how great a part, of semiology) could and should be turned upside down. Instead of taking language as the richest province in the land of signs, he mistook all the other provinces for what they are not: languages, that is, territories of coded sign units dominated by manifest conventional meaning. When all is said and done, Barthes was a very gifted semiologist who had no clear idea of what he was doing.

This is especially true in the case of his longest book, *Système de la Mode* (1967)—a living proof that semiotics, dutifully applied, is capable of anything, even of turning such a witty essayist as Barthes into a perfect bore. With fashion he entered in principle a different semiotic universe in that here the immediately perceptible data—clothes—*are not already institutional signs* readable as indices, as they were in all the other instances just mentioned (even the rules of wrestling or cycle racing could be so considered). But though they are not signs in this institutional, openly coded sense, clothes are certainly interpretable as indices, that is, as bearers of many a connotation. Moreover, Barthes accentuates this aspect by focusing, not on the garments themselves but on photograph captions in fashion magazines ('the *written* fashion') on the grounds that these verbal elements are the normal indicators of what is fashionable, casting upon the sartorial stuff a grid of discrete categories,

---

[12] Mounin, *Sémiologie*, pp. 194–95.

each of them fraught with numerous but ordered connotations. Barthes scrutinized some fashion magazines of the late-fifties and took their technical description of fashion in a given season as a factor of 'structuration'; such description, he wrote, did not aim at isolating items for the sake of their aesthetic value but at making 'intelligible in an analytical way the reasons that turn a collection of details into an organized set'; for, as he put it, 'it is meaning that sells'.[13]

A problem naturally arises: given the goal Barthes set himself —a structural analysis of the fashionable sartorial repertory in a specific 'cycle' (fashion in a certain year, actually)—how are the words in the descriptions used in fashion journals that belong to the 'vestimentary code' to be distinguished from those words that are also part of the sentences describing garments, yet are not *pertinent* to the fashion code under consideration?

Barthes went about it as though the structural analysis of the sartorial corpus ruled out calling on the judgement of normally fashion-conscious people (consumers or producers of fashion) to elucidate problems of pertinence. The corpus had to 'speak' by itself. Moreover it had to be regarded in strictly *synchronic* terms, as indeed natural languages are when analysed as systems. But these methodological decisions prove quite crippling when it comes to solving the problem of pertinence.

Jonathan Culler has singled out a good instance of the difficulties involved. He seized on a case of piping, a caption that reads 'Une petite ganse fait l'élégance'. Barthes claimed that 'petite' was not a coded unit because its opposite, 'grande ganse', did not figure in the corpus of fashion in the year under study. But perhaps, notes Culler, it did not precisely because large pipings were *unfashionable* that particular season.[14] If so, Barthes' decision not to resort to intercode comparison turns out to be a typical structuralist overstatement of the synchronic —in plain English, a disregard for the time factor. Together with his no less questionable refusal to consider the social

[13] Barthes, *Système de la Mode*, Paris 1967, pp. 10, 26. Barthes said later (Tel Quel, Aut. 1971) that the focus on written fashion followed Lévi-Strauss's advice to stick to homogeneous corpora.

[14] J. Culler, *Structuralist Poetics: Structuralism and the Study of Literature*, 1975, p. 34–5.

dimension—fashion as actually experienced in public taste (even without going into deeper sociological analysis of the kind long ago pioneered by Simmel and represented nowadays by the Veblenian work of Quentin Bell[15]), this amounted to an unwise neglect of the need for clearly determining the pertinent traits in the discourse of fashion: pertinent, that is, for the system of connotations the semiologist wants to lay bare.

Thus the analysis of the 'vestimentary code', said to have taken years of Barthes's labours, proves to be largely self-defeating. It is only the second, shorter part of *Système de la Mode*—'the rhetorical system'—that gives the book life—and restores to us our dear old semioclast. There he is, stressing how fashion, besides presenting culture as though it were nature (just like social myths), mounts the 'spectacle' whereby 'men make what is insignificant signify'. Or contrasting fashion in traditional society, where garments, while signalling the social status of their bearers, did not disguise their semiotic role under 'functional' rationalizations, with bourgeois society, where the opposite occurs. Or again, portraying the 'fashionable' woman with the help of sociological snapshots worthy of the best moments of *Mythologies*.[16] Listen to the critical bite of this sharp and highly perceptive tirade on the inbuilt sexism of the fashion mentality: 'when fashion allows a woman to have a job, her occupation is neither completely noble (it is not quite the thing for a woman really to compete with men) nor absolutely inferior. It is always a 'clean' job: secretary, window-dresser, librarian; and this job always remains part of those callings which can be designated as 'self-abnegatory' (as, in the past, those of nurse or companion for an elderly lady). The woman's identity is thus defined as being in the service of man (the boss), of Art, of Thought, but this submission is always sublimated by pleasant working conditions and rendered aesthetic by exhibiting an image.[17]

All in all, however, *Système de la Mode* constitutes the summit of Barthesian semio-technics. No book of his is so patently the work of the dutiful structuralist, the painstaking

[15] G. Simmel, *Philosophie der Mode*, Berlin 1904.
[16] Barthes, *Système de la Mode*, pp. 287, 269–70, 263.
[17] Ibid., p. 256. Translation borrowed from P. Thody, *Roland Barthes: A Conservative Estimate*, London 1977, pp. 101–02

scrutinizer of a corpus, the slave to an abstruse taxonomic terminology. Here the semiocrat—a technician of semiology fully besotted by a scientistic mirage—clearly prevails over the 'Argonaut', the far more modest bricoleur of interpretation spotting combinatorial or simply recurrent elements in the mental and emotional underground of Racinean tragedy, without boasting of bogus 'codes'. From this point on, there was to some extent a split (instead of a mere alternance), in Barthes's semiotic soul, between the semiocrat and the Argonaut. A split that began with *S/Z*.

Criticism as Kitsch: from *S/Z* to *Empire of Signs*

As far as I remember, even in Barthes's ultra-fashionable seminar, at Rue de Rennes facing the church of St Germain-des-Prés, his hair-splitting, scholastic semiotics of fashion only got a lukewarm reception. The wedding between those two very Parisian wonders, haute couture and structuralist haute culture, proved less than fascinating. Some unkind wits went as far as suggesting that while it became more or less obvious that structuralism had failed to explain fashion, fashion might very well be able to explain structuralism. At any rate, almost everybody was relieved to see Barthes turn his semiological gaze (in 1968–9) to more familiar if largely unexplored ground and tackle, in his next and second lengthiest analytic enterprise, the work of Balzac.

S/Z (1970) may be reckoned a feat of structuralist hubris: two hundred-odd pages of Barthes on thirty pages of Balzac. Until then, all structuralist analytical machines bore on *universes*: the jungle of kinship systems, a plethora of Amerindian myths, the tragic microcosm of Racine, the world of fashion, the repertoires of narratology. *S/Z* changed the focus: it is one continuous book (Barthes's sole work of its kind) on one single text, *Sarrasine*, a Balzac novella of 1830 later incorporated into the *Comédie Humaine*. No wonder it became a kind of mythical paradigm of structuralist potency.

Barthes nails his colours to the mast on the back cover. His intention is to contribute to (among other things) 'the structural analysis of narrative' and the 'science of the text' by impersonating the four roles of work on the text acknowledged in the

Middle Ages: there was the *scriptor*, who copied a written work without any addition; the *compilator*, who added to the text, but added nothing by himself; the *commentator*, who added something original but only in order to clarify the text; and finally the *auctor*, who put forward his own ideas, though always supporting them with arguments from others. Barthes confesses to some slight variation: besides gathering around Balzac's *Sarrasine* 'the ideas of our culture', he says he has commented not to make intelligible but to ascertain 'what is the intelligible'; and he ends his back-cover presentation on a manifesto-like note by hailing the 'pluralization of criticism' the collective building of a 'liberating theory of the Signifier'. We hear distinctly the fanfares of the *Tel Quel* group, ever fond of wedding structuralism and libertarian catchwords. (*S/Z* was published by Editions du Seuil in the series sponsored by the journal and directed by its head, the bouyant Philippe Sollers, on whom Barthes was to write his penultimate, unimportant book: *Sollers Ecrivain*, 1979.)

Sarrasine is one of the least distinguished '*scènes de la vie parisienne*' within Balzac's *Human Comedy*. The first part of the narrative takes place at a brilliant reception given by the opulent and mysterious foreign family of Count Lanty at their magnificent *hôtel particulier* in the Faubourg Saint-Honoré. During the reception the narrator's partner, the marchionness of Rochefide, is intrigued by a bizarre and repulsive Methusela who proves to be very close to the Lantys. Ruffled by a clumsy contact with the decrepit creature, the marquise drags her escort into a boudoir dominated by a beautiful picture by Vien representing Adonis. When the narrator informs her that Vien painted Adonis after a *female* nude, a sculpture, she becomes very curious about it. The narrator plays upon her curiosity in order to get a rendezvous with the ravishing marquise. Next day, at her home, he tells her the life-story of the old man: he is no less than Zambinella, a castrato, who decades earlier had made a fortune out of his singing and his looks in mid-eighteenth-century Italy. There a young French sculptor, Ernest Sarrasine, fell deeply and tragically in love with him, or rather (as he then believed) with her. Madame de Rochefide finds it all positively disgusting, to her lover's dismay.

The story of Sarrasine's ill-starred passion forms the bulk of Balzac's text, though many would prefer the sparkling prose of the beginning, describing the Lanty party. Barthes chopped *Sarrasine* up into 561 unequal pieces called 'lexias'. The latter by no means correspond to the episodes of the tale, nor indeed (unless by accident) to paragraphs or sentences. Complaining that structural analysis of fiction has stopped 'at large structures', Barthes set out to 'follow the capillaries of meaning'— hence the breaking up of the text into 'galaxies of signifiers'.

But, of course, as in every structuralist interpretation, dividing is not enough: one must also classify. Barthes's grid for *Sarrasine* comprehends five 'big codes': the code of riddles, or *hermeneutic* code (for example, the uncanny wealth of the House of Lanty; the identity of the old man at their party; that of a picture of Adonis, which the narrator tells the marquise is really a portrait, and so on); the code of *semes*, that is, of connotations conveyed by sudden 'flickers of meaning' hinting at the signification and significance of a given character, place or name; the code of *symbols* (presumably less 'flickering' than the connotations of the 'code of semes'); the code of *actions*, which Barthes calls *proairetic* because it also comprehends the weighing of options before acting, named proairesis in ancient rhetoric; and the code of all the *cultural references* contained or implied by the text.

Lexias and codes give Barthes food for thought in ninety-odd rambling 'digressions' that harbour the more theoretical moments in *S/Z*. The taxonomic gusto and the gestures towards a science of the text still smack of the semio-technics of *Système de la Mode*. At the same time, however, Barthes enjoins us to think of *structuration* rather than of structure, and multiplies warnings to the effect that his codes, besides holding no hierarchy among themselves, are far less systematic than it may appear (appear to believers, that is: for to the sceptical reader they are anything but systematic—they are not even properly distinguished from one another). At any rate, to Barthes, the real thing is now the 'ludic' energy built into the profusion of signifiers (digression LXXI). The author of *Critical Essays* was very keen on eliciting *conditions* of signification; the author of *S/Z* has exchanged this circumspect concern with fundamentals for a much more playful outlook: meaning becomes unabashedly labile; interpretation, an endless series of capricious *glissandi*.

It is true that in *S/Z* Barthes does not indulge, heaven be praised, in the naïveties of narratology, the generative mirage that was by then inducing critics such as Claude Bremond, Greimas or Todorov to play the poor man's Chomsky in an unyielding field. But neither is he keen on simply pitting the individuality of the text (so treasured by stylistic criticism) against more generic categories. True, *S/Z* (digression XXIII) invites us to forget worn-out distinctions between the arts and to start asserting in their stead 'the plurality of the texts'. Still, one should not mistake this for any Goethean praise of the *individuum ineffabile*. From the outset (digression II) Barthes states that one should get rid at once of the idea of textual 'wholeness' and of what is external to it (so much the worse, therefore, for the 'cultural code': it is obviously admitted only on sufferance). Can one think of a better prop for aesthetic individuality than the age-honoured idea of wholeness?

Yet Barthes does not stop here. The very first page of *S/Z* demotes the individuality of texts in favour of their 'play', a play governed 'by the infinite paradigm of difference'. The same critic who, in 1966, godfathered Todorov et al's 'structural analysis of the narrative' (and turned the eighth issue of his journal, *Communications*, into a canon of narratology) was now patently much closer to the post-structuralist tendencies of *Tel Quel*—a group, quite significantly, then falling under the spell of the philosopher Jacques Derrida, the Columbus of the post-structuralist America. There was a strong chameleon-like streak in Barthes's intellectual personality.

Narratology apart, perhaps it is in Todorov that we may find the best way of understanding what Barthes was up to in the late sixties. At the time, Todorov drew a distinction between three traditional approaches to the interpretation of literature: projection, commentary, poetics. Projection read through literary texts in order to talk about the author and his or her social milieu. Commentary tried to stick to the text (as in the standard French practice of *'explication de texte'*). Finally, poetics sought general principles as enacted (though not simply exemplified) in particular works. Against all three, *reading*—a kind of commentary geared to structures—mediates between the text's individuality and the concern with general principles held by poetics. Now reading brings us quite near to that trans-individual textual 'play' envisaged by Barthes: for in reading, 'each literary text is at once a product of pre-existing categories and a transformation of the whole system', of what Todorov calls the 'generic system' of each text.[18]

So much for Barthes's aims in *S/Z*. What about the results? I suspect they are more meagre than most critical comments would suggest. To begin with, the relaxation of structuralism into the misty notion of a 'plural structuration', however appealing to tolerant, undogmatic minds, takes a heavy toll in terms of methodological consistency. It often makes Barthes's comments, both in the lexias and the digressions, exceedingly woolly and sloppy. On the other hand, this lack of discipline is far from ensuring an unbiased view, especially when Balzac's art is conceptualized. For all the genial beckoning to a 'collective' criticism called to sort out 'playfully' a profusion of signifiers, the book reflects a rather narrow-minded obsession with the 'illusions of realism'. Throughout the commentary, realism is shown to be no more than a convention (or a set of conventional devices, working as indices of a will-to-realism within artistic ideology). As for Balzac, he is just the obedient servant of such a doctrine and his work is interesting when the realist betrays his own creed and is caught red-handed building verisimilitude with the help of art, not life.

But the trouble with this relentless (and quite belated) denunciation of realism is that it is lop-sided on two scores. First, since at least Ernst Robert Curtius (*Balzac*, 1933) and Albert Béguin (*Balzac visionnaire*, 1946), nobody has equated Balzac with the cliché of the photographic 'realist novel'. Barthes's abuse of realism hits a straw-man rather than Balzac's actual fiction and to a large extent seems to result from a lack of any sustained discussion or utilization of modern, especially non-French, Balzac scholarship. (This happens only too often with structuralist critics: under the pretext of methodological novelty, they tend to overlook their predecessors' work—much to their own peril.) The absence of a sustained discussion of Béguin's work (a distinguished forebear of 'thematic' criticism) is all the more amazing since he was decisively helpful in the publication of *Writing Degree Zero*, turned down by Gallimard and then accepted by Seuil on the recommendation of the Swiss Béguin, who thus introduced Barthes to what was to become the leading structuralist publisher.

[18] See the essay 'Comment lire?' in T. Todorov, *Poétique de la Prose*, Paris 1971. Quote from p. 246.

Second, Barthes's utterly conventionalist view of realism as a style, though close to erstwhile relativist views such as Jakobson's,[19] falls short of modern reappraisals of this thorny issue. In the best-known of them, Ernst Gombrich's *Art and Illusion* (1960), the critical rejection of the 'innocent eye' thesis by no means entails a rash liquidation of the concept of realism and resemblance. Far from it: although he displays the most learned awareness that representation is never a replica, Gombrich builds his masterful study upon the idea that representational art is fuelled by a make-*and-match* process, by definition at a far remove from any wholesale dropping of mimetic concepts. Throughout, his book stresses the ambiguity of forms under the veil of illusion—but it does not sneer at the visual art equivalents of Stendhal's famous metaphor of the novel as a mirror by the road. On the contrary, Gombrich sees the history of art since the late eighteenth century as a fight against the sway of *schemata* in representation. Fine recent scholarship such as Linda Nochlin's *Realism* (1971) does not balk at stating that the major weapon in the struggle against conventional schemata was 'the empirical investigation of reality'.[20] This means that realism is not an empty label—and as in art, so in literature.

Barthes, on the other hand, treats realism as a mere confidence trick. Realism is but a rhetorical deception working through a number of *'effets de réel'*, technical devices geared to entice us into a tacit agreement with the ideology of verisimilitude. Malraux, acting as a popularizer of Wölfflin, insisted that all art is born out of art, not nature. Barthes sticks to this with a vengeance and, in the event, loses sight of a great deal of what is relevant for an understanding of the mechanics and the achievement of realist *trends* (which are as such perfectly compatible with non-naturalist styles such as Balzac's—or Stendhal's—own brands of romanticism).

We have seen how Barthes defined the 'degree zero of writing' with the 'transparent' prose of Camus in mind. Therefore *some* kind of realist literature seems to be tolerated in the

---

[19] See Jakobson's 1921 essay in R. Jakobson, *Questions de Poétique*, Paris 197, pp. 31–39.
[20] See L. Nochlin, *Realism*, Harmondsworth 1971, p. 20 and all of her excellent definitional chapter 1.

Barthesian dispensation. Unlike Balzac's, Camus's prose was not valued by the young Barthes in spite of its realist intentions but precisely *because* of them. True, its model ceased to be invoked after *Writing Degree Zero*, no doubt because Barthes made the deplorable decision to replace Camus by Robbe-Grillet as the modern novelist par excellence. But he never formally abjured it—which only increases our right to avail ourselves of this critical standard of a transparent narrative (is it not alive and well in a writer such as Handke, for instance?) and to use it as evidence that realist prose is not necessarily tantamount to a stereotyped moral vision, like the one assigned by Barthes to Balzac, and indeed to the whole classical and romantic heritage—a notion, anyway, hardly tenable after his own account of Racine. Is it not telling that Barthes's overcooked anti-realism should land in a quagmire of contradictions provoked by his own work?

At bottom, Barthes's unremitting war against realism was a piece of *Kulturkritik*—a corollary of his wish to break with 'the kerygmatic civilization of meaning and truth'.[21] If you assume that meaning boils down to the dogmatic Truth of a doctrinal Revelation (*kerygma*), it becomes easier to surmise what Barthes means by that lofty phrase, 'a liberating theory of the Signifier'. The trouble, of course, is that there is no cogent reason for conflating meaning and sacral Truth; and the kindred assumption that as things stand signifiers are in the clutches of a bunch of nasty signifieds in league with a highly repressive *kerygma* is far from self-evident either. Yet it is on these rickety planks that Barthes rests his actual reading of *Sarrasine*. For all his priestly structuralist talk about 'plural signification' and 'infinite (circular) transcribability'[22]—the endless shuttle between 'codes'—as the sole seat of true (read 'free') meaning, the fact remains that his lexias and digressions are heavily skewed towards a few definite biases. These in turn amount to no more than a mix of formalist foibles plus a rather jaded version of Oedipal blasphemy.

Let's take a quick look at how this Freudian formalism, or formalist Freudianism, works on poor Balzac. Examples of unwarranted formalist tenets abound in *S/Z*. In digression

---

[21] Barthes, *S/Z*, London 1975, p. 76 (digression XXXII).
[22] Ibid., p. 120 (digression LIII).

XXXII, Barthes would have us believe that the 'hermeneutic code', the one where narrative puzzles are posited and solved, is a formal contraption 'just like rhyme', structured by a pattern of expectation and fulfilment. This is all very well—but the actual story, the specifics of its plot, go straight overboard. They are treated as mere motivating nuisances, like those that so annoyed Shklovsky in the days of nascent formalism; and it is doubtful whether this is an adequate manner of coping with the wealth of meaning—including *moral* meaning—usually involved in the plots of great fiction.

Sometimes the formalist superstition takes itself so seriously that it reaches a kind of involuntary ridicule. Digression LVIII, for instance, recalls the episode in the novella when the infatuated Sarrasine brushes aside the warnings of an Italian pressing him to give up Zambinella or face mortal danger, since his/her protector, Cardinal Cicognara, would certainly be less than charitable to a rival. Thereupon Barthes earnestly instructs us not to be fooled by the narrative illusion: Sarrasine, says he, is by no means free to accept or refuse the Italian's warning, for 'if he were to heed it and to refrain from pursuing his adventure, there would be no story. In other words, Sarrasine is forced by discourse to keep his rendezvous with la Zambinella: the character's freedom is dominated by the discourse's instinct for self-preservation.' Please don't rub your eyes: it's really so. You might think that this odd, indeed Pickwickian, way of putting it is tongue-in-cheek—but unfortunately the very sententiousness ('the discourse's instinct for self-preservation') gives the lie to this hypothesis. Now while Barthes is being foolish in arguing like this, he is certainly not alone. Indeed it is standard structuralist wisdom to reason as though characters, let alone authors, had no will of their own—and to endow plot, language or whatever with a mysterious power of decision. Language, narrative, structure, does the willing that we, in our beclouded naïvety, insist on crediting people (real or imaginary) with . . .

But I mentioned a mix of formalism and Oedipal lore; so let us end with the second element. *S/Z* takes one trait of Balzac's novella—the castrato—and suffuses castration symbols everywhere. Castration is contagious, says Barthes. Zambinella's dream of femininity is said to pervade the whole tale. Barthes deploys a whole panoply of arguments and analogies to convince us that all the main characters, from Sarrasine down to

136

the marquise, are in one way or another affected by sexual denial or sexual inversion. The Lanty children, in particular, become tokens of a womanhood devoutly wished by Zambinella—the castrato. One of them, Marianina, is indeed a quintessential girl. But her brother Filippo, equally handsome (he makes one think of Antinous), is an adolescent whose looks, says Balzac, suggest a future full of 'male passions'; even at his tender age, he already makes the heads of young women turn.

Yet Barthes will have none of this nonsense. He decides that Filippo, too, belongs to the femininity that Zambinella could not reach in himself but achieved in his/her symbolic children, the Lanty youngsters and their beautiful mother. Why? Simply because, since Filippo 'plays no part in the story' he must be in the text in a purely symbolic capacity. Which one? Well, 'to say of a boy that he is beautiful is to make him feminine'—and if on top of that you compare him, as Balzac does, to Antinous (Hadrian's Apollo-like favourite), then you might as well lay your cards on the table. Filippo, according to Barthes (though not Balzac), has an 'ambiguous physique'; therefore his sole 'semantic existence' is to be placed 'in the women's camp, on the side of active castration.'[23] Let no one mislead you by recalling that in the romantic age comparisons of youthful beauty of either sex with well-known pieces of classical art were a staple device in the portrayal of characters; that nobody found broad-breasted Antinous, either in his colossal statue in the Vatican or in his bust in the Louvre (not to speak of a well-known relief at the Villa Albani in Rome) androgynous instead of virile; that in ancient art he was often portrayed as (among other deities) Hermes[24] but never as Hermaphrodite; and that in any case the context makes clear that Balzac was thinking in

[23] Ibid., pp. 37–38 (lexia 22 and digression XVIII).
[24] The so-called Antinous of the Vatican turned out in particular to be a Mercury. It was among the best-known and copied classical statues. Bernini told the students of the newly founded French Academy, in 1665, that when he was in difficulties with his first statue, he turned to it 'as to the oracle'. See R. Wittkower (*Sculpture—Process and Principles*, London 1977, pp. 191–93) who shows that Bernini still had the same 'Antinous' in mind as he drew studies for one of the angels originally planned for the S. Angelo bridge in Rome (the Angel with the Superscription, in the church of S. Andrea della Fratte; there is a second version in situ executed by Bernini—see Wittkower, *Sculpture*, pp. 195–200). In literature, of course, Antinous was more than once depicted as sexually inverted, long before Marguerite Yourcenar's *Mémoires d'Hadrien*

terms of physique, not of character. Above all, don't let Balzac himself deceive you by 'euphemisms' (Barthes dixit): 'vigorous eyebrow', 'male passions'—the critic knows better, and if he tells you that Filippo is effeminate, you had better believe him—otherwise how can he read his pan-castration theme into *Sarrasine*?

For *Sarrasine* is allegedly so castration-ridden that it gives a revealingly feminine ending to the name of its melancholy hero (Ernest Sarras*ine*) besides concealing in it a *z* (as in Zambinella)—a patently phallic letter. Not for nothing had Barthes come across the novella by reading a Freudian study: Jean Reboul's 'Sarrasine ou la castration personnifiée' in *Cahiers pour l'Analyse* (1967). Reboul, in turn, had his attention drawn to Balzac's text by a passing reference in the foreword of Bataille's *Le Bleu du Ciel*. Prior to his Italian sojourn, the stubborn, inexperienced young sculptor had been 'castrated' in Paris by Bouchardon, one of the first great post-baroque masters of his art. As young Sarrasine was motherless, Barthes jumps to the conclusion that Bouchardon, by lodging and helping him,

---

(1958), perhaps the best, most sensitive modern rendering of the theme. As distinct from the wide diversity of the Antinous iconography in antiquity (Antinous was practically the sole ancient individual, except for rulers, statesmen and philosophers, whose face got so reproduced), post-classical literature, especially without reference to this rich plastic and numismatic tradition, does tend to stress inversion, from Shelley's 'sullen effeminacy' line to Symonds and other decadents. One of the most prolific but also most mediocre among the latter, the camp 'magus' Joséphine Péladan, turns Antinous into the virgin homosexual lover in *Le Vice Suprême* (1884), where Antinous's also inverted mistress, the Princess d'Este, was modelled on Cristina, Princess Belgiojoso, the Paris lionne under Louis Philippe who was a carbonara, and a translator of Vico; Henry James's Princess Casamassima is said to be based on her; for a truer portrait, see Ludovico Incisa and Alberica Trivulzio's biography, Milan: Rusconi, 1984. Yet even in decadent subliterature Antinous's main appearance is not in an effeminate capacity but as a marble bust with emeralds: Mario Praz (*The Romantic Agony*, New York 1956, pp. 313–14, 346) explains the role of green-eyed youth in the symbolism of literary sadism. On the other hand, the pederastic parti-pris in the interpretation of Antinous's iconography does not belong to Antiquity (nor to the images Balzac could have in mind) but to some eloquent pages in the pathbreaking *History of Ancient Art* (1764) of Winckelmann, the father of neo-classical aesthetics in the visual field and a well-known tormented homosexual. On the ancient iconography of Antinous, see C. Clairmont, *Die Bildnisse des Antinous—ein Beitrag zur Porträtplastik unter Kaiser Hadrian*, Rome 1966.

replaces not his father but his missing mother.[25] Now mothers in Barthes do tend to be castrating, the personal sources of this rather one-sided interpretation being amply described in *Roland Barthes by Roland Barthes* (1975). Thus Bouchardon cannot but repress Sarrasine. How? By killing him with work and study, with no sexual compensation.[26] Once in Italy, however, Sarrasine will fall into another repressive trap: he will 'refuse to see' that Zambinella is no woman, partly by ignorance (he does not know that in Italy at that time women were not allowed on the stage, and Zambinella is an opera singer), but partly—and much more significantly—because, having been 'castrated' himself, he is powerfully attracted by a taboo: the cursed love of homosexuality.

The whole far-fetched interpretation revolves around repression. What disgusts the pretty marquise is precisely what Balzac, underneath all his blind loyalty to established morals, has shown behind the façade of his novella: (a) there is repression and (b) what is repressed is not normal sex. Delighted by the latter aspect, Barthes opens *S/Z* with a full-page reproduction of the *Endymion* of Girodet (1767–1824), inspired, according to the narrator in *Sarrasine*, by Vien's *Adonis* in turn modelled on the statue of Zambinella by Sarrasine. Girodet was a minor neo-classical artist much in vogue during the post-Napoleonic Restoration. A Davidian painter influenced by the romantic light of Prud'hon, 'the French Correggio', he managed to keep his male sleeping beauty 'as remote from the hard and vigorous rhetoric of David as from the genuine lyricism of Prud'hon', to use the wise words of Fritz Novotny.[27]

Delacroix once made a point of stating that in order to be a true romantic one had to know the difference between a Prud'hon (or a Gros) and a mere Girodet.[28] The latter's langorous Endymion, as a figure, seems to be indebted to an angel in one of Canova's papal tombs at St Peter's[29] (the superb Angel of Death in the monument of Clement XIII Rezzonico, the Venetian pope who died in 1769 when under duress from

[25] Barthes, *S/Z*, p. 97 (lexia 172).

[26] Ibid., pp. 102–03 (lexias 185 to 189).

[27] F. Novotny, *Painting and Sculpture in Europe 1780 to 1880*, Harmondsworth 1960, p. 12.

[28] H. Honour, *Romanticism*, Harmondsworth 1979, p. 22.

[29] H. Honour, *Neo-Classicism*, Harmondsworth 1968, p. 150.

the Bourbon kings to banish the Jesuits). But there is some poetic justice in Balzac's mention of Vien, not Canova, as the source of Girodet's archandrogynous Endymion: for Vien, the frivolous 'premier peintre du roi' in the 1780s, is much closer in spirit to the facile piquancy of Girodet's erotica, a good specimen of neo-classical kitsch.

As for Barthes, his placing of this effigy of unmanliness on the threshold of *S/Z* underscored the whole drift of his reading as a vindication of artificial femininity. One must admire his cleverness at it. Balzac has his picture of Adonis lit gently by an alabaster lamp. This is sufficient to set Barthes on an ingenious digression (xxix): he claims that the soft light of the Lantys' boudoir bathes the Zambinella-like Adonis just as the moon embraces her beloved Endymion; therefore, the lamp-moon, albeit feminine, is cast in an active role, while Adonis, a male, basks under her in sleeping passivity. Although a female, the lamp-moon penetrates Adonis-Endymion, possessing him; although masculine, the painted hero acts sexually as a woman, like the castrato in *Sarrasine*. Reinforced inversions of this kind are exactly what drive structuralists to analytical ecstasy. Now here is an inversion about . . . 'inversion'! Adonis has been marshalled to strengthen Barthes's panegyric of androgyny. One can doubt how much his stress on universal penis-envy advanced the cause of the liberation of the Signifier; but no one will fail to recognize in *S/Z* a rather forced alliance between gay power and structuralism.

Nevertheless, sexual politics apart, we still have to assess the critical yield of the book—'Barthes's *summa*', as Jonathan Culler has it. To Richard Howard, one of Barthes's English translators, the digressions in *S/Z* are 'exact'.[30] Maybe this word now has two meanings, one for the private use of structuralists and the other common to the rest of us. Or again perhaps we should agree with Graham Hough: since the structuralist flood, expressions such as *'homologie rigoureuse'* are French for a vague resemblance.[31] Be that as it may, despite occasional insights, *S/Z* is marred by a wilful over-interpretative attitude. Now I hope that after our comments on *Sur Racine* nobody will hold me capable of denying Barthes (or anyone else) the right

[30] Barthes, *S/Z*, p. XI.
[31] See his article in the *Times Literary Supplement*, 9 Dec 1977.

to 'try on Balzac the languages of our time'. Hence the use of psychoanalysis does not bother me—rather, it is its misuse in bullying the text of Balzac into meaning what it does not say, and does not seem to imply in any plausible sense. As it happens, while Barthes's skilful handling of Freudian concepts in *On Racine* did cast much light on several of his tragedies, his insistence on castration connotations in *Sarrasine* ends up by revealing more about Roland Barthes than about Balzac's novella—and that is, after all, the whole point of it.

Barthes himself warns that to reduce a text 'to the unity of meaning, by a deceptively univocal reading, is . . . to sketch the castrating gesture' (digression LXXIII). Yet, curiously enough, he makes this contention straight after endorsing a glaringly univocal and reductionist interpretation: having pointed out that the 'grouping of codes' in 'the movement of reading' constitutes a *braid* (text-tissu-*tresse*), he calmly quotes Freud: 'We know the symbolism of the braid: Freud, considering the origin of weaving, saw it as the labour of a woman braiding her pubic hairs to form the absent penis.'[32] Astonishingly, the critic swallows up the crudest Freudianism. But this in turn may be seen with the help of Freud: for is it not a wonderful slip on Barthes's part to have endorsed such a blatant sexual reductionism as he flattened Balzac's story into a tale about the ubiquity of castration-fear and castration-wish? Reboul, Barthes's source, thought that Sarrasine's gruesome disappointment as he finally realizes the truth about Zambinella also 'castrated' him[33]—a plausible remark, given the utter despondency of Sarrasine. But Barthes cannot leave things at that. He wants the narrator and the marquise to be castrated/castrating too; castration is like measles—something highly contagious. However, this insistence betrays a single-mindedness that ends by 'sketching a castrating gesture'. As Barbara Johnson puts it, Barthes 'erects castration into the *meaning of the text, its ultimate signified*'.[34] Moreover, Johnson has no difficulty in showing that both enamoured males in Balzac's novella—Sarrasine and the narrator—are narcissistic, and that actually the text of *Sarrasine*

[32] Barthes, *S/Z*, p. 160.

[33] Jacques Reboul, 'Sarrasine ou la Castration Personnifiée', *Cahiers pour l'Analyse*, 7, 1967.

[34] B. Johnson, *The Cultural Difference: Essays in the Contemporary Rhetoric of Reading*, Baltimore 1980, p. 11.

skilfully presents the sculptor's blind passion as a true *hamartia*, a tragic error of vision; for when the castrato demolishes Sarrasine's boastful masculinity we have been enabled by several details in the narrative to understand that the self-centred kind of love offered by him was indeed a 'castrating affection', in that it thoroughly cancelled out the true otherness of the other.[35] In short, Balzac's text has more to it than Barthes's one-sided reading would allow; Barthes, by reading too much into it, misses it out.

Whereas Barthes was naturally entitled, as every critic is, to concentrate on a peripheral work by a great novelist, the unobjective thrust of a great deal of his interpretation does not succeed in setting *Sarrasine* at the centre of Balzac's achievements—our final impression is of an extravagant analysis of an inconsequential text. The contrast with the labours of anti-formalist criticism in reinterpreting the Balzac of the major novels could not be greater (I refer, of course, to Lukács's *Studies in European Realism*, 1948; but I also have in mind Harry Levin's *The Gates of Horn: a study of five French realists*, 1963). For all the noise about revolutionary methodologies, structuralism seemed unable to cope with the strategic task of renewing and expanding our understanding of one of the giants of post-classical literature.

Right at the beginning of *S/Z* Barthes draws a polarity between readerly and writerly texts (*le lisible* et *le scriptible*). The antithesis hinges on two different modes of text consumption, and is not intended as a clear-cut division between two kinds of literature. In readerly texts, one goes from signifier to signified in a straightforward, automatic way; readerly texts pre-determine meaning, so that the reader's job is overly simplified: in fact, the reader is 'left with no more than the poor freedom either to accept or reject the text' (it's the bare 'contract of readership', French for Coleridge's 'willing suspension of disbelief'; Sartre brilliantly described it in *What is Literature?*). In a sneer at *Cinquième République* politics, Barthes says that in readerly literature, reading is but a referendum.

Writerly texts, by contrast, call for an active reader. Reading becomes thoroughly self-conscious and amorously playful;

[35] Ibid., pp. 9–10.

readers, transformed into virtual co-authors, make love to signifiers freed from the tyranny of fixed signifieds. Taking over from the previous author/writer dichotomy, which focused on the producer rather than the consumer of texts,[36] the writerly/readerly difference commands the theoretical field in the later Barthes—and in the process, largely blurs the distinction between producing and consuming as far as the meaning of texts is concerned.

In an essay of the early seventies entitled 'From Work to Text'[37] Barthes draws a related antithesis. Unlike 'works', 'texts' can be properly handled only in active language production; they are not bound by literary genres; they postpone infinitely the signified by dint of a wild play of freely floating signifiers; their eminently 'plural' meaning is not rooted in any truth-basis; they call (like Umberto Eco's *'opere aperte'*) for a collaborative reading; their author enjoys a 'ludic', not a paternal (authoritative) status. Works, says Barthes (indulging in one of the worst weaknesses of modern humanists—the drawing of unwarranted, misleading analogies borrowed from science) are closed Newtonian systems; texts are, of course, Einsteinianly open . . . They are also connected with libidinal utopias. Textuality, thy name is *Lustprinzip*. Not for nothing have essays such as these earned Barthes the nickname of being the first 'obsédé textuel'.

Almost point by point, Barthes's textolatry opposes 'new criticism's' concern with an 'ergocentric' perspective, that is, the primacy of work over author and the stress on a stable 'verbal icon'. But then Barthes seems never to have heard about new criticism. Moreover, when it comes to upstaging the author and the 'intentional fallacy', he does it with a vengeance. The same book (in fact a collection of essays felicitously assembled by Stephen Heath), which contains 'From Work to Text', *Image-Music-Text* (1977), also includes Barthes's celebrated piece on the death of the author. *S/Z*, quite naturally, already scorned the author as 'that somewhat decrepit deity of the old criticism' and decreed rather solemnly that 'the very being of writing . . . is to keep the question, Who is speaking?,

[36] L-J Calvet, *Roland Barthes: Un Regard Politique sur le Signe*, Paris 1973, p. 172.
[37] In Barthes, *Image, Music, Text*, London 1977.

from ever being answered.'[38] 'The Death of the Author' states that 'to give a text an author is to impose a limit on that text'; it further proclaims, 'the birth of the reader must be at the cost of the death of the Author.'[39] 'Author' here is a theological echo with deplorable teleological habits, because the author always strives to confer finality—in both senses of the word—to the text, that is, to present it far more as a 'work' than as a true 'text'. Barthes then reduces the author's self to a kind of byproduct of writing: 'Linguistically, the author is never more than the instance writing, just as *I* is nothing other than the instance saying *I*: language knows a 'subject', not a 'person', and this subject (is) empty outside of the very enunciation which defines it.'[40] A few years later, *Roland Barthes by Roland Barthes* insists on this strange authorcidal theory, reducing the writer to no more than 'an effect of language'.

In his major works after *S/Z* Barthes returned to what he had done in *Michelet* and *On Racine*: once again examining oeuvres rather than specific texts, he published *Sade/Fourier/Loyola* (1971). What was he up to in focusing on 'the bad, the mad and the sad', in the apt Browning-like phrase of Philip Thody?[41] Barthes sets out to detach their work from its ideological under-pinnings. He is not interested in Sadism, socialism or the Counter-Reformation; all he wants is to look at the writing of these ideologists. To do so, he proposes to 'steal' their language (as he puts it) from their ideas. But once this is done, what do we get—a network of obsessional images, as in Michelet, a set of figures symbolizing power, passion and guilt, as in Racine? Not exactly. Barthes sees the nasty Marquis, the great Catholic ascetic and the wild Utopian, who believed in the copulation of planets and earnestly expected that his communal paradise would transform sea water into lemonade, as 'logothetes': creators of original discourses. Hence he seeks to catch the particular grammar of each of their logoi. He is, of course, alive to what is common to his odd trio: for, underlying Sade's minute catalogue of sexual exploits, postures and permutations, Fourier's maniacal blueprint for a strictly harmonic civilization

---

[38] Barthes, *S/Z*, p. 211 (digression xc) and p. 140 (digression LIX).
[39] Barthes, *Image, Music, Text*, p. 148.
[40] Ibid., p. 145.
[41] Thody, *Barthes*, 1977, p. 127.

and Loyola's fastidious spiritual exercises, there is the same tendency to order, count and classify (or better said, to over-order, overcount and overclassify). Barthes's work consists of an attempt to unravel some basic rules beneath their taxonomies—a structuralist job, to be sure.

As might be expected, he writes more interestingly on Sade, a hero of French avant-garde culture since the surrealists (who of course also loved Fourier). The old neologist in Barthes (he thought neologism was a token of libertarianism) relishes dubbing the units of Sade's 'porno-grammar' 'erotemes'. At the same time, he keeps the fanciful style of overinterpretation displayed in *S/Z*. Witness his digression on the 'scriptural sperm' of the wretched Marquis, who was threatened with being denied pen and paper in his prison: 'castration!' cries Barthes: the inactive Sade grows fat 'as a eunuch'.

In practice, however, as Philip Thody noted, Barthes does indulge in comments on the thought of his three authors. He deems Fourier's 'harmonism'—a society defined by the free play of instincts, but where differences of opinion would have no place—better than 'the modern state', where a 'pious organization of leisure' is just a figleaf for 'a pitiless censorship over pleasure'. Shades of Marcuse and 'repressive desublimation', one might think; hollow libertarian clichés with a poor sense of the cultural reality of our permissive liberal society. By 1970, in stark contrast with the dignified silence of Lévi-Strauss, Barthes was sending hints of approval towards the spirit of May 1968. After all, the students worshipped the statue of Fourier.[42]

Perhaps we should see Barthes's yoking together of Sade and Fourier as a ritual gesture, an act of allegiance to an antinomian tradition in French literary thought. Only three years after *Sade/Fourier/Loyola*, the novelist Pierre Klossowski (a key figure in the launching of the Nietzsche revival so closely associated with post-structuralism, and one of the few true living masters of French prose) published his own *Sade et Fourier*. Klossowski's argument runs as follows: Sade saw that modern institutions seek to preserve individual freedom by

---

[42] Perry Anderson (*In the Tracks of Historical Materialism*, London 1983, p. 98) rightly deplores the persistence, in Marxist thought, along with the Saint-Simonian chimera of 'replacing the government of men by the administration of things', of Fourier's angelic idea of an 'abolition of the division of labour'.

substituting the exchange of goods for the (feudal) exchange of bodies. In reality, however, the circulation of money ensures an allocation of bodies in the interest of the social status quo; hence the repression of bodily exchange ends up by bolstering what boils down to disguised prostitution. Sade's secret societies highlight this predicament: they practise prostitution with a vengeance, on a monstrous scale (by the extent of their oppressive methods). Thus Sade, who like Nietzsche had no esteem for sociality and regarded mankind as just the raw material of outstanding individuals (the Sadist 'monsters'), wished to push modern society to its extreme logical development as a repressive order. Fourier, by contrast, was a socialist and an optimist. He replaced Sade's grim world of sex and power with an ideal of sensuous bliss based not on perversion but play—and in so doing, re-instated what Sade tried to denounce: the innocence of exchange.[43]

Klossowski's essay is worth mentioning because it is an elegant instance of the genre to which much of Barthes's own musings on Sade and Fourier belong: the old French genre of *experimental morals*, an (often tongue-in-cheek) exercise in moral thought periodically carried out in the land of great moralists by prominent writers from Anatole France to André Gide, and from Sartre or Camus to Jean Genet or Michel Leiris. Most structuralisms in the 1960s were closely related to modern stages in this tradition, at least since surrealist dissidents such as Bataille and Artaud. If this seldom emerges in academic discussions of structuralism, the reason is that most 'innovative' pundits in literary departments are now athletes of methodology with an increasingly scant literary culture.

Fourier's post-Sadean restoration of exchange in Utopian thought emboldens Barthes to praise money, flying in the face of proverbial Catholic, Marxist and Freudian distrust. Ultimately, however, Barthes's own ideal is too narcissistic to agree with any communal Eden. In *Roland Barthes by Roland Barthes*, he goes so far as to defend prostitution not, as did Sade, because it reveals the truth of the social order but because it allows one to go about one's own pleasure without bothering to think of one's partner. At bottom, Barthes wanted to combine Sade and

[43] P. Klossowski, *Les derniers Travaux de Gulliver suivi de Sade et Fourier*, Montpellier 1974, especially pp. 41, 49, 54, 57, 62 and 67–70.

Fourier: he would like to have sensuous bliss not in a communal, but in a deeply individualistic (and mildly perverse) society.

We shall presently see more of this as we discuss his later, overtly hedonistic texts. But before entering his crusade for personal pleasure, Barthes discovered the 'happiness' of the *sign*. Where? In Japan. There he was, as made plain in a pretty Skira book, *Empire of Signs* (1970), overjoyed as a semiologist. In Japan, Barthes found a glorious alternative to 'Western semiocracy', that is, to the kerygmatic dominance of Meaning as Truth. Japanese culture seemed to him the realm of semiosis as freedom. 'The Japanese sign is strong but empty,' he writes. What need is there for semioclasm in a culture where religion is all ritual and no God; where militants fight for the fight's sake; where towns are centreless, faces do not hide a personality, and the food invites everyone freely to compose a personal menu; where politeness is an *art pour l'art* practice and poetry a minimalist artistry, whose form is far more important than its content? Barthes did not see in Japan another symbolic, another metaphysical grounding. Rather, he craved the fissure (and fission) of the symbolic, of *all* the symbolic: he rejoiced in the nature of the Nipponese sign, which is (or so he thought), the void—the utmost degree zero of meaning.

Unfortunately, orientalists are not convinced. One of them, Professor Stephen Reckert, takes issue with Barthes's interpretation of the Sino-Japanese ideogram reproduced on page twelve of *Empire of Signs*. Barthes assumes that such an ideogram means 'emptiness'. Reckert explains that it corresponds to the verb 'to miss', or alternatively to the adjectives 'absent' or 'inexistent' (or more generally to the negative prefix 'in-' or 'un-') or again to the preposition 'without'—but not at all to 'empty'.[44] This little episode seems to encapsulate the whole spirit of the book. Frankly speaking, the trouble is that Barthes is not making sense of Japan—he is just making *use* of its culture as a *machine de guerre* against a (highly garbled) picture of the West. As one of the book's best reviewers put it, 'it is a mere accident that the world Barthes discovers . . . purports to

[44] Stephen Reckert, 'Império dos signos ou imperialismo dos significantes?' *Publicações Dom Quixote*, Lisboa, 1982, pp. 60–61.

be Japan. It could have been England or Bali or any country with a dense enough tradition of manners and art, where the visitor who does not share its conventions and code can still relish the style of what he finds'[45]—which makes it only too easy to understand why the Japanese public basically ignored Barthes's paean to their culture. In a more jocular vein, the veteran critic of *Le Figaro*, Robert Kanters, said that Barthes's ideal in *Empire of Signs* was patently to be able to write in Japanese without actually understanding the language[46]— maybe the best description yet of the campaign for the 'liberation of the Signifier'.

Taken together, the fanciful overinterpretations of *Sarrasine*, the brazen misconstruction of Japan and the whimsical *Kulturkritik* ensconced in *Sade/Fourier/Loyola* put semiological criticism—the 'interpretive trip' version of structuralism— in a definitely kitsch light. The weighty terminology and the pretence of higher wisdom create a visible chasm between critical intention and critical achievement. Structuralism is here at its most wildly analogical and irresponsible. No wonder it often beckons us to the more 'inventive' shores of post-structuralism, where the idea of accountable knowledge seems positively amiss. Semiology on a spree tried to demoralize standards of objectivity in the name of the holy right to dissent and debunk—but in the end, all that it achieved, through many tiresome clichés, was a discrediting of dissent. In so doing, it also rehearsed several main tenets of the humanist counter-culture, or of the subtler immoralist tradition, in a manner both strident and mollified. Lacking the sharp eye and the bold panache of his former semioclastic self, the *contestataire* structuralist of 1970 was all bark and little bite: Barthes was writing as an epigone of Barthes. On the eve of his final decade, he seemed eager to trade the duties of interpretation for other, more exciting uses of non-fictional writing.

[45] Hidé Ishiguro in the *Times Literary Supplement*, 12 August 1983.
[46] Quoted by Thody, *Barthes*, p. 123.

148

A Hedonist Apostasy: the Later Barthes

> *Je voudrais bien savoir si la grande*
> *règle de toutes les règles n'est pas de*
> *plaire. . . . Veut-on que tout un pub-*
> *lic s'abuse sur ces sortes de choses, et*
> *que chacun ne soit pas juge du plaisir*
> *qu'il y prend?*
>
> Molière,
> *Critique de l'Ecole des Femmes*, VI

In January 1977, well cured of his 'dream of scientificity', Barthes delivered his inaugural lecture at the Collège de France. He put forward a humble wisdom, based on the wish to 'forget' and 'unlearn'. '*Sapientia*,' he said, means less knowledge than 'flavour'. Two years earlier he told an interviewer that in linguistics he had never been 'anything but an amateur' (Mounin would promptly agree); and he called his intellectual autobiography, *Roland Barthes by Roland Barthes* (1975), 'the book of my resistance to my own ideas'.[47]

In the same vein, he re-defined semiology. No longer a linguistics writ large, it was now to focus on 'the impurity of language, the waste of linguistics, the immediate corruption of the message: nothing less than the desires, the fears, the appearances, the intimidations, the advances, the blandishments, the protests, the excuses, the aggressions, the various kinds of music out of which active language is made.'[48] In the inaugural lecture, from which these words are taken, he actually paints semiology as the debunking of linguistics' severance of language from discourse—something he now deems fallacious and even dishonest (an 'imposture'). Semiology changed, he says, because of the effect of May 1968 on the intellectual community.

The new direction taken by Barthes was hedonism: 'a discredited philosophy, repressed by centuries', as he put it in an interview.[49] There had, of course, been intimations of hedonistic reading in Barthes before its theoretical canon, *The Pleasure of the Text*, was published in 1973: *S/Z* with its gestures

[47] Barthes, *Roland Barthes by Roland Barthes*, London 1977, p. 119.
[48] Barthes, *Selected Writings*, pp. 470–71 (from the *Leçon*).
[49] Barthes, *Le Grain de la Voix*, Paris 1981, p. 194.

towards a joyful 'pluralization' of criticism; *Sade/Fourier/ Loyola* declaring the text 'an object of pleasure'; much of the *New Critical Essays* (1972) and of *Barthes by Barthes*. But the liberation of hedonism—the ideological rationale of the later Barthes—was proclaimed by the short book (one hundred-odd pages in a small format) of 1973.

Underlying Barthes's full conversion from structuralism to hedonism one notices a distinct shift in his main conceptual allegiances, from the austere structuralist categories of Saussure and (by Paris standards) of Lévi-Strauss to the labile notions of Lacan and Derrida. Therefore, a brief excursus on Lacan will help us to better understand Barthes's last books. (Derrida will be dealt with at greater length in Chapter 5.)

Until 1982, when he died, there were only two persons in the world able really to understand the theories of Dr Jacques Lacan: himself and God. Lest anyone think I am exaggerating, let's reproduce two often-quoted jewels from the Master's shimmering prose. The first comes from the beginning (p. 2) of *Ecrits*: On the mirror image: 'The fact is that the total form of the body by which the subject anticipates in a mirage the maturation of his power is given to him only as Gestalt, that is to say, in an exteriority in which this form is certainly more constituent than constituted, but in which it appears to him above all in a contrasting size that fixes it and in a symmetry that inverts it, in contrast with the turbulent movements that the subject feels are animating him.'

The book becomes no less obscure as it goes on. Take, for example, a brief quote from the very end (p. 835)—and this time, to exonerate Lacan's heroic translators, in the original French: 'Le sujet donc, on ne lui parle pas. Ça parle en lui, et c'est là qu'il s'appréhende, et ce d'autant plus forcément qu' avant que du seul fait que ça s'adresse à lui, il disparaisse comme sujet sous le signifiant qu'il devient, il n'était absolu-ment rien.'

One thing, however, can be said without risk: Lacan was conspicuously the theorist who provided the bridge between Saussurean structuralism and the 'negative dialectic' of main-stream post-structuralism, the fief of Jacques Derrida, where the imprint of Hegel and Heidegger is just as important as the mark of Saussure. Lacan 'Saussureanized' psychoanalysis by loftily decreeing that the 'unconscious is structured like a language'[50]—a highly fallacious oracle, since, as Benveniste has shown in masterly fashion, there are weighty *differences* between the unconscious and language. First, unlike the unconscious, language is something that is learned. Second, whereas the linguistic sign is, as we saw, essentially 'arbitrary', that is, unmotivated, Freudian symbols are by definition deeply motivated. Third, the unconscious is one and universal—its dreams and neuroses are made up of a 'vocabulary' common to every individual in all cultures while language, *precisely as system*, is articulated into *several* different natural languages.[51] Cognitively, therefore, Lacan's celebrated dictum is almost worthless. Obviously the unconscious makes much use of language, its rules and figures (how could it be otherwise?); but this by no means implies that it is 'structured like a language'. Actually the real function of Lacan's sentence is ideological: it was the main prop in a bold move to get rid of the positivism and biologism of classical Freudian thought, thereby aligning psychoanalysis with the much more 'culturalist', that is, non-naturalist tenor of the new *'sciences humaines'*. As Edouard Morot-Sir realized, the Freud of Lacan's 'return to Freud' was above all a gospel 'purified from his links with last century's outmoded epistemologies'.[52] It only remains to be seen whether the 'outmoded' was replaced by anything better than the merely modish—but that is another question, which need not concern us now.

At any rate, Lacan's borrowings from Saussure were always far from orthodox. The Lacanian 'law of the Signifier' stems from an alleged 'incessant sliding of the signified *under* the signifier.'[53] But this is to assert the primacy of the signifier in a spirit utterly foreign to Saussure's sober polarity: with Lacan, the signified goes overboard and the polarity is destroyed. Thus ultimately the unconscious is no language—it is just one of the faces of the linguistic coin, obscurely endowed with a dense, dim margin of symbolic meaning. No wonder Lacan was so keen on the poetics and ontology of absence—on Mallarmé and Heidegger.

[50] J. Lacan, *Ecrits: A Selection*, London 1977.
[51] Benveniste, *Problems*, chapter 7.
[52] E. Morot-Sir, *La Pensée Française d'Aujourd'hui*, Paris 1971, p. 102.
[53] Lacan, *Ecrits*, p. 154.

We have already met (see pp. 112–114) the ontology of absence in the poetics of Bataille and Blanchot—a key source for Barthes and much late and post-structuralism. Lacan's fondness for the Mallarméan theme of de-realizing poetics is at the root of his peculiar 'linguistic approach' to psychoanalysis: a linguistic approach that invokes Saussure's structuralism yet has no structures—and therefore provided French theory with a powerful rationale for going *post*-structuralist.

We saw how the Lacanian unconscious is far from being structural in the linguists' sense. On the other hand, it is eminently *verbal*—a bottomless cornucopia of word-playing. Lacan's whole work has been seen as a sequel to the *oral* tradition in French psychiatry, which made young Freud so admire the sheer brilliance of Charcot's lectures. His mutli-volume *Séminaire*, in particular, consists of a transcript of oral teaching patently enamoured of its own verbal wit; it reads as a relentless (and in the end, quite tiresome) improvisation of puns, as though Freud's main heuristic tool—free association—had been reduced to *word* association.

This comes as no surprise when one remembers Lacan's strong links with surrealism. Whilst his attempts at a systematic application of Saussurean perspectives to analysis came rather late in the day (in two papers from the 1950s, 'The Function and Field of Speech and Language in Psychoanalysis' and 'The Agency of the Letter in the Unconscious since Freud'), he met several leading surrealists considerably earlier, in the late twenties. The surreal poets René Crevel and Paul Eluard gave their blessing to his view that the writings of 'Aimée', the self-punitive paranoaic about whom Lacan wrote (in crystal-clear prose) his doctoral thesis (1932), had true poetic value. Lacan himself contributed articles to the surrealist review *Minotaure* (19). His second wife was the former Madame Bataille, née Sylvia Maklès, a school-mate of the sisters Kahn, the future Mrs André Breton and Mrs Raymond Queneau; and he is said to have inspired Salvador Dali's boisterous paranoia-mongering.

Like Jung, in whose Zurich clinic he spent some studious summers around 1930, Lacan was an expert on psychosis: schizophrenia and paranoia were staple subjects in his psychiatric background. Whenever I recall the hieratic solemnity of his dicta as an esoteric lecturer, held in awe in crowded rooms by high-brow Paris (Althusser, Barthes, Foucault, Derrida), or when, browsing through the journal of his school, *Scilicet* (1967–), I see that only the Master's articles are signed, I cannot avoid the impression that Dr Lacan did not restrict himself to inspiring Dali: he, too, was a skilful performer of fake paranoia —only this time, it was presented as 'theory'.

But this does not mean that his utterances did not matter. Indeed, the cult thinker, the Freudian guru, used the language of paranoia to convey the dogmas of the structuralist and then post-structuralist. Who, for instance, did more than Lacan to reinforce the structuralist taboo on the subject as consciousness and transparent selfhood? Lacan poured contempt on American ego psychology, a psychoanalytic trend developed by 'The New York troika', as he dubbed them: Rudolph Loewenstein, Ernst Kris and Heinz Hartmann. Now Loewenstein had been Lacan's analyst throughout the thirties until as a Jew he sought refuge in America during the war—which makes it tempting to construe Lacan's later hostility to Loewenstein's brainchild, ego-centred Freudianism, as an aggression born of a sense of abandonment.

But since his seminal paper on the mirror phase (1937) Lacan had already redefined ego-making as a process far removed from stable selfhood. He saw the original ego as formed in the child's play with its own mirror image. This process of self-identification, however, does not represent anything like a stage in the way to psychic maturity; rejecting Freud's developmental views, Lacan denounced all unity of the ego as a dubious and precarious achievement, foredoomed by the essential in-completeness of man. Scattered through the *Ecrits* and the *Séminaire* there is a bitter quarrel with the famous Freudian motto 'Where id was, there ego shall be'—though characteristically Lacan, in his unconvincing fundamentalism, would have us believe that Freud's sentence does *not* mean an ideal rule of the ego and goes so far as to suggest (in *Séminaire XI*) that it should be paraphrased as 'here, in the realm of dream, you are at home. . . .'

Furthermore, the self's dynamic was for Lacan a function of drives deeply contingent on the other's desire. Alluding to Hegel's insightful stress on the craving for recognition as a key factor in human interaction, Lacan stated that *'the first object of desire is to be recognized by the other'*. But he gives it quite a twist: desire for the other's regard becomes desire for the other's object of desire. Thus the child's desire, in Lacan, is less for the mother than for what she most lacks and wants: the phallus (oddly enough, this stark Freudian machismo did not prevent French feminism, or the nouveaux philosophes, from adopting Lacan).

So far so good. By severing drives and desires from instinctual urges, Lacan ruthlessly debiologized psychoanalysis; he kept as great a distance from crude biological determinisms as the so-called 'cultural school' of neo-Freudians (Erich Fromm, Karen Horney, H. S. Sullivan). But unlike the culturalist Freudians, his own dropping of instinct did not lead to a more sociological approach to the psyche. Lacan set great store by the other (*'l'inconscient, c'est le discours de l'autre'*); yet his main focus falls consistently on the abstract otherness of an impersonal symbolic order (a 'Name-of-the-Father' imposing denials on a feeble, egoless subject); he pays scant attention to concrete others, that is, true individuals exchanging reactions and emotions. In one of the first important English-language articles on him ('The Cabinet of Dr Lacan', New York Review of Books, 25.1.1979) the noted Freudian, Richard Wollheim, remarked that Lacanian theory has no room for individual experience, and is accordingly very poor, by Freudian standards, in case histories.

Instead of turning his debiologized Freudianism to social interaction, Lacan plugs the unconscious into language or, better still, into rhetoric. He sees censorship and repression, the classical Freudian mechanisms, as symbol mills, ever churning out metaphors and metonymies. Desire, once displaced through fascination with the other, becomes a playground for metaphoric repression. The self's accession to the symbolic marks its acceptance of the father's name as a prime object of desire (the phallus, coveted by the mother) that is also the source of the Law as an instance of repression, that is to say, culture. Desire is caught up in the Law as a fly in a spider's net: even when the Law is permissive, and allows or commands pleasure, the subject is less free than compliant (if the Law says *'Jouis!'* (enjoy yourself), the subject will translate it into *'J'ouïs'* (I hear)). Consequently desire is irretrievably affected by denial and cannot help substituting one object for another, forever and forever; and this endless chain of substitutions makes the unconscious intensely prolific in tropes.

The Name-of-the-Father thesis encapsulates the basis of

Lacan's outlook. We saw how the father's name denotes the phallus transmogrified into a general sign of the other and the other's desire. It identifies Freud's sexual theory with, or reduces it to, an almost Jansenist Christian view of salvation through repression. For culture and society to obtain, we need a symbolic order. The Name of the Father—the Super-Other—is the hub of it all: it guarantees meaning by being the linchpin of the symbolic. Then the whole theory is clinched by a crowning pun: the *Nom du Père* is also a *Non du Père*, a transcendental denial of the individual's 'imaginary' as a realm of desire. Therefore the phallus/father points to a fundamental, irredeemable lack ('manque').

The religious overtones are unmistakable. Lacan came from a Catholic background. His doctoral thesis was dedicated to his brother, a Benedictine monk. He predicated the unconscious on a dark view of man as a creature defined by want and imperfection. Freud held no rosy idea of man, and died with many forebodings about the fate of civilisation—but in his therapeutic enlightenment he kept his faith in a modicum of bliss, based on an alleviation of instinctual repression. By contrast, Lacanian man seems definitely cursed, a melancholy child of the Fall.

Lacan has been the most influential post-Freudian since Jung. There are similarities between them, not least in the way these two experts on psychosis repressed the naturalist aims of classical psychoanalysis and refurbished it as a humanist lore. Jung did it by means of a deliberate absorption of religion and mythology; Lacan, by dint of a prolonged intimacy with modernist literature. Yet the cultural tone of Jung's quest for spirituality could not be further from Lacan's literarization of psychoanalysis. In his own high-minded way Jung was as optimistic a prophet as his antithesis, the over-sexualizing Wilhelm Reich. Not so Lacan, the archdenier of fulfilment, for whom all desire was bound up with the tragedy of lack and dissatisfaction. Jung condemned modern civilization for its soullessness but for Lacan civilization tout court was rubbish: *'cloaca maxima'*, he called it. In this grim pessimism he was a true contemporary of Sartre, the metaphysician of humanity as a pointless passion. Lévi-Strauss became disillusioned with history, but Lacan despaired of humanity as such—an echo of existentialist nihilism quite alien to the romantic optimism of mainstream surrealism, a movement detested and decried by Sartre. Lacan, of course, substituted a quiescent mood for the Sartrean revolt—but the nihilist ground was much the same.

The price of meaningfulness—of meaning—is, in Lacan's terms, repression and denial. Culture (the symbolic) is a forbidding Law, a merciless Order of the Other. Psychosis alone, by refusing to stabilize a symbolic order, opens up a flux of baseless signifiers. But we have seen that for Lacan the unconscious, 'structured' as a language, is dominated, indeed overwhelmed, by the 'primacy of the signifier'. Does this mean that the 'linguistic' unconscious mimes psychotic processes? Inhabiting a shadowy psyche, unconnected with any discernible reality principle, the Lacanian unconscious amounts to an uncanny id of language—the stuff of 'unrepressed' signifiers. Just as Hegel spoke of a Bacchic dance of the concept, Lacan enthused over the drunken signifier and its 'decentred' subject. As we saw, Lévi-Strauss postulated a 'floating signifier' that engenders a perpetual surplus of meaning ever ahead of the advances of knowledge. But Lacan promotes a fission of this floating signifier: he tends to conflate sign and signifier, and then surrenders all signifiers to a fog of ever-elusive meaning. That is why his theories had such an appeal for post-structuralist literary criticism and its fierce reference-phobia (and Lacan's greatest impact by far was in literary quarters—understandably enough).

The Lacanian theme—the hypostasis of the signifier—plays a central role in Derrida's strategy of *deconstruction*, as we shall see (Chapter 5). Both Barthes and Derrida (along with Althusser and Foucault) attended Lacan's crowded seminars in the sixties.[54] The later Barthes paid explicit tribute to Derrida and Lacan. For intance, he connected his dropping of structuralist matrices in *S/Z* to the Derridean concept of difference.[55] As for Lacan, he credited him with the central concept in *The Pleasure of the Text*: the notion of bliss or ecstasy (jouissance). On the one hand, there is natural, organic pleasure, ruled by deprivation and fulfilment. On the other, there is bliss, a Bataillean short-lived excess (like orgasm) akin to loss and self-

[54] Cf. J. Passmore, *Recent Philosophers*, London 1985, p. 138.
[55] See 'A conversation with Roland Barthes', in *Signs of the Times* (Cambridge: Granta, 1971), quoted in Culler, 1975, p. 242.

dissolution. *The Pleasure of the Text* often speaks of pleasure (beginning with the book's title) when what is meant is more than pleasure, that is to say, bliss; but that, explains Barthes, is just because French does not have a generic word encompassing forms of hedonic experience.

Barthes claims that true pleasure has always been repressed as a philosophical banner: only marginal thinkers such as Sade or Fourier upheld it, and even in Nietzsche hedonism was only half-vindicated, since it was still tinged with pessimism. In our own time there is much lauding of desire, very little of pleasure. Yet it cannot be sheer coincidence that genuine materialists in the past, Epicurus, Diderot and again, Sade or Fourier, were all hedonists. Barthes's worst grievance is that official left ideology, 'forgetful of Marx's and Brecht's cigars', is suspicious, or scorns every 'residue of hedonism'. *The Pleasure of the Text*—which *Le Monde*'s critic, Bertrand Poirot-Delpêche, called 'Barthes's Kama Sutra'—intended to redress the balance.

Ostensibly, however, its aphorisms deal with literary criticism —they are recipes for proper reading. According to Barthes, there are two kinds of agreeable texts. The pleasurable text brings euphoria out of a 'comfortable' reading that corroborates one's given cultural standards; blissful texts, by contrast, unsettle our cultural expectations, disturb us to the point of boredom, subvert our normal relation with language: they break pleasure, language, culture 'into pieces'. Bliss often comes in a 'drift' disrespectful of wholeness—which again sounds pretty close to Lacan's almost Kleinian love for unconscious fission, the split self, shattered meaning.

The pleasure/bliss dichotomy in turn implies 'two reading regimes': one (adequate to the traditional pleasant text) fastens on the plot and neglects the play of language; the other dwells on the latter. Barthes contends that if we decide to read a modern text quickly, it will deny us our gratification, while if, on the contrary, we undertake a slow reading of a Zola novel, it will fall from our drowsy hands. (I have tried this on *Lois*, by Sollers—a text praised by Barthes—and I must confess it wasn't the book that fell: it was me, bored to death.) As the French like to say, *c'est à dormir debout*. Yet Sollers, Severo Sarduy and the insufferable Guyotat are precisely what Barthes mentions as modern texts, sources of bliss.

Blissful textuality, *'happy Babel'*—offers us meaning produced *sensually*: *'signifiance'*, Barthes says, borrowing one more gratuitous neologism from Julia Kristeva, the high priestess of a very Lacanian (in)discipline, 'semianalysis', or semiotics taught to speak Lacanese. Kristeva, a brilliant Bulgarian scholar, settled in Paris and married Sollers, the leading editor of *Tel Quel*. Barthes's debt to her stressed his own kinship with the *Tel Quel* group, the temple of post-structuralism. But Barthes's old gurus, Bataille and Blanchot, are not too far away either: for whereas the pleasure-text is sayable, textual bliss is by definition *ineffable*—as dead silent as the ecstasies of Orphic literature. Lacan had also warned that bliss could only be uttered between the lines. And Barthes is only too glad to comply with the Lacanian subsumption of signified under Signifier: he is at pains to remind us that, in his hedonist poetics, bliss 'lifts' the signified, so that all value goes to the 'sumptuous plane of the signifier'.

However, Barthes adds a touch of immoralism by contending that the rule of textual pleasure is 'perversion'. Writing, says he, is an Oedipal fantasy: 'the writer is someone who plays with his own mother's body.' His notion of a blissful textuality comprehends 'one's body's own ideas', just as it includes a kind of 'writing aloud' yielding a 'stereophony of deep flesh'—something not very distant, one senses, from the 'somatic' concept of style we met in *Writing Degree Zero*. Yet for the reader the text is a spider's web, a fabric in which the subject gets lost. These 'masochist' overtones had already led Barthes, in the early seventies, to praise literature's power 'to astonish us'[56]—a revival of Cocteau's slogan (*étonnez-moi!*) few would have expected from him.

The Pleasure of the Text is Barthes's first full-blown post-structuralist work. Not surprisingly, Nietzsche is invoked throughout its slim pages. As a statement in aesthetics, these scattered fragments (inaugurating a felicitous technique continued in *Barthes by Barthes* and *A Lover's Discourse*) put us before something quite original: an attempt to vindicate modernist literature, that is, radical avant-garde, 'Joycean' writing, by means of the very concept—the classical idea of *delight* as an

---

[56] See his foreword to Chateaubriand's *Vie de Rancé*, included in Barthes, *New Critical Essays*, London 1980.

end of literary art—consistently abhorred by all avant-garde poetics.

Shortly before Barthes's unabashed conversion to hedonism, T. W. Adorno gave the Frankfurt school his summa, an *Aesthetische Theorie* (1970) starkly inimical to hedonist art. To Adorno, modern art justly glories in defeating the 'culinary' aesthetics of delight. Now it might be argued that by separating demanding bliss from easy pleasure Barthes reinstates much that resembles Adorno's unpalatable norm. Yet a still better case could be made for saying that Barthes seeks to free modernism or at least neo-modernism from all puritanism, including its own original revulsion against 'pleasantness' in art. Barthes's writings after *The Pleasure of the Text* fully confirm a shift away from the aesthetics of difficulty, still so influential in his choice of literary models in the 1973 book. I cannot but agree with Susan Sontag: in the end, he came to speak of literature 'as the embrace of subject and object' and in so doing disposed of the dour aesthetics of absence[57]—and what a good riddance it was. The real trouble with *The Pleasure of the Text* is that Barthes seems to equate textual delight with the suspension of criticism and judgement, as though individual joys in reading entail the collapse of every horizon of shared values and objective valuation.

After pleasure, love. *A Lover's Discourse* (1977), Barthes's lyrical text, is a casual 'dictionary' where several fragments on passion, mostly prompted by a reading of Goethe's *Werther*, are placed loosely as entries in alphabetical order so as to avoid 'the temptation of meaning', that is to say, of a theoretical totality. The book contains an attack on the disparagement or neglect of love as such in three powerful belief systems: Christianity, psychoanalysis, Marxism. Barthes also takes arms against both the Socratic and the romantic love ethics because both enjoin sublimation, while the prize merit of love is for him the 'withdrawal from all finality'. His critique of romantic passion lies at the antipodes of Denis de Rougemont's 'neo-classical' strictures in *L'Amour et l'Occident*: unlike de Rougemont, Barthes sides with passion, but wants it de-sublimated—just the opposite of the chivalry of *amour courtois*, whose mystique had been rekindled during surrealism by Breton's eulogy of *l'amour fou*. As

[57] S. Sontag, Introduction to Barthes, *Selected Writings*, p. xxxvi.

so often, Barthes's own intellectual ancestry belongs rather to the heretic surrealism of Bataille, whose writings on eroticism (as well as his fictional erotica) were bedside reading for structuralists.

Sometimes Barthes displays a psychological insight worthy of Stendhal in *De l'Amour*, as for instance when he describes the complex set of emotions involved in jealousy and, above all, in what he says about the dialectic of concealment and expression in a lover's behaviour. Here passion becomes a (cryptic) message from lovers to loved ones; infatuation requires, creates its own spectacle and so, for all a lover's struggle to hide his feelings, 'the sign always wins'. *'Larvatus prodeo'*—'I come forward pointing at my mask': the motto of Roman actors, which Descartes liked to quote, also defines—Barthes says— the fate of lovers, doomed to betray themselves. The semiotic critic turned erotologist rejoices at every awareness of sign.

A golden thread links *A Lover's Discourse* to *Barthes by Barthes* and *The Pleasure of the Text*: narcissism. And in narcissism is grounded Barthes's resolute pitting of *discourse* against language. *'Language is fascist'*, Barthes states in his Collège de France inaugural lecture: it is totalitarian because it *compels* speech (of a certain kind). Discourse, the voice of the self (no matter how different from the subject myth of the doxa), is all there is to redeem words from the grip of 'sociolects'. Yet at bottom the lover is ensnared in the impossible dream of saying the unsayable. No more than writers can lovers 'write themselves'; to write is to mourn one's sincerity. Writing and loving, writing and living, are ultimately incompatible. In order to save in words what is adored, a lover has to walk towards language, turning away from the object of love. Once again, in love's writing, we find the predicament of Orpheus.[58]

The later Barthes was writing in the *libertine* tradition—a recurrent element in French literature since the early modern sceptic Epicureans such as Saint-Evremond, Théophile de Viau or Cyrano de Bergerac challenged the moral order of the Grand

---

[58] The Portuguese Barthesian José Augusto Seabra—one of the finest interpreters of Barthes's thought—showing the recurrence of the Orphic motive in all his oeuvre, relates it convincingly to another mythical streak in the Blanchot-Barthes line: the Moses situation of the writer, who walks towards a Promised Land (the utopia of his imaginary, in Lacanian terms) without ever reaching it. See Seabra, *Poética de Barthes*, Oporto 1980.

Siècle. There was a kinship between the libertine litterati and the important philosopher Gassendi (1592–1655), who opposed both scholasticism and Cartesianism.[59] Molière and La Fontaine, among the French classics, were not untouched by libertinism, which in the next century came back in full force in the fictions of Laclos and Sade. Romantic libertines such as Gautier handed on the torch to Baudelaire and the symbolists and decadents, most of whom were 'heretic' sensualists (Verlaine and Rimbaud come readily to mind). Then the tradition was carried on by some great immoralist writers, from those brought up in the second symbolist generation, such as Gide, to the maverick existentialist, Genet, who restored the old alliance between libertine and *maudit* forged by Sade and Rimbaud in their own peculiar ways. This placed libertine writing in a moral landscape very different from the innocent sensualism of the first libertines.

Between Gide and Genet, however, there came the age of avant-garde, dominated in France by surrealism. Now surrealism marked a curious watershed as regards libertinism. The rebelliousness of Breton and his friends, for all the homage paid to Sade and Rimbaud was far less perverse and *maudit* than once appeared to be the case. Surrealism soon departed from the nihilism of Dada, its avant-garde cradle. The dadaists were anarchic destroyers; the surrealists, visionary neo-romantics. As is now increasingly recognized,[60] they deftly transformed the coarse nihilism of Dada into the optimism of a 'Cartesian' romanticism—an exaltation of the power of mind. But although surrealism never thought of itself as an idealism or a mysticism, and actually took pains to dissociate the surreal from the supernatural, keeping its 'immanent beyond' poles apart from the transcendental, the drive towards differentiation from its dadaist origins did so to speak spiritualize the movement. In the process, the link with the libertine stress on countermorality, especially as this became twisted in the nihilist mould, was considerably weakened. To a large extent, mainstream

[59] In the study of the philosophical counterpart of libertine literature in its origins, J. S. Spink's *French Free-Thought from Gassendi to Voltaire*, New York 1960, still commands the field.
[60] For studies on surrealism which stress its differences from dadaism, see M. Nadeau, *History of Surrealism*, London 1967 and R. Cardinal and R. Short, *Surrealism: Permanent Revolution*, London 1970.

surrealism remained much more libertarian than libertine. It was left to *dissident* surrealists, like Bataille, to join forces with genuine sacrilegious literature.

As a critic, Roland Barthes began by writing on Gide[61] and ended with an empathetic analysis of Sade. The immoralist and perverse components of the headier brands of libertinism were always among his literary predilections. That literature is a conveyor of shocking countermorals was not an odd possibility for him—it was a matter of course. Indeed, one of the most conspicuous traits in his intellectual profile was his ability to combine this aspect of 'content'—his loyalty to 'nasty' libertinism—with a long allegiance to the formalist poetics of the avant-garde. Now uniting these two lines—libertine counter-culture and modernist formalism—was tantamount to some novelty in French literary criticism, for all previous critics, even when sympathetic to key areas in the modernist canon, had shied away from more radical avant-garde techniques (thus Blanchot, for all his loyalty to Mallarmé, never got close to radical literary language of any kind).

Yet, by the end of his career, Barthes was veering in another direction. He stuck to the modern libertine challenge to bourgeois morals and liberal culture, but started tentatively to take the edge off its more dogmatic, sectarian sides. In *Barthes by Barthes* he provocatively asked whether 'a bit of sentimentality' would not be 'the utmost transgression'. *A Lover's Discourse* contends that today 'it is no longer the sexual which is indecent, it is the sentimental—censured in the name of what is finally only another morality.'[62] Notice the form of the reasoning: a Nietzschean immoralism (the quip about moralities) is employed to turn the tables on the doxa of modernist counter-culture itself, which takes pride in its sexual liberation yet represses as moral kitsch every manifestation of sentiment. *The Pleasure of the Text* denies culture *and its destruction* the privilege of harbouring the erotic.

At the same time, Barthes was also mellowing on the issue of form. Despite his attachment to the work of avant-garde purists such as Sollers, his hedonist breviary acknowledged that every text, no matter how radically autonomous its language, 'needs a

---

[61] See the 1942 essay 'On Gide and his journal' in *Barthes: Selected Writings*.
[62] Barthes, *A Lover's Discourse: Fragments*, London 1979, p. 177.

shadow: *a bit* of ideology, a bit of representation, a bit of subject . . . ; subversion must produce its own *chiaroscuro*.'[63] Again, we retain modernist taboos (for example, mimesis: the 'bit of representation') on sufferance, as it were—but the progress away from formalist prejudice is no less visible for it.

So much so, that structuralist or post-structuralist fans do not find it easy to forgive him for his later allergy to models and systems, his 'regressive' admissions of mimesis and feeling, or his alleged numbing of critical intelligence through the humane mood of his last books: *Barthes by Barthes, A Lover's Discourse* or *Camera Lucida* (1980), an essay on photography which is bold enough to be openly sentimental about the loss of one's mother and to allow photos a direct mimetic value—a double blasphemy, in terms of the modernist creed. Barthes's own image is now often a victim of Barthesian puritans.[64] It would seem that it takes the quiet courage of Philip Thody—the man who dared to write 'a conservative estimate' of Barthes, and produced the most sensitive and sensible discussion of him in English or indeed in any language—to recognize that as a writer-thinker Barthes deserves to be reckoned, alongside fine clarets, among that rare category: the older, the better.[65]

From Fruit to Onion: Barthes's Critical Theory

Although I have commented on Barthes's beliefs, our discussion of him has focused up to now on his performance as a literary theorist (in *Writing Degree Zero, The Pleasure of the Text* and other essays), as a critic (*Michelet, On Racine, S/Z*, etcetera), and as a semiologist (*Mythologies, Système de la Mode*). Admittedly the later Barthes, in books like *Barthes by Barthes* and *A Lover's Discourse*, was moving away from criticism or semiology; but even here I have tried to consider the place of these texts in the evolution of his work as a whole rather than using them to build a portrait of Barthes *as an ideologist*. Drawing such a portrait will be the task of our

[63] Barthes, *S/Z*, p. 32.

[64] See the strong reservations of two more-Barthesian-than-Barthes ultras, Annette Lavers 1982, chapter 15 and Jonathan Culler, chapter 10.

[65] Thody, *Barthes*, p. 157.

concluding remarks on him. But before doing so, we must consider his position in the *theory of criticism*, certainly one of the areas where his contribution to structuralism proved widely influential.

In 1963 Barthes published two important articles on criticism: one, entitled 'The Two Criticisms' for *Modern Language Notes*; the other, 'What is Criticism?', for the *Times Literary Supplement*. These twin essays, both included in *Critical Essays* (1964), together with an article from 1960, 'History or Literature?', which became three years later the final part of his book on Racine, and the pamphlet *Critique et Vérité* (1966), form the core of his critical theory—as can be guessed from these dates, very much an offshoot of his own 'structuralist activity' at its peak.

Barthes distinguished between two kinds of criticism: academic and interpretive. Interpretive criticism refuses to kneel in 'homage to the truth of the past'; it looks at literature in a bold quest for 'intelligibility for our time'. Hence its unashamed espousal of current ideologies: existentialism, phenomenology, Marxism, psychoanalysis. By 'academic' criticism Barthes meant research in literary history conducted in the tradition established in the Sorbonne of the Belle Epoque by Gustave Lanson (1857–1934). By 1960 this type of literary study cut a rather dowdy figure alongside the main families of modern criticism: the stylistics of Spitzer or Auerbach; Russian formalism; the Richards–Empson school of literary semantics; American new criticism; the creative Marxist readings of Lukács and Benjamin; Cambridge moralist criticism of the *Scrutiny*, that is, Leavisite kind; the Chicago neo-Aristotelians, and the Franco–Swiss group of 'thematic' critics.

These schools of modern criticism each held very different ideologies. But all of them practised one form or another of focusing on the text for its own sake. 'Close reading' might be less than a method—but it was a shared approach. In his TLS article Barthes berated Lansonian criticism precisely for its neglect of the duty of 'immanent analysis'. Ever intent on regarding the text as an epiphenomenon, as a mere reflection of an author's life and milieu, criticism, always on the lookout for determinisms, lost sight (argued Barthes) of both the *functions* and *significations* of literature. By insisting on seeing texts as *products*, it forgot how to perceive them as *signs*. Nor was this its only sin. It also erred in two other respects. It showed great reluctance to accept the symbolic and connotative dimensions of literary language; and it persistently disguised its own ideological biases under a cloak of common sense. As a whole, therefore, traditional criticism was impugned by Barthes on three accounts: reductionism, insensitivity to symbolism and ideological hypocrisy.

Interpretive criticism, on the contrary, remains aware that criticism is but a *metalanguage* of the object-language literature; hence its natural inclination to immanent analysis, to attentive 'microscopies', as Jakobson liked to say. Indeed, interpretative criticism feeds on the 'friction' of two relations: that of the critical metalanguage with its literary object, and that of the latter with the world. However, Barthes hastened to add, the second relation by no means placed criticism at the mercy of an external criterion of reality or objectivity. As a metalanguage, criticism should not aim at the discovery of truths but of *validities*. For example, no true critic is supposed to decide on matters such as whether Proust's Charlus is Proust's friend Count Montesquiou or not—all he or she has to do is to integrate into the chosen code of interpretation the largest possible amount of Proustian language. Thus interpretive criticism, acknowledging that literature is *a language*, seizes on the form and rules of this sign-system instead of pursuing its 'message'.

Barthes's overall position has a lot in its favour. Pre-structuralist criticism in France (though much less so elsewhere) was prone to collapse the work into crass yet fanciful biographical or sociological determinants. It also frequently showed little concern for the wealth of connotation and symbol inherent in literary language. And again, its common-sense stance hid many a doubtful or downright prejudiced belief; Barthes would have had no difficulty illustrating his charge that until very late in the day Lansonism worked with a rather shallow psychology, using Ribot but largely ignoring Freud.

Nevertheless, owing to the rather anaemic state of his target —withered Lansonism—by the mid-sixties, much of Barthes's critique amounted to flogging a dead horse. What misled many into the opposite impression at the time was the fact that Barthes's essays on Racine caught the eye of one of Lansonism's last Mohicans, Raymond Picard, who attacked him in a vigorous libel, *Nouvelle critique ou nouvelle imposture*, in 1965. First published in a Lille academic journal, Picard's strictures were printed in book form in a polemic series, *Libertés*, edited for the Pauvert publishing company by Jean-François Revel, whom we already mentioned as a critic of Lévi-Strauss. On the strength of his own well-researched *La Carrière de Jean Racine* (1956), Professor Picard scored several points by showing that Barthes evinced—to put it mildly—a less than full command of Racine scholarship; but he then spoiled his case with a silly a priori dismissal of Barthes's explorations of sexual overtones in Racine's tragedies ('Racine is not D. H. Lawrence') and by harking back to tiresome Lansonian jibes at 'impressionism'— the standard accusation levelled by Lanson himself against rival critics, especially Jules Lemaître.

Picard's pamphlet was not his first shot in the controversy. He had already given Barthes's 'The Two Criticisms' a rough ride when reviewing *Critical Essays* for *Le Monde*. To that extent, the opening salvo did come from the 'old' critics. Yet Barthes's *On Racine* already contained some disparaging remarks about academic studies of classical literature (not without some unfairness towards fine literary historians such as Antoine Adam or Paul Bénichou). Structuralist strongholds such as the *Tel Quel* coterie tried to present the whole quarrel as a clash between left and right, with Picard cast in the role of a benighted reactionary from both a literary and a social point of view. This, however, was a far cry from the truth. After all, as P. Thody impartially observed, Pauvert and Revel, the publisher and the editor of Picard, had just issued books by Sade, Russell and Bakunin and therefore could scarcely pass for models of moral or social conformism in the 1965 *république des lettres*. Converts to structuralism almost everywhere like to refer to the battle of the nouvelle critique as a dramatic Manichaean combat between right and wrong—but in reality the whole issue showed anything but a clearcut division between structuralist insight and old critical error.

Moreover, in trying to extract a modicum of real critical light from the heat and dust of the polemic, it is hard to avoid the suspicion that Barthes's unqualified veto on critical concern with determinisms—his call for a blunt replacement of a 'criticism of determinations' by a 'criticism of functions and significations'—was a bit cavalier. To begin with, Barthes reduced the search for the external motives of literary creation to a caricature. He poked fun at a stodgy biographism which played sleuth, tracking down atomistic details ('was Charlus Montesquiou?') at most only peripherally relevant to the artistic structure of the text. But Barthes, of all people, should have known better; for, as we have seen, in *On Racine* he made great use of a kind of psychological interpretation (Mauron's deft psychoanalysis of Racine) which had much to say about the structure of plays such as *Andromaque, Britannicus* or *Bajazet*, and yet also cogently related some basic patterns of Racinean tragedy to major aspects of the poet's life-story and psyche.

In 'History or Literature?' Barthes claimed that the only legitimate literary history was a *structural* one, focusing on 'the literary function', that is, the role played by the literary, its conventions and techniques, in society and the collective mentality (he had in mind Lucien Febvre's advocacy of an *'histoire des mentalités'*). Short of which, said Barthes, all we get is a bunch of monographs—a 'chronicle' rather than a true history. In other words, he was pitting the lesson of modern historiography, in the style of the *Annales* school (indeed, in its original publication, 'Histoire ou Littérature?' was an *Annales* article), against the drabness of Lansonian positivism; and he stressed that the sole rewarding history of literature was *sociological*, dealing with *institutional* elements instead of vainly trying to grasp what the mind of an author was like. But the point is, Barthes never allowed an historical approach to literature beyond the mapping out of the 'literary function'. As hinted by the disjunctive in his title, history *or* literature, as soon as he turned from the prospect of an institutional history of literature to the problem of literary *creation*, his recipe was limited to 'immanent analysis' of the text as a sign, shorn of every concern with it as (also) a product. And so rigid was the Barthesian separation between history and interpretative analysis that even a fellow-structuralist, Gérard Genette, thought it necessary to qualify it with a reminder that at least room should be allowed for a 'history of forms', the object of a structural literary history capable of studying something more than the 'literary function'.[66]

Now there seems to be no visible reason for severing the

---

[66] Cf. G. Genette, 'Littérature et Histoire', in Genette, *Figures III*, Paris 1972.

the scrutiny of literary sign-structures so sharply from historical research into causes and effects. Why should we confine the historical perspective in literary criticism to the institutional dimension of verbal artworks? Why on earth should it be wrong to look at them *also* as an effect of a unique constellation of antecedent conditions and intervening variables? Why is it not possible for rational criticism to be at once *interpretive* and *explanatory* in the causal sense? Those who tend to ask such questions can hardly disagree with Robert Weimann, an outstanding East German theorist of literary history: for him, Barthes ended up by drawing 'a deplorable antithesis between literature as product and literature as sign (or structure).' In Weimann's view, this regrettable move was at bottom a tribute to the ingrained structuralist habit of positing an antinomy between system and history.[67]

It should be added that Lansonism as an intellectual project was far less stupid than the zealots of the nouvelle critique like to suggest. In fact, Lanson's programme can be seen as a culmination in a series of plausible theoretical advances in French criticism since the aftermath of romanticism. A brilliant recent study by Antoine Compagnon, *La Troisième République des Lettres* (1983) recalls how Lanson saw his own literary history as occupying a strategic place at the end of almost a century of pathbreaking critical steps.[68] First François Villemain (1790–1870), following Madame de Staël who in turn followed German romanticism, claimed that literature was *an expression of society*. Then a far greater critic, Charles-Augustin Sainte-Beuve (1804–69), carried on Villemain's plan and added to it an important specification: he kept the idea of literature as a historical phenomenon, but saw the work as the product of an individual *temperament* instead of regarding it as directly reflecting society (hence his goal, 'a natural history of minds'). Next came H. Taine (1828–93)—whom we have already met as a forerunner of Saussure—who proposed to ground Sainte-Beuve's temperament in *social, ethnic and historic determinisms* (the famous triad of race, milieu and

[67] R. Weimann, *Structure and Society in Literary History: Studies in the History and Theory of Historical Criticism*, London 1977, p. 154.

[68] A. Compagnon, *La Troisième Républiques des Lettres: De Flaubert à Proust*, Paris 1983, especially pp. 174ff.

'moment'). Finally, Ferdinand Brunetière (1849–1906) com-
plemented Taine's set of causes by isolating within the Tainean
'moment' the effect of *genre*, that is to say, of the ongoing
literary system, on the making of new works.

Such is Lanson's assessment of French criticism's analytical
capital in 1895, the year in which he first published his monu-
mental *History of French Literature*. Lanson conceived of his
own efforts as a kind of re-adjustment from Brunetière back to
Sainte-Beuve: he liked to qualify Brunetière's 'Darwinian'
stress on the weight of the impersonal evolution of genre
by emphasizing the 'residual' importance of the individual
equation.

However, Lanson did not simply return to Sainte-Beuve,
because, he wrote, 'instead of using biographies to explain
works, Sainte-Beuve had employed the works to build biographies'. A 'positive' literary history would do nothing of the
kind: it would keep a firm grasp of its prime object, literature.
In a sense, this led Lanson to another departure from his
immediate predecessors—this time from Taine—in an important point of method. In his own research, Lanson substituted
the unearthing of *sources* for Taine's privileged factor, milieu.
Now the quest for literary sources was in principle much more
empirically grounded than the vague determinist hypotheses of
Taine. Nevertheless, for all these rectifications, Lanson stuck to
the historist-positivist idea of causality in literature, and emphatically opposed his brainchild, scientific literary history,
which soon became a glory of the Sorbonne, to the rhetorical
criticism of Emile Faguet (1847–1916), the anti-Tainean of the
Collège de France.

Interestingly enough, Lanson later inserted literary history
midway between two rival academic schools of historical knowledge. On the one hand, Charles Seignobos (1854–1942)
defined history (like the German historists) as 'the science of
what happens just once'. On the other hand, a Durkheimian
economist and methodologist, François Simiand (1873–1935),
campaigned for a 'history of institutions'. When his friend
Durkheim pressed him to take sides on the Simiand-Seignobos
debate (1903), Lanson did not fudge the issue. He set great
store by a history of literary institutions (and not just of literary
events) and thus seemed to agree with Durkheim and Simiand.
But against the sociologists he insisted that *each literary fact*

was unique of its kind. Moreover, he warned that the subject matter of literary history was different from the object of historians because, unlike historical documents, literary texts were *alive*.

Compagnon[69] aptly notes that by thus refusing to opt for one or the other of the contenders Lanson was in fact trying to save his new-born discipline from being swallowed up by the two academic imperialisms of the age: history (a central force in the refurbishing of the Sorbonne during the first decades of the Third Republic) and sociology (a lay sect of great moment in the post-Dreyfus era). This was very likely so, and yet does not detract a bit from the soundness of Lanson's theoretical considerations.

Lanson had more than one failure of taste and critical performance (his rejection of Mallarmé on the grounds of 'literary anarchy' is a case in point). But as a whole his critical theory has much to recommend it. True, it is entirely lacking in sophisticated approaches to interpretation and 'immanent analysis'— but neither does it preclude them, in its way of devising an explanatory literary scholarship. Can we say as much of structuralism, when it comes to accepting the legitimacy of (and even the need for) causal enquiries about literature? Lansonians were never very adept at grappling with structure and sign in literary texts. But at least their critical creed did not bar close reading. Their concern with history neither encouraged nor forbade attention to structure. What about those critical persuasions whose love of structure and system militates against remembering what works of art, verbal or not, never cease to be: social sign-machines, enduring historical artefacts?

Barthes used to deny that he held an anti-historical critical outlook. Anti-genetic, yes; anti-historical, no (he writes in his intellectual autobiography)—and anti-genetic precisely because the myth of origins mistakes history for nature. But I am afraid this is a rather unconvincing disclaimer. None of his analyses is conspicuous for sustained historical depth and his rare brief attempts at seeing French literature in historical perspective are definitely not among his best pages. In *Writing Degree Zero*, long before he was inoculated by structuralism against historical interpretations, he suggested that the belief, based on

[69] Ibid., p. 163–73.

an instrumental concept of language, that the aim of literature is communication was destroyed after 1848 by the realities of class war, which forced the bourgeoisie to realize that language is not always persuasion feeding on dialogue. That is why writers such as Flaubert and Mallarmé broke with the central myth of classical French writing, which the romantics failed to abolish: the fallacy of the instrumentality of language. Any reader of Lukács or Lucien Goldmann will feel uneasy about assuming such a direct correlation between politics (and politics wildly oversimplified) and literary change: there are scores of missing mediations in this picture. Barthes fares much better when he turns to sheer historical characterization without historical analysis, as in the short text in *Critical Essays* "Literature and Metalanguage" (1954), where post-romantic, self-conscious literature is said to have undergone several mutations: the overscrupulous ideal of craftsmanship (Flaubert); the 'heroic' endeavour to merge literature and poetics (Mallarmé); the indictment of literary good faith through the wilful intensification of polysemy (surrealism); and finally, contrariwise, the rarefaction of meaning in a kind of 'white' writing (Robbe-Grillet's nouveau roman).

Accompanying his outlawing of every view of literature as product is Barthes's strong antipathy towards *expressivism* in all shapes and sizes. That literature is not expression is the first dogma of the Barthesian creed. Now this was not entirely new in French literary thought. As Professor Thody reminds us, there was an anti-expressivist tradition stretching from Proust and Valéry to Camus,[70] all of whom may be reckoned among persistent opponents of the classical dictum, *oratio vultus animi* —the sentence is the face of the soul.

But Barthes gave a new twist to the anti-expressivist line by his determination 'to shake the assumption that the sign is natural', as he put it in an interview for *L'Express* (May 1970). Indeed, the idea that the myth of expression belongs to the disguise of history as nature, which it is the task of semioclasm to debunk, is a leitmotiv in Barthes's whole work. Expression is rejected because it runs counter to that crucial self-awareness of the sign Barthes spots in places as diverse as Brecht's theatre, the world of wrestling, 'Flaubertian' writing (in the sense of

[70] Thody, *Barthes*, p. 46.

deeply thoughtful literature) and—at a slightly less conscious level—in the dialectic between restraint and avowal displayed in a lover's behaviour. Even Barthes's views on acting—on the performing styles of Louis Jouvet, Helene Weigel, Alain Cuny —reflect his anti-expressivist bias: for all these actors, he says on different occasions, share an unwillingness to 'translate' thought and emotion into language. Jouvet's insistence on clarity of diction, his stark refusal to let the text be maimed by expressionistic performances; Cuny's hieratic manner of playing Thésée in *Phèdre*; or again, Weigel's famous Mother Courage, numbed by catastrophe and an inability to understand the meaning of events, were for him true paradigms of theatrical artistry[71]—and he applied the same standard to his appraisal of singing stars, as shown in the interviews collected into *The Grain of the Voice* (1981).

"What is Criticism?" suggests a sort of complicity between expressivist aesthetics and naive psychology. The Lansonians, according to Barthes, constantly assume that psychological elements in a given literary work *resemble* bits and pieces of its author's life or experience. But, as psychoanalysis has shown, a work of art often *negates* its psychological roots in its creator, through a mechanism of compensation. In short, expressivism not only neglects the self-consciousness of art: it also rests on a simplistic view of the psyche.

I have stressed the anti-expressivist rage in Barthes because, though not part of his critical theory proper, it underlies a still more general trait of both his aesthetics and his views on criticism: his *denial of inner meaning*, subjective as well as objective. Subjective inner meaning, of course, collapses with his ban on expression. But Barthes also refuses to countenance any assumption that 'objective' inner meanings are present in the texts themselves, waiting to be discovered, deciphered or unveiled by us. The metaphor for fallacious inner signification comes from Barthes himself: 'If until now we have regarded the text as a species of fruit with a kernel (an apricot, for example) the flesh being the form and the stone the content, it would be better to see it as an onion, a construction of layers (or levels, or systems) whose body contains finally no heart, no kernel, no

---

[71] Once more, I owe the analogy between Barthes's anti-expressivest aesthetics and his way of judging performances to Thody, *Barthes*, pp. 56–7.

secret, no irreducible principle, nothing except the infinity of its envelopes which envelop nothing other than the unity of its own surfaces.'[72]

The first impressive use of the onion metaphor in post-war thought was, I think, made by the late Hannah Arendt, who in her celebrated work *The Origins of Totalitarianism* described totalitarian regimes as Stalinist police states where real power dwells in the heart of the bureaucratic onion, in the KGB rather than in the outer, visible surface of the state. Barthes does it the other way round: he makes the onion into the symbol of a *centreless* structure. Ironically, a metaphor devised to grasp the quintessence of oppression became an emblem of the liberation of the signifier.

Throughout his work, Barthes insists that we *project* meaning onto signs instead of extracting it from them. Semantic bliss lies in openness to interpretation. His eulogy (in one of his *Mythologies*) of the Eiffel Tower, which 'means everything' by constantly inviting new interpretations of its powerful symbolic energy, is a case in point. *Empire of Signs* opposes Japanese theatre, where faces are masks devoid of all expressiveness, hence open to all 'readings', to the despicable 'expressive' make-up of our bourgeois stage. And *Camera Lucida* prefers photos to movies because before the stillness of the photographic image one can indulge in endless interpreting rêveries. Above all, the momentous distinctions drawn by the later Barthes between *readerly works* and *writerly texts* may be said to hinge upon the presence or absence of an objective inner meaning: works are 'readerly' in that they impose a contract of readership based on stable sense, allowing the reader no more (in the words of *S/Z*) than 'the poor freedom either to accept or reject the text'; true texts, on the other hand, are 'writerly' in that they grant us plenty of room to revel in *ad libitum* interpretations.

Critique et Vérité praises the ancient oracles because their concise cryptic sentences were 'open to several meanings', uttered as they were 'outside any situation—except the situation of ambiguity itself'. The last words are telling. Barthes is not just underscoring the fact that at its most important literary

[72] Barthes, 'Style and its image', in S. Chatman, ed., *Literary Style: A Symposium*, Oxford 1971, p. 10. Novalis used the same simile.

meaning is seldom univocal—rather, he is relishing ambiguity
for its own sake—hence his impatience with the possibility that
contexts might clarify the obscurity of texts. By willing texts
into Delphic oracles, *he makes ambiguity into an a priori*,
unscathed by the intelligibility normally provided by one of the
standard means of elucidating meaning—the appeal to the
speech context. As stated in *Critique et Vérité* (p. 51), 'the work
proposes, man disposes': what endows literary texts with a
power of permanence is not their eternal single meaning, but
their capacity to *suggest* different meanings to different people
over different ages.

Criticism, says Barthes, is no 'translation': its business is not
to get a clearer meaning out of an obscure one, for nothing, he
adds, could be clearer than the works themselves. *Critique et
Vérité* states that the true relationship between criticism and
work is that *'between a meaning and a form'*. Here if anywhere
Barthes evinces his full loyalty to the formalist canon: literariness is form in its pure state; content comes from the world. The
critic, speaking the 'languages' (that is, the ideologies) of his
age, reads meaning *into* the texts. Yet texts in themselves are
blank and empty, shining as the enduring, structured vessels of
an ever-changing content.

That is why, according to the doctrine of "The Structuralist
Activity" (1963), a key text in *Critical Essays*, the crucial task in
criticism is not so much to assign meanings to works as to
ascertain *how* meaning is possible. Barthes establishes at this
point the conceptual grounding for one of his most influential
distinguos; the severance of *poetics* from *criticism*. Whilst criticism interprets by actually projecting meaning onto literary
form, poetics contents itself with pointing out the conditions
of meaning—the rules and conventions of signification. The
second and last part of *Critique et Vérité* urges the emancipation
of poetics (alternatively called the 'science of literature')
from interpretive criticism. But Barthes enriched the formalist
stance by making gestures towards a Chomskyan perspective:
he postulated a 'generative' model of 'literary competence' akin
to the concept of linguistic competence in Chomsky's transformative grammar.

To be sure, the notion of poetics as a 'science of literature'
vanished from the later Barthes. As the spirit of Derrida
overshadowed his Chomskyan similes of the sixties, the idea of

literature as rule-bound production made room for an uncanny identification of theory and writing,[73] dominated by the typical post-structuralist ideal of a broad proliferation of meaning through a profusion of signifiers. To the accomplished Barthologist, Stephen Heath, the shift from a 'scientific' concern for structure to a joyful expectancy of wild *structurations* came as early as the period between, on the one hand, Barthes' introduction to the *Communications* issue on narratology, published in the same year (1966) as *Critique et Vérité*, and, on the other hand, the turning-point of *S/Z*.[74] The change of perspective included a shift of focus from a whole textual *corpus*—in quest of its generative matrix—to the closer reading of *particular* texts, such as the micro-analysis of Balzac's novella.

Up to a point, the Chomskyan metaphors of the previous, structuralist Barthes were replaced by the concept of *intertextuality*, which, alongside his debt to Derrida, marks Barthes's most significant borrowing from *Tel Quel* doctrine, in this case from the semiotics (more Lacanian than Saussurean) of Kristeva. With each text seen as an intertext, a mirror of other texts, both past and future, literary semiosis—the process of literary sign-making and signifying—was to be regarded as an *open* structure, a structure governed less by (deep) rules than by ever-missing elements: structure became a work-in progress forever in thrall to an undetermined future.

In the theoretical and critical prose written under the joint spell of Derrida and Lacan, this insistence on the radical openness, the gap-like nature of structure, lent an almost magic aura to a specific word, *béance*—the gaping chasm of constant absence which undermines all meaning. I can think of nothing better than Friedrich Hebbel's old dictum—'there is no surface, just depth; there is no depth, just the abyss'—to encapsulate this post-structuralist mood.

Not surprisingly, the later Barthes was one of the main authorities invoked as a plethora of tortuous analyses set out to demonstrate that literature is overcrowded with countless instances of *mise-en-abîme* techniques. *S/Z* defines the intertext

[73] Cf. Barthes's interview 'La théorie' in the little-known journal VH 101, 2, Summer 1970; quoted by S. Heath, *Vertige du Déplacement: Lecture de Barthes*, Paris 1974, p. 79.

[74] Heath, *Vertige*, pp. 88 and 91.

as the infinite of its reprises[75]—an eminently 'writerly' horizon, begotten by the Derridean dissemination of signifiers. This futuristic slant, incidentally, put Kristeva's concern with intertextuality miles away from the old humdrum search for 'sources'—a Lansonian chore treated by structuralists and post-structuralists alike with the utmost contempt.

As early as 1967, Barthes, commenting on his *Système de la Mode*, was already suggesting that Saussurean categories were best employed to study 'the reified and mythical objects of mass culture'.[76] He also referred, in a more general vein, to an adequacy between structuralism and the classical or popular work, hinting at the 'Aristotelian' (that is, pre-modern) bent of Saussurean theory. Rule-bound sign-worlds obedient to stable codes came to be seen as the very opposite of *the aesthetics of transgression* nurtured by *Tel Quelism*—an ideal which Barthes found embodied in *Sarrasine*, with its 'lawless, disordered (*déréglée*) circulation of signs, sexes and fortunes'.

For the structuralist Barthes, the glory of criticism lay in colonizing the Americas of poetics: the critic, therefore, should not be after meaning, because he or she should first lay out the pure grammar of signification. But for the post-structuralist Barthes criticism did not deal with meaning either, since the swarming, enfranchised signifier was always running well ahead of its demoted signified. Thus the critic most closely associated with the view that the stuff of literature is signs—indeed, signs galore—ultimately put *an unbridgeable distance between sign and sense*. The literary sign as form instead of sense—such is the core position of Barthes's view of criticism, both during and after structuralism. Nothing more eloquently betrays the kinship between literary structuralism and its forerunner, Russian formalism.

This fact alone casts a strong light on the influence of Barthes on modern French criticism. Indeed, if the history of the *nouvelle critique* may be told largely in terms of the eclipse of meaning and the loss of reference, this is, to a great extent, Barthes's fault. Nobody else, not even Jakobson, encouraged so many to believe that 'meaning is nothing but the possibility

---

[75] Barthes, *S/Z*, pp. 211 (digression xc).
[76] See his interview with Raymond Bellour in *Lettres Françaises*, March 1967.

of *transcoding*,[77] regardless of any reference to something beyond (though not exactly outside) language and the languages of culture; no one was so reckless in offering groundless suggestions that 'generative' models could be drawn for *literature* as well as language; no other critic was so prodigal in giving his blessing to the misfired endeavour of narratology to establish an algebra of story-telling which was oblivious to the major differences between narratives in their degree of artistry and their moral scope or moral depth.

Robert Scholes once called the 'regional', less theoretical forms of structuralist criticism, such as narratology, 'low structuralism'.[78] Now low structuralism, more than anything else, introduced the gospel of sign and structure, code and text into the academic world, quickly dislodging older trends in modern criticism. There is some controversy over the actual extent of its academic triumph; but few would doubt its smashing victory in the Latin countries, its penetration into several prestigious American universities (with Yale and Cornell of late turned into bulwarks of 'deconstruction') or again, the embattled mood with which nouvelle critique models managed to build solid bridgeheads in British academe (as witnessed by the 'Cambridge affair' in the late seventies, the presence of Marxist-structuralist critics such as Terry Eagleton in Oxford and the sprinkling of structuralist and deconstructionist devotees in the new universities). When, in a very recent debate in Paris, the distinguished structuralist Gérard Genette tried to refute the assertion—made by the literary historian, Marc Fumaroli—of a hegemony of the nouvelle critique in French universities over the last decades, his disclaimer met a polite but widespread skepticism.[79]

Now whether high or low, full-blown theory or just jargon-laden 'practical criticism', structuralist criticism quickly developed some extremely questionable habits of mind. Above all, it has held in abomination what Roy Porter so aptly dubbed the 'ET heresy':[80] ET here being not Spielberg's engaging

[77] A. J. Greimas, *Du Sens*, Paris 1970, p. 13.
[78] R. Scholes, *Structuralism in Literature: An Introduction*, New Haven 1974, p. 157.
[79] See 'Comment parler de la littérature?', in *Le Débat*, 29, March 1984.
[80] See his article in the *London Review of Books*, 20 Dec. 1983.

extra-terrestrial creature, but Extra-Textuality, that is, every-thing that pertains to a pretext, a pre-text, or a context which prompts or props up the making and reception of a literary text. ET phobia has in fact become the staple response of both the Jakobsonian and the Barthesian modes of criticism—the two most powerful influences in what now passes for advanced literary theory.

Half a century ago, a critic such as F. R. Leavis uttered shrill complaints about the stultification of literary studies by dint of an immoderate scholarly concern with the social *contexts* of (past) literature, to the detriment of fresh reassessment of its human content. Nowadays the situation is clearly the reverse: criticism wilts not because of context-indigestion, but because most of it is text-besotted—the textual obsession blinds criticism to the decisive importance of the social ground of literature, both in its origin and in its life through history. Nor does one need to add that in the process the human wealth of literature gets lost once again, though for reasons quite oppo-site to those castigated by Leavis.

Many a thoughtful mind worries in our time about the decline in what we might term the 'humanistic coefficient' in current ways of dealing with art, theory and literature. Paradoxically, however, the eclipse of the humanistic in our approach to such studies seems to be in league with some of the most cherished beliefs of the *humanist* mind—especially when it embraces avant-garde ideology. Consider, for example, the traditional emphasis put by the ideology of modern art (and literature) on the ideal of *experiment*. Mainstream modernism in art and literature has notoriously insisted on the right—nay, the duty—to look for the 'new form'; and it has quite often justified such an urge by invoking the legitimacy of the experi-mental attitude in both art and sciences.

Yet the scientific analogy underlying the modernist plea for experimental art is far from well-founded. The modernist tra-dition, which now largely constitutes the ideology of our art world, likes to compare itself to science because it takes science to be an experimental method. Nevertheless, as Sir Ernst Gombrich has shrewdly remarked, in practice, the hectic experimentalism of modern and post-modern art apes the ex-perimental method but forgets 'its function', which is, of course, to detect mistakes, thereby separating truth from error. 'The word experiment, Gombrich warned, became a vogue word to be used indiscriminately for any departure from tradition.' As a result, 'there is no (longer) bad art and good art, only anti-quated and advanced art.'[81] This in turn is backed by a purblind belief in automatic progress—a curious survival of the histori-cist creed, right in the middle of the general discrediting of social historicisms. Thus the humanist ideology—the same cast of mind whose entire outlook thunders against the evils of progress and indeed against the whole course of modern civil-ization and the central role of science therein—borrows its own aesthetics from the prestige of science and sticks to a spurious progressivism in its attempts to legitimize sterile experiments and stale avant-garde sects. The consequences are there for anyone to see. They amount, as Professor Gombrich wisely and bravely put it, to an 'unintentional breakdown of standards'. Those very standards that were precisely—in taste, skill and knowledge—the pride of yesterday's humanisms.

If I were to label the two phenomena grasped by Gombrich's critique of the modernist dogma, I would call them *fake experimentalism* (experimental method 'minus its function', in Gombrich's words) and *crypto-historicism*. What we face is a covert historicism, a historicism *qui n'ose pas dire son nom*, acting as a prop to a fake experimentalism—the cult of experi-ment severed from any concern with standards of truth or excellence. But let us leave the criticism of modernist aesthetics at that, and turn towards literary criticism. What happens when this kind of modernist ideology is injected into critical theory?

As we have recalled, the experimentalist myth is a figleaf for the defining feature of the bulk of modern art: *formalism*. The late Hans Sedlmayr used to say that modern art had three main characteristics: purism, constructivism, primitivism. Under modernism, each particular art strove to be purely itself: thus modern painting tried to be just painterly by eschewing literary elements, while modern architecture divested itself of sculptural ornament ('ornament is crime', in Loos's famous warcry) and modern music dropped programme-music. As for modern liter-ature, it began by purging itself of rhetoric (as witnessed in the *'poésie pure'* slogan) and ended by renouncing mimesis.

[81] See Gombrich, 'Experiment and experience in the arts', in R. B. McConnell, ed., *Science and Human Progress*, London 1983, pp. 166 and 169–70.

'Constructivism' was conspicuous in the modernist stress on form and technique, geometry and abstraction. 'Primitivism' denotes the taste for the absurd and the near-mystic quest for states of primeval innocence—briefly, everything that comes together when we assemble the traditions of Dada, surrealism and expressionism.[82] Now the point is: of these three character-istics, at least two—purism and constructivism—could only foster formalist trends, both in style and in aesthetics; and even primitivism often privileged formal values over preoccupation with content.

In our time of senile modernisms, neo-formalist trends in criticism espoused versions of modernist doxa and took over a large part of the academic study of literature (now the habitat of ninety per cent of literary criticism) by institutionalizing teach-ing and research based on the massive employment of *ready-made methods*. Hence the oft-noted unhealthy swelling of 'literary theory' and critical methodology in the curricula. Pro-longed exposure to literature proper dwindles, whereas literary theory and critical methodology are swallowed up by the ton. This grotesque predicament is aggravated by the fact that most students in today's mass universities do not seem to bring to higher learning a decent literary culture acquired *before* their graduate years, as was still the case with the tiny bands of literature students when the subject was trusted to philology-trained dons who knew little or no literary theory but a lot about poems, novels, plays and essays.

The gross irony is that the rule of theory and method, far from reinforcing objectivity in current discussion of literature, leads straight to a collapse of relevance and accuracy in critical discourse. More than ever, critics and interpreters theoretically and methodologically tend to project their own *à la page* views onto the texts, regardless of what they say or imply. More and more, texts are misread by being read into.

No wonder that when structuralism was still in its prime, a true scholar such as Marcel Bataillon already found it wise to call his presidential address to the Modern Humanities Research Association 'Défense et illustration du sens littéral.'[83] Since then, how many literal meanings have been mugged, kidnapped,

---

[82] See H. Sedlmayr, *Die Revolution der Modernen Kunst*, Munich 1955.
[83] M. Bataillon, *Défense et Illustration du Sens Littéral*, Leeds 1967.

180

disfigured or openly slaughtered! Structuralism, or its progeny, has even devised a special technique to do away with it: its name is 'deconstruction', the wilful murder of literal meaning, killed by the systematic (and unwarranted) postulation of its very opposite as the secret of the text.

'New' criticism, then, is often a kind of *ventriloquism*—a charge which, incidentally, comes from no foe of structuralism: for it is the considered opinion of structuralist criticism expressed by none other than Claude Lévi-Strauss,[84] once again dead right when it comes to the follies of modernism and its epigoni. Curiously enough, Lévi-Strauss says that the ventriloquism of structuralist critics stems from their failure to follow the lead of art historians such as Panofsky and ask the historical record (that is, the historical *context*) to back up their textual interpretations. A case of physician, heal thyself? Perhaps—but in anthropology at least there is often no historical record; and be that as it may, Lévi-Strauss puts his finger on the ET phobia: the structuralists' allergy to the (social) context of literature.

The ET phobia survived structuralism rather well. Now that the 'scientistic dream' of Saussurean semiotics rests in peace, few people still think of devising generative models for literariness and each of its genres. The ghost of the ever-elusive 'genotext' (Kristeva dixit) has been laid. As Geoffrey Strickland has reminded us,[85] had Benveniste's sensible theorizing been heeded, it would never have been afoot in the first place. For as Benveniste saw, in linguistic analysis, as soon as we get to the level of the sentence, we enter the realm of what lies *outside language*. Sentence meaning implies reference to the discourse situation. Logically speaking, this peculiarity should have forbidden from the start every attempt to produce: (a) a 'linguistics of literariness' based on the phonological model of finite units and a few rules of exclusion and combination; and (b) an ET–phobic theory of literature, since a full account of literature requires a semiotics of *discourse* (and hence of reference), not just a semiotics of language.

[84] See Lévi-Strauss, *Structuralist Anthropology II*, chapter xv, 2; originally an answer to an inquiry on structuralism and literary criticism made by the Italian journal *Paragone*, no. 182, 1965.

[85] G. Strickland, *Structuralism or Criticism? Thoughts on how we Read*, Cambridge 1983, pp. 16–19. For Benveniste's text, see *Problems*, chapter 10.

True, the post-*S/Z* Barthes often spoke of discourse as the hub of post-structuralist analysis. But he clearly failed to integrate a theory of reference within his final, post-Saussurean perspective. Why? Strickland rightly notices[86] that Barthes chose to neglect Benveniste's careful distinction between levels of linguistic analysis. In his well-known essay "Analyse structural des récits" (*Communications*, 1966), Barthes contended that 'the same formal organization (*sic*) most probably governs all semiotic systems, whatever their substance and dimensions.' This was written in the teeth of Benveniste's 'levels' essay, to which Barthes actually refers to justify the—thoroughly opposite—view just quoted. For what did Benveniste mean, but that different semiotic 'systems' (or more properly, levels) do *not* possess the same formal organization?

There is no question that Strickland has spotted a blind alley in Barthes's thought—and a classic case of structuralist misconstruction of linguistic theory. But there is an alternative, and not necessarily contradictory, way of accounting for the continuous distaste for reference in Barthes's critical theory, even given his infatuation with 'phonological' models. I submit that Barthes's failure to acknowledge reference stems from the fact that, even after dropping structuralism, he remained attached to the *metalinguistic fallacy*: to the belief that literature is a 'metalanguage' whose object is itself, so that it is basically pointless to look elsewhere when trying to understand its works. Nevertheless, strange as it may now sound, the true object of literature is not itself—it is the human experience of the world. Literature is seldom about language or literary devices and conventions other than in an occasional or instrumental sense; but it is constantly about 'life', however real or imagined. Matthew Arnold or, for that matter, good old Dr Johnson were, in this respect, wiser than Roland Barthes or the formalist critics.

Having cut off his discovery of literary discourse (as opposed to literary 'codes') from an exploration of the rich referentiality of verbal artworks, Barthes was bound to fall back on an increasingly self-indulgent kind of critical prose. He was indeed the main practitioner and proponent of 'creative' criticism. In the exercise of this mode, the truth that great criticism is an art

---

[86] Strickland, *Structuralism or Criticism?*, p. 135.

degenerates into the perverse idea that it may be creative writing, shorn of the duty to further the objective interpretation (and no less objective explanation) of imaginative literature (Aristotle's *logos phantastikós*). Denis Donoghue once suggested that the key to the spread of esoteric deconstructionist readings is that they enable the academic critic to feel superior to both his authors and his students[87]—a sad instance of crypto-elitism among the humanist clerisy. But the root of such an evil lies in Barthes's complacent characterization of creative criticism—a narcissistic licence that found prompt acceptance, in America, among such critics as Geoffrey Hartman.

In his essay, *Writing and the Experience of Limits*, Philippe Sollers pits 'textuality' against 'literature'. In 'literature', he says, meaning obtains because it amounts to a surplus-value, extracted from 'productive', 'transgressive' reading. Ergo, textuality gets rid of meaning because it is not exploitative. A *Tel Quelian* conceptual hotch-potch at its most typical, blithely fusing Marxist and Bataillean categories without any respect for sense or context. But the drift of this wild analogy unmistakably bears the mark of Barthes, in that textuality is exalted whereas meaning is debased. Sign triumphs over sense: old formalism reigns, ill-disguised by the ritual smattering of Marx and Nietzsche.

Disappointment is hard to avoid: thanks to the formalist binge, structuralist and post-structuralist criticism has never lived up to the challenge of deciphering the moral import of so much of the best contemporary literature. The *'obsédés textuels'* never wrote a memorable word about Svevo or Musil, Canetti or Solzhenitsyn, Sciascia, Handke or Milan Kundera. And this is perhaps the worst indictment of structuralist criticism and its sequel.

A Farewell Glance

So much for an assessment of Barthes *as a critic*—which, in his case, inevitably means assessment as a critical *theorist*. Let us now conclude by briefly underlining some of the defining

---

[87] See his cogent attack on deconstruction in the *New York Review of Books*, 12 June 1980.

elements of his intellectual personality, in order to situate Roland Barthes in contemporary French thought. A good way to start is to recall the emphasis he put, from beginning to end, on the artificial character of cultural signs, literary or otherwise. We have seen how French structuralism tended to mystify the thesis of the arbitrariness of the sign, by presenting as an earthshaking discovery of Saussure what was at most the crowning point in the long history of a classical concept. Now Barthes was precisely *the theorist who bestowed upon the arbitrary sign a sort of moral virtue*. Stephen Heath claims that throughout his writing, Barthes yielded to a *'vertige du déplacement'*, obeying a passion for shifting levels, in hot pursuit of new configurations. Accordingly, he conceived of semiology as an 'infinite science', a 'vertiginous spiral of metalanguages'.[88] Increasingly, he allowed the sign no respite: Barthesian signs were never granted the right to rest in a given meaning. Besides being radically arbitrary, utterly unmotivated, the sign became restless and unsettling, a homeless cultural artefact ever geared towards an unknown elsewhere. Since the late sixties, Barthes stepped up his onslaught on *'the referential illusion'*;[89] but his debunking was by no means directed only against mimetic claims in fiction: it was intended against all kinds of sign reference. The signifier set free from the signified got rid, by the same token, of every referent. As in Russian formalism, 'objects' ceased to matter.

Now what does this restless, homeless sign, this wandering signifier, readily bring to mind, if not—of all concepts—the Sartrean *pour-soi*? Have we not seen that the Sartrean consciousness was a Flying Dutchman, a knight-errant unable to pause, incapable of dwelling on any object? Maybe, then, Barthes remained to the very last loyal to his first philosophical love, Sartre's left existentialism. At any rate, there seem to be grounds enough for saying that, by endowing the arbitrariness of the sign with a fierce 'ethical' temper, by depicting as sinful and impure every meeting (let alone matching) of sign and reference, Barthes was ultimately *'existentializing' the*

---

[88] Heath, *Vertige*, p. 58.
[89] See his influential essay, 'L'effet du réel', in *Communications*, no. 11, 1968, p. 88.

the Saussurean view of the sign.

Philip Thody has very perceptively detected a 'puritan' streak in Barthes, for whom all received meaning is sin:[90] meaning is to be conquered, not received; it must be, against all odds, the reward of virtue, not an unearned gift from semiotic Grace. Even so, there is no end to the tribulations of the meaning-seeker: no final, consoling meaning in which to rest and bask. Now we can integrate this puritan streak, not without its roots in Barthes's Huguenot upbringing, with the impact on his intellectual background of that other lapsed Protestant, Jean-Paul Sartre. The Sartrean in Barthes gave us a highly tensional, moralistic interpretation, fraught with existential Angst, of the Saussurean stress on the autonomy of the sign. Barthes's semiotics may never speak (unless in disparagement) of consciousness and conscience—but it certainly reeks of existentialist pathos.

To be sure, there is ultimately nothing of the rigorist about the outlook of Barthes the *moralist*—a soul conspicuously more akin to Montaigne than to Pascal, closer to Epicurean self-enjoyment than to moral rigour. Those who, like Susan Sontag, choose to highlight the *aestheticism* of Barthes, his natural leaning towards elegance at all costs in thought as well as style, are by no means in error. But then, it is well-known that Sartreanism, too, for all its advertised ethical aims, contains strong aestheticist elements. Is it not a *rhetoric* of option, an art pour l'art of 'engagement'? Barthes simply injected the high moral pitch of the Sartreanism, originally concerned with subjects and consciousness, into the register of semiotics, the land of signs. The conceptual weaponry changed—but the existentialist pathos is the same.

Moreover, it turned out to be a perfect mould for formalist aesthetics. Indeed, only by keeping in mind his peculiar Sartre-anization of Saussure can we explain, if not justify, some of Barthes's glaring inconsistencies about the relationship between art and reality. Take for example that grand *non-sequitur* in *Critical Essays*, the statement that literature has an inevitably 'unrealistic status' because reality can only be grasped through language. We can grant the premiss and still object to the conclusion. Why in fact must the linguistic mediation be

[90] Thody, *Barthes*, p. 132.

necessarily, automatically, a distortion or a lie? Plainly, the assertion of unrealism is for Barthes a normative statement, not an accurate description of the complex interplay between knowledge, language and world. Therefore, non-realism and de-realization are made into a priori concepts with, consequently, little analytical value.

Literature is declared unrealistic because of language; language in turn is declared non-referential because the sign cannot 'sin' by taking root in meaning and reference. The thorniest epistemological problems are simply ignored. The *pour-soi* sign must never be allowed to end its Flying Dutchman curse. What could better serve the formalist war against content than sign without sense, language torn away from reality? From the outset, the Sartrean incubus delivered Barthes's very personal semiology into the hands of formalism. That is why French structuralism, instead of pursuing the sensible semiotics of Mukařovsky, ended up by resuming and prolonging the doubtful tenets of the hard-liners among Russian formalists.

What about the ideologist in Barthes, apart, that is, from the literary theorist? First, let us ask ourselves what *kind* of thinker he is. Annette Lavers claims that he, like Bataille or Blanchot before him, was primarily a 'literary anthropologist': a moralist reflecting on the human condition by means of what is officially 'literary theory'.[91] Susan Sontag, in her preface to the American translation of *Writing Degree Zero*, stresses that only if criticism is equated with a whole variety of discourse, both theoretical and analytical, about culture and the *Zeitgeist* can Barthes be called, in fairness, a critic—which boils down to considering him a *cultural critic*.

The literary critic as (counter)cultural prophet is a well-established figure in modern literature. The first half of our century found a superb instance of the literary cultural critic in the person of Walter Benjamin (1892–1940), doubtless one of the foremost essayists of the West. It might therefore be useful briefly to compare Barthes with Benjamin. Both, after all, were famously engaged in literature as a source of 'intelligibility for our own time', as it is put in *Critical Essays*; both were sworn enemies of the bourgeois doxa; and both were great writers, though it would be difficult to find equivalents in Benjamin for

[91] Lavers 1982, p. 62.

some of the slightly annoying mannerisms of Barthes's prose. Above all, both were partial to the freedom of the sign, as shown by their worship of Brecht's alienation effects and, in Benjamin's case, by his love of surrealist montage and decontextualized quotations. Yet, somehow Barthes lacks the stature of Benjamin. Two differences between them seem to account for this.

First, of the two, only Benjamin was a true Western critic, by which I mean a mind able to cope with modern literature from a cosmopolitan point of view. While Benjamin's purview included a broad range of French and Russian authors besides, of course, German literature, Barthes' was patently less comprehensive. His critical corpus—Racine, Voltaire and Sade; Chateaubriand, Balzac, Stendhal, Michelet; Baudelaire and Flaubert; Proust and Gide; Sartre and Camus; Robbe-Grillet and Sollers—evinces two main gaps. One, poetry (he wrote on Baudelaire but not on his poems; on Racine, but not on his verse). One must agree with Henri Meschonnic: Barthes turned away, as it were, from modern poetry.[92] The other gap is foreign literature, with the single exception of Brecht. Like Foucault (but unlike Lévi-Strauss), Barthes was profoundly parochial in his intellectual reach. It is no wonder that the catholic-minded Benjamin was a gifted translator, whereas Barthes never showed any familiarity with other living European languages.

The second main difference is far more decisive and has to do with the very substance of their criticism. Like Barthes, Benjamin adopted more than one element of the ideology of literary modernism. Actually, he played a vital role in the history of modernism by combining avant-garde taste with two other streams of thought, Freudianism and Marxism,[93] transforming the resulting blend into a powerful—if highly biased— indictment of the culture of modern 'bourgeois' society. To this extent, Benjamin placed himself right at the core of that *war of modernism against modernity* that inspired most of the avant-garde, lending its code of values a strong *antinomian* character.

However, Benjamin did not follow the formalist drive of modernist aesthetics. He never took to anything like Shklovsky's 'objectless' art, nor in any way divorced sign from meaning. On

[92] H. Meschonnic, *Pour la Poétique*, Paris 1970, p. 111–12.
[93] On Benjamin, see my *Western Marxism*, pp. 117–30.

the contrary, his main essays, from the book-length *Origin of the German Tragic Drama* (1928) to his later studies on Baudelaire and Kafka, are exercises in the retrieval of complex human experiences of meaning, value and vision. For Benjamin, literature, modernist or not, remained the bearer of a rich moral message. For Barthes, it had become the plaything of the wanton sign, unburdened of all serious relation to the quandaries and perplexities of life. Can this be unrelated to the fact that, unlike Barthes, Benjamin retained a sharp awareness of the social context of texts? As good a close-reader as anyone, he never severed literature from its historical tegument.

The difference in the tone of their criticism could hardly be greater. In Benjamin the countercultural ethos kept a noble Utopian halo, which may often be read as an echo of neo-romantic messianism, yet speaks for the high seriousness of his determination to scrutinize literature as a criticism of life. This is poles apart from the nihilistic flavour of Barthes even—or especially—at its most libertarian. Significantly, the later Barthes showed an explicit sympathy for nihilism. The *Pleasure of the Text* accepts Nietzsche's diagnostic of nihilism ('the debasement of higher ends') only to resist Nietzsche's strenuous plea for a cure.

The greatest countercultural sage of structuralism remains Lévi-Strauss. But Roland Barthes had a crucial role in the movement: he was, so to speak, the liaison officer between structuralism and existentialism—an intellectual trend which, despite being openly challenged by the structuralists, shared many a trait with its haughty successor in Parisian haute culture. The above-mentioned Sartreanization of Saussure is, I suggest, the main evidence for the persistence of existentialist undercurrents throughout Barthes's work. Maybe one can go so far as to suggest that whilst Lévi-Strauss's chief quarrel is with industrial civilization as such, Barthes as an ideologist features rather as a modernizer of the *anti-bourgeois* literary revolt—a persistent theme in French literary thought, which runs from Baudelaire to Sartre.

'We stifle under bourgeois evil' the young Barthes wrote in an article on Sartre's minor play *Nekrassov*. His acceptance of much Freudian lore, after Sartre gave notoriously short shrift to the concept of the unconscious, could be taken as a measure of his 'modernization' of the anti-bourgeois ideological kit. But his

5

Structuralism into Post-structuralism: an Overview

Schüler—   *Kann Euch nicht eben ganz verstehen.*
Mephistopheles— *Das wird nächstens schon besser gehen,*
                 Wenn Ihr lernt alles reduzieren
                 Und gehörig klassifizieren.

Goethe, *Faust*, Part One, vs. 1942–45.

Redefining Structuralism

While Lévi-Strauss represents a thorough-going structuralism, Barthes, as we saw, constituted a clear-cut case of evolution towards post-structuralism. Much the same contrast could be made between the two other tetrarchs in the original structuralist constellation: Lacan died without any discernible major movement away from the positions he held in the sixties; Foucault, having never accepted the structuralist label in the first place, dropped even the 'archaeological' concern with unconscious cognitive structures that made him akin to the movement in its flourishing years. (Of course, the tetrarchy becomes a pentarchy if we choose to include Althusser, exponent of structuralism within the Marxist camp.)

Let us now sketch a concise redefinition of *structuralisme* and its succession. Naturally, almost everything hinges upon the meaning of two notions: structuralism and post-structuralism. Let us try and put some order on their fluid connotations.

Structuralism first, of course. As we saw, a minimal definition of structuralism presupposes the rejection of atomist views. Structures are never mere aggregates, accidental bunches of elements and their properties; structuralism, therefore, is a molar, not a molecular, view of reality. But this molar outlook, though necessary for structuralism to obtain, is not sufficient. We saw how Piaget added to wholeness two other defining aspects: self-regulation and transformation. In other words, a structural system does not use elements external to it, nor are the outcomes of structural processes external to the system. Thus we get a richer meaning, for now 'structure' denotes a reality at once molar, transformative and homoeostatic (that is, self-stabilising). Yet this last aspect raises a problem in that self-regulation seems to apply much more to systems like the pattern of Piaget's genetic cognitive psychology than to the structures studied by structuralist social science. In Lévi-Straussian anthropology, in particular, homoeostasis turns out to be far less important than entropy.

At this juncture one should also bear in mind the shift from a biological to a formal, or mathematical, concept of structure— a shift by means of which the idea of organism, as a ruling metaphor, was displaced by a concern with far more abstract models. Here lies no doubt a major difference between sociological structuralisms: while 'palaeo-structuralisms' (such as anthropological theory under Radcliffe-Brown; sociological theory under Parsons) made constant use of biological analogies, French structuralism opted for an entirely different approach: it tried very hard to adapt a linguistic paradigm to social science. In so doing, Lévi-Strauss vowed to link the concept of structure to the notion of *sign*. Other traits of structural anthropology, both methodological, like binarism, and substantive, such as the overrating of synchrony, do not seem as essential to the principle of modern structuralism as the conjunction of these three attributes: structure is something molar, transformational, and semiotic (it is part and parcel of a sign-process).

Now if we take the methodological crux of (French) structuralism to be model theory within a purported semiotic paradigm, then it obviously comprehends the work of Barthes as well as that of its founder, Lévi-Strauss. It would also embrace Lacan —but not Foucault, whose indifference to the lessons of modern linguistics was quite genuine. Nevertheless, it would be wise to consider at least two other general stances, this time substantive rather than methodological.

First, what I feel tempted to call—borrowing an image from Lévi-Strauss himself—*the kaleidoscope thesis*. Structuralism tends to perceive reality as a kaleidoscope: a host of colourful different shapes, the glimmer of which conceals a ground of identity, a matrix composed of just a few, recurring elements. In Lévi-Strauss, this is intimately connected with the resolute *universalist* thrust of his thought. In a curious essay, the anthropologist Stanley Diamond tried his hand at a psycho-historical interpretation of the founder of structural anthropology by drawing on the contrast sketched by Sartre (in his *Anti-Semite and Jew*, 1946) between two Jewish religious types: the prophet and the priest. The 'prophetic sense' is authentic because it is existential and liberating, focused on unique situations, as in Martin Buber and the Hasidic tradition. The 'priestly sense', on the other hand, is 'inauthentic' because it represses the quest for Jewishness under a 'passion for the universal' which cannot but fall back on ritualized codes.[1] Now with all respect for Sartre, we can retain his characterization (and apply it to Lévi-Strauss, as does Diamond) but drop his evaluation. I for one find that one of the best things in classical French structuralism is precisely its healthy embrace of a universalist perspective. Talk of inauthenticity almost always proved no more than nonsense; but the renewal of a concern for human universals in social theory was badly needed—and provided the fuel for the 'kaleidoscope' thesis.

Second, structuralism seems pervaded by a *mantic outlook* as regards signs. As Barthes put it (in *Critical Essays*), it rejoices in pointing at the place of meaning *without naming it*. Like a cryptic soothsayer, the Pythian oracle of Barthes's own example, structuralist analysis loves to spot meaning as an obscure vibration, a dim discharge of deeply enigmatic sense. Hence the mystique of the signifier, the obsessive dream of non-denotative languages. As Geoffrey Thurley has shrewdly realized, structuralism is a 'linguistic' version of the high modernist rage against mimesis and content.[2]

But the point is, how many of the structuralist masters subscribe to the kaleidoscope thesis and the mantic outlook? The answer comes quickly to mind. Lévi-Strauss evidently takes the kaleidoscopic view of the social world as a host of images

---

[1] S. Diamond, 'The myth of structuralism', in I. Rossi, ed., *The Unconscious in Culture: The Structuralism of Claude Lévi-Strauss in Perspective*, New York 194, pp. 318–5.

[2] G. Thurley, *Counter-Modernism in Current Critical Theory*, London 1985, pp. 7–11.

ultimately reducible to a few sets of rules; after all, it is his simile. When it comes to the mantic side of structuralism, his position is far less clear-cut. We saw him taking pains to distinguish structuralism from formalism, deliberately avoiding reductionist formalisms such as Propp's morphology of the folktale. It cannot be said that in his own myth analysis he just 'pointed at the place of meaning without naming it'. Nevertheless, he often discussed kinship, myth and other intellectual social constructs as though they were referentless machines spreading their taxonomies and transformations in a way largely uncaused by, and unresponsive to, external factors. Barthes first upheld the kaleidoscope thesis (in books like *On Racine* or *Système de la Mode*), then dropped it from *S/Z* onwards. Foucault, as a radical historist, never swallowed the postulate of identity underneath the kaleidoscope. On the other hand, both Barthes and Foucault not only displayed a mantic posture but made it still more radical, as we shall presently see. As for Lacan, he was a kaleidoscope thinker (language was to him the One Big Structure of the unconscious); and he was also a highly mantic theorist, who conceived of the signifier as something hermetically sealed off from the impurity of denotation.

Post-structuralism: Anti-structuralism or Neo-structuralism?

The kaleidoscope thesis and mantic semiotics enable us to settle the thorny issue of ascertaining whether *post-structuralism*, chiefly as embodied by the later Barthes, Derrida and Foucault, is a sequel to or a break with mainstream structuralism of the early and mid-sixties. Or, to put it otherwise: is *post-structuralism a neo-structuralism or an anti-structuralism*? Those who regard it as a break with structuralism generally stress 1968 as a watershed. They can support their view with statements from both Barthes and Foucault that acknowledge the impact of the gauchiste and libertarian upheaval of May 1968 upon their work. We have seen Barthes, in an insurrectional mood, speak of the need for 'liberating the signifier', and Foucault stressed the kinship between his critique of power and the neo-anarchist temper of the students' revolt. At the zenith of the May *évènements* as well as in their aftermath, the silence of Lévi-

Strauss, Lacan and Althusser sounded very eloquent (the latter, sharing the communists' deep embarassment over a quasi-revolution that was almost as much against them as against the bourgeois Fifth Republic); at any rate, as a graffito on the walls of the Sorbonne read 'structuralism is dead', it seemed only too natural for the leaders of classical French structure theory to sulk. In December 1969, confronted with a restless Vincennes student, Lacan did not mince his words: 'What you as a revolutionary aspire to is a master. You will have one.'[3] Thus structuralism gave short shrift to the libertarian rhetoric of *soixante-huitards*—and those who pampered it soon ceased to describe themselves as structuralists (Barthes) or underscored in every way their distance from structuralism (Foucault).

However, things are not so simple. To begin with, the silence over 1968 was shared by at least one central figure in post-structuralism, Derrida. On the other hand, post-structuralism (beginning with Barthes and Derridean deconstructionism) was from the outset fraught with Lacanian themes. The best evidence for this is the philosophical gospel of post-1968 gauchisme, Guy Lardreau and Christian Jambet's book *L'Ange* (1976). This weird work attempted to ground an 'ontology of revolution' by legitimizing the deeds of Mao—the ideal of a cultural revolution, espoused in Paris by the *Gauche prolétarienne* (a tiny sect far more gauchiste than proletarian). Lardreau and Jambet broke with the libertarianism of the philosophers of desire (Deleuze and Guattari). As good Lacanians, they saw rebellion frustrated by impulses deeply conditioned by the Law of an unsuppressible other (*le nom/non du père*, the ever-castrating instance of the Father). Ergo, there is only one way to escape social pessimism, to justify revolution and to reconcile the realism of Lacan with the bold wisdom of Mao: historical change must come from a withdrawal from the chains of desire. Hereupon enters the Angel, symbol of a sexless transcendence. The authors likened the ascetic sects of early Christianity, with their proto-Catharist ethos of libertarian purity (no sex, no labour), to the Chinese cultural revolution.

Just as Marcuse, in *Eros and Civilisation* (1955), tried to win Freudianism over to Utopian revolutionism in spite of Freud,

---

[3] Cf. *Magazine Littéraire*, 121, February 1977.

Lardreau and Jambet tried to draw from Lacanism, in spite of Lacan, a brief for revolution without Utopia. One might of course ask why we need revolutions which cannot even bring about Utopias, but our point is that Lacanism bestrode structuralism *and* post-structuralism, thereby seriously vitiating the assumption that the latter is in essence an anti-structuralism. If Lacan was, as he undoubtedly was, one of the tetrarchs of structuralist theory and yet still cast such a big shadow over the evolution of Barthes, the work of Derrida and the core of the world view of the nouvelle philosophie (of which *L'Ange* provided the extreme leftist incarnation), then there must be at least one important bridge between structuralism and its succession in French thought.

As we saw, Lacan was also a staunch paladin of the mantic glance: he was unswervingly on the side of the blank signifier. So overall, the Lacanian leitmotiv offers considerable support for the claim that post-structuralism is at bottom a neo-structuralism. However, none of this seems to weaken the relevance of the kaleidoscope thesis as a defining element of most major classical French structuralisms (Lévi-Strauss, Lacan, Althusser, Barthes in the sixties). Therefore it is also true to assert that, to a far from negligible extent, post-structuralism, in the thought of Derrida, Foucault, Deleuze and Lyotard, turned out in fact to be anti-structuralist as well.

Thus we can say that post-structuralism, insofar as it is an intellectual landscape mainly formed by the thought of Derrida and Foucault (and of the later Barthes in literary criticism), is at once a neo-structuralism and an anti-structuralism. In the main, the 'neo' strand amounts to developing and deepening the mantic outlook of the movement.

Since his philosophical début, Derrida has insisted that structuralism as the legacy of Saussure is the thought of radical difference—something that, as such, Saussure himself both realized and failed to establish in a consistent theoretical way. For Derrida, this Saussurean outlook (Jakobson: phonemes are 'purely differential and contentless signs') deserves a full-blown speculative expansion (Heidegger: 'for us, the business of thinking is difference qua difference[4]). The big mistake, explains Derrida in "Force and meaning", the leading essay of

[4] M. Heidegger, *Identity and Difference*, New York 1969, p. 37.

his seminal *Writing and Difference* (1967), is to think in terms of *form* instead of thinking in terms of *force*. Form-thinking is bound to be static and Apollonian; only force-thinking apprehends difference and becoming. Derrida uses this Nietzschean *distinguo* against Saussurean structuralism because the attempt to detect structures in cultural processes already implies a fateful superposition of form upon the realities of force as dynamic, infinite difference.

The Derridean radicalization of the principle of difference entails two broad strategies: (a) it implies dropping once and for all the 'kaleidoscope' idea that structure is an identical ground, a core beneath the multiple surfaces (the transformational approach); and (b) it also implies sticking more than ever to the 'mantic' severance of signifier from signified—the purist, Mallarméan view of language and, by extension, of other cultural codes. Consequently, by Derrida's logic, deconstructionism is true structuralism, that is, structuralism come true—the fulfilment of Saussure's central insight. By the same token, 'post-structuralism' is a red herring as a label. Structuralism was adumbrated in Saussure and promised by Lévi-Strauss—but it has been delivered by deconstruction. Strictly speaking, the neo-structuralism of Derrida is not at all a post-structuralism; rather, it is a 'propter'-structuralism, a kind of theory developed *because* of some structuralist core assumptions (above all, the recognition that meaning rests on difference) and against some others (above all, the attempt to stabilise the play of difference in a fixed master-structure). The unforgivable sin, for Derrida, consists less in searching for structure than in the illusion that structure has a centre.

In discussing Barthes, we noticed how in French literary culture the mantic poetics of Mallarmé, rekindled in the literary anthropology of Bataille and Blanchot, prepared the way for the acclimatization of key tenets of formalist criticism, especially as regards the ideal of a contentless, objectless art. Now Foucault has also linked his endeavours to the 'formalist culture' of our century, a stream of thought that he found basically congenial to Marxism, though in open defiance of dogmatic Marxism; as for French structuralism, he called it a 'minor episode' within the broad span of such 'formalist culture', which in his view might well be as significant in our time as romanticism and positivism were in the nineteenth century.[5]

Foucault's spontaneous homage to formalism allows us to connect him, too, with the mantic spirit of structuralist/post-structuralist thought. The connection is of particular moment because, unlike those of Lévi-Strauss, Lacan, Barthes or Derrida, Foucault's main subjects were neither sign systems nor social institutions envisaged as social codes; his analyses did not bear on myth, fashion, textual fabrics, the unconscious as language or kinship structures as a means of communication. As a result, they were not—any more than Althusser's—predominantly couched in semiotic concepts. All the same, and for all his occasional hints at the social roots of the discursive practices he scrutinised, Foucault always tended to dwell on them for their own sake, regardless, that is, of their social referents. In other words, more often than not, he dealt with attitudinal codes towards insanity, systems of cognitive a prioris, regimes of punishment and sexual ethics in a *formalist vein*, invariably choosing 'immanent analysis' against more contextual approaches.

That is why Foucault's occasional references to class struggle in relation to the madhouse or the prison often sound hollow: it is not so much that they are factually wrong—more importantly, they are conspicuously beside the methodological point of his kind of analysis. Like the structuralist's, Foucault sought meaningful relations, not causes and effects, in whatever he undertook to study at length. Although he very rightly criticised deconstructionists for being unable to see anything outside the text, he, too, had little concern for social context and still less for specifiable causal mechanisms. In this sense, he too displays the mantic cast of mind. Thanks to him, formalism annexed power structures to its domain.

To the historian of ideas, the arresting aspect of the powerful formalist streak in structuralism and its dialectical sequel, post-structuralism, is perhaps the combination of this formalism with a Nietzschean standpoint. We have just seen Derrida base his critique of 'kaleidoscope' structuralism on Nietzschean premises, his form/force antithesis being a translation of the celebrated Apollonian/Dionysian opposition; while the centrality of Nietzschean motives in Foucault's work has been

---

[5] Cf. his interview with Gérard Raulet in *Telos*, 55, Spring 1983, pp. 196–97.

emphasised by most of his commentators. Now Nietzschean formalism is an odd creature in that, within humanist culture, formalist thought did not originally stem from the *Lebensphilosophie* tradition to which Nietzsche belonged, as a maverick thinker beside a Dilthey or a Bergson. Thus, as we saw, one of the main influences on Russian formalist criticism was the formal tradition in art history, brought to completion by Wölfflin—a distinctly un-Nietzschean affair. To be sure, Russian formalists blessed futurist art, and the impact of Nietzsche's anti-decadentism on futurism in general can hardly be overrated. But little if any of this ingredient of their favourite poets' world-view was transposed into the formalists' theoretical work. By contrast, their acquaintance with Husserlian phenomenology eased their conversion to the definitely Apollonian concepts of Saussure.[6]

It was only in interwar France, via Bataille, that literary formalism (stemming from Mallarmé) and Nietzschean ideas (the mystique of vitality and transgression) merged. But Bataille, like his disciple Blanchot, was not even a literary philosopher, as Nietzsche himself had been: he was regarded as a man of letters dabbling in some sort of wild philosophical anthropology. Therefore the penetration of the new hybrid, Nietzschean formalism, into philosophy did not happen until the days of Foucault and Derrida—not surprisingly, two fervent admirers of Bataille. Nietzschean formalism has since became a trademark of post-structuralism.

Presumably the best-known instance of Foucault's Dionysian allegiance is his comment on Descartes's first *Philosophical Meditation* in *Histoire de la Folie*.[7] Foucault strives to demonstrate that Descartes's famous 'evil genius' hypothesis actually amounts to an arbitrary expulsion of madness from thinking. While the cogito is held by Descartes to comprehend doubt, dreams, daydreaming and illness, no room is allowed for insanity in the certainty of self-conscious mind. Foucault's discussion quickly became a locus classicus of the indictment of rationalism as sheer epistemological 'arrogance'. Derrida challenged Foucault on this strategic point. In *Writing and Difference*,

---

[6] Cf. Elmar Holenstein's study, *Jakobson ou le structuralisme phénoménologique*, Paris, 1974.

[7] Cf. Foucault 1961, pp. 54–57 and Merquior, *Foucault*, pp. 21–31.

he objected to Foucault's attempt to make his stand on the side of madness.[8] Any discourse on madness has of necessity to speak the language of reason, argues Derrida; therefore, Foucault's claim to bypass rationality for the sake of the rights of insanity proves perfectly vain. Reason, according to Derrida, cannot be evaded; all we can do is deconstruct it, undermining its pretence of clear, stable meanings—a mirage derived from 'logocentrism', that is, the Apollonian attempt to centre the play of signs on fixed signifieds, under equally false principles like 'truth' and 'objectivity'.

Here we seem to be facing two different ways of assessing the status of reason. Foucault's position boils down to the classical irrationalist disparagement of epistemological concerns with valid, critical knowledge. Derrida's attitude is more nuanced. He, too, questions the rationalist claim of cognitive validity and demonstrable truth; but he wants to recast reason rather than just ditch it. 'There is no Trojan horse against reason', he wrote: one cannot escape its net. But if you think that, by stating—against Foucault's romantic transrational stand—that our thought is ineluctably ensnared in reason, Derrida is defending the use of logic and analytic reason, you are very much mistaken. He wishes to use rational language and at the same time to circumvent it through the unspecified idiom of a 'higher' form of reason—a modern equivalent, as it were, of what Hegelian dialectics purported to be.

Indeed in *Writing and Difference*, he says, cryptically, that the idiom of philosophy—all philosophy—is necessarily Hegelian. So in the end what he seems to be advocating in place of the young Foucault's misology is the language of the concept (as Adorno did against Heidegger)—as for logic and rationality, they are only accepted on sufferance. Ultimately, Derrida deplores the fact that we cannot dispense with reason, since the inbuilt rationality of language is precisely what foists upon us the metaphysical assumptions that meaning is the presence of stable signifieds. Because logos dwells in language, we can neither reject nor rely on such logocentric premises. All we can do, according to the *Of Grammatology*'s 'flying instructions' is to put our contaminated statements 'under erasure'—an abominable mannerism inaugurated by Heidegger to speak not

[8] J. Derrida, *Writing and Difference*, Chicago 1978, chapter 2.

of metaphysics but of Being.

In sum: whilst Foucault appeared simply to follow Nietzsche's own open irrationalism, Derrida seemingly used Hegel-like arguments concerning the nature of philosophical discourse to reach the same impeccably Nietzschean conclusions: there is no truth, no objectivity, no disinterested knowledge. Their opposition, therefore, involves their means, not their ends. Their common goal as the two main leaders of post-structuralist French thought is quite clear: it consists in a determination to break the structuralist kaleidoscope by dint of two very different ways of wielding the same weapon—*the unholy alliance of Nietzsche and formalism.*

A Handful of Critiques

French structuralism, as suggested in the preceding sections, is a 'molar' view of social or cultural phenomena best described not as an approach stressing systemic self-regulation but as a semiotic model of kaleidoscopic transformations. The model is semiotic because it insists on presenting the stuff of culture as if it were made of signs and codes, and within semiotics it followed or tried to follow the lead of Saussurean linguistic analysis. Together with its loyalty to the modern linguistic paradigm, the accent on transformation rather than self-regulation lent its concept of structure a formal instead of an organic sense. But the structuralists' peculiar way of dealing with sign-like or code-like phenomena soon evinced another major characteristic: the tendency to treat structure as 'blind' to external referents, or of 'speaking of meaning without naming it'—what we, following Barthes, dubbed the mantic streak in structuralism. This mantic leaning was strong enough to be handed over to post-structuralism, in which it was enhanced. For, needless to say, one could sustain the mantic note either by remaining sign-besotted (as in Derrida) or, alternatively, by setting little store by semiotics (as in Foucault). But in either case, the original structuralist view of reality as a bunch of kaleidoscopic images underpinned by a few invariants was ruthlessly rejected.

So much, then, for our synthetic, admittedly too schematic, *description* of structuralism and its half-prolonging, half-denying sequel in post-structuralism. What can we say by way of a brief *evaluation*? A global assessment of the work of Lévi-Strauss and Barthes was offered at the end of the chapters devoted to them. Specific appraisals of their main books and theoretical contributions were also given. It now remains for us briefly to examine the claims of some of the most serious, or at least influential, lines of criticism addressed to structuralism. Then, we should be ready to sketch a final appreciation of the post-structuralist scene.

One of the earliest critiques of structuralist theory, voiced from the mid-sixties in the pages of *L'Homme et la Société*, stated that structuralism was an *un-historical rationalism*. This derives from the veteran humanist Marxist, Henri Lefebvre, who called structuralism a new Eleatism, an anti-history phobia propounded by a scientism deeply akin to the technocracy of the Gaullian age.[9] Lévi-Strauss was the new Parmenides of Elea: the enemy of Heraclitean, dynamic views of society, best represented by Marxism. Lucien Goldmann then framed the same basic Marxist criticism within a broad historical perspective. Building on Lukács's ideas on irrationalism as an ideology endemic to 'decadent' bourgeoisies, Goldmann depicted bourgeois thought as alternating between rationalism and irrationalism. The progressive bourgeoisie of the age of revolution embraced reason. Nevertheless, as soon as their class rule was threatened in the nineteenth century, they went over to irrationalism. Similarly, in our own century, under social pressures that came to the fore with the Depression and world war, the bourgeoisie turned once more to irrationalism, in the age of existentialisms. Finally, with the affluence of the fifties and sixties, the capitalist order recovered confidence— bourgeois thought could safely return to rationalism. This, however, did not prevent the bourgeois world view from lacking a *historical* rationality, since the flag of social progress was no longer in its hands but in those of Marxism, the philosophy of the working class. Hence the rationalism-minus-history of Lévi-Straussian social theory.[10] Both Lefebvre and Goldmann

[9] Lefebvre, '*Claude Lévi-Strauss et le nouvel éleatisme*, in *L'Homme et la Société*, 1, July–Sept. 1966; and 2, Oct.–Dec. 1966; repr. in Lefebvre, *Au-delà du Structuralisme*, Paris, 1971.

[10] L. Goldmann, 'Structuralisme, Marxisme, Existentialisme', in *L'Homme et la Société*, 2, 1966, pp. 105–24.

make the charge of Eleatism, but Lefebvre stressed the scientistic, non-humanist face of structuralism; Goldmann, by contrast, pressed still further its unhistorical cast of mind.

The trouble with the unhistorical rationalism critique is twofold. On the one hand the idea that structuralism engineered a shift to an unhistorical mood in contemporary western theory scarcely holds water. Many a prior school of thought had dodged history well before Lévi-Strauss's praise of cold societies and historyless intellect. Neither Husserl nor Heidegger cared much for historicity; yet they—and not Croce or Lukács—turned out to be the two consuls of their age in continental philosophy. (Heidegger actually talked of the historicalness of existence against the abstract timelessness of Husserlian conciousness; but he was at pains to specify that this had little to do with historical processes in the broad social sense.) Their counterpart as the major influence in British philosophy since the war, Wittgenstein, was not exactly a devotee of Clio either (indeed, Oxford 'linguistic' philosophy, Wittgenstein's brainchild, was to be memorably scolded[11] precisely for its lack of historical consciousness). In literary criticism, the situation on the eve of the structuralist wave was also far from favourable to historical-mindedness. With Walter Benjamin and Erich Auerbach dead and half-forgotten, American new criticism and the '*critique thématique*' imposed distinctly non-historical paradigms.

Furthermore, even at the high point of twentieth-century historism, that is, before World War II, social theory had often defined historical knowledge in a curiously a-chronic way. For instance, to Alfred Kroeber, the greatest inheritor of *Historismus* within anthropological thought, the historical approach did not deal with time sequences; rather, it strove towards 'descriptive integration' geared to the grasp of patterns. And the English Croce, R. G. Collingwood, writing in the twenties, set Clio against Chronos by declaring that history was 'the mind's triumph over time'. Time, he argued in *Speculum Mentis* (1924), was real; but real only as the correlative of an equally real opposite, the 'extemporal' knowledge whereby the mind at once knew its own change and was 'lifted above change'.

---

[11] Cf. Gellner's *Words and Things: An Examination of, and an Attack on, Linguistic Philosophy*, London 1959.

Overall, then, there is little basis for presenting structuralism as the initiator of a new anti-historical mood in western thought. On the contrary the structuralist vogue came after roughly a quarter of a century of musings over 'the crisis of historism', to quote Karl Heussi's soul-searching critique of 1932; a crisis in which, in more than one respect, the assault on *historicism* conducted by authors as widely different as Popper, Loewith, Eliade and Berlin was just a minor, if decisive, episode.[12] By 1960, the animus against history was anything but a novelty.

On the other hand, with the benefit of hindsight, it is easy to realize that structuralism was far less 'rationalist' than it originally appeared. Impressions to the contrary derived chiefly from Lévi-Strauss, the *Kulturkritiker* who never berated science. But he was an exception, not the rule, in his defence of analytical reason (even Althusser, the champion of scientism among structuralists, extolled dialectics over and above analytical reason). Barthes and Lacan never showed any particular respect for natural science models. Foucault, the odd man out among the structuralist tetrarchs (for he never accepted the label) subtly introduced the English translation of *Les Mots et les Choses* by stressing the need for valuing the 'informal knowledge' of the human sciences as against the traditional epistemological emphasis on hard science. As a whole, in its general outlook as well as in its methods, structuralism did not side with science but with its adversary, humanist culture. In fact, it finished as a humanism with a vengeance.

So much so, that it was rebuked—by a second major strand of criticism—*for not being scientific enough* (if at all). Thus Philip Pettit, writing in the mid-seventies, but still concentrating on structural anthropology, found that, except in linguistics, the structuralist model did not yield truly scientific results, though it at least provided the means for organizing analysis beyond mere ad hoc observations.[13] Pettit included Chomsky's generative grammar (alongside phonology) in the narrow circle of structuralist scientific achievements. But structural linguistics was far from satisfactory to Chomsky himself.

[12] See K. Popper, *The Poverty of Historicism*, London 1957; Löwith 1949; Eliade 1959; and Berlin, 'Historical Inevitability' (1954) now ch 2 in Berlin 1969.
[13] Pettit, *The Concept of Structuralism*.

Chomsky shared at least three views with Saussureans in social science such as Lévi-Strauss. First universalism: Chomsky's linguistic *competence* works as a human universal, just like the Lévi-Straussian 'mind'. Second, the idea that mind is not, as in the traditional philosophies of the subject, transparent. As Chomsky wrote in *Language and Mind* (1968), both rationalists and empiricists, both the sons of Descartes and the scions of Locke and Hume, held 'the unquestioned assumption that the properties and contents of the mind are accessible to intuition.'[14] In Chomsky's theory, however, as John Cottingham aptly puts it, 'we have no privileged access to the contents and workings of the mind, any more than we have in the case of any other phenomenon to be studied by science.'[15] Third, the 'kaleidoscope' thesis: in Chomskyan linguistics, deep structure stands to surface grammar just as the few core invariants of the kaleidoscope stand to the colourful images that meet our eyes; deep grammar offers invariants. Chomsky's later work, such as *Rules and Representation* (1980), discussed rules which work much closer to the surface level than in his previous transformational research; yet this evolution did not affect the heart of the matter: the kaleidoscope was preserved.

However, for all these significant areas of agreement, Chomsky regards structuralism as a whole as no more than an 'inductive taxonomy'—something definitely inferior, in explanatory power, to his own transformational linguistics, geared to elucidate the mechanism of sentence-making. To Chomsky, structuralism stuck to the myth of the museum: the error of regarding mind as a storehouse harbouring mental objects called meanings, instead of taking a dynamic point of view and seeking to account for language as a *productive* activity which is causally explainable.[16]

The same basic objection, this time directed against *non-linguistic* structuralism, was taken up Ernest Gellner, who sees the structural method as valid insofar as 'we are shown the generation of one world from materials drawn from another

---

[14] N. Chomsky, *Language and Mind*, New York 1968, p. 22.

[15] J. Cottingham, *Rationalism*, London 1984, p. 128.

[16] For an accessible presentation of Chomsky's position vis-à-vis structural linguistics (distinguishing between its branches), see Chomsky, *Language and Responsibility*, Sussex 1979, pp. 106–19.

. . . independently identifiable world.' According to Gellner, such is the case in phonology. Yet in most structuralist analyses of myth or literature or ritual one fails to detect signs of a similar achievement. 'There does not seem to be even any attempt to locate some deeper level so as to explain the surface in terms of it. Instead, elements plucked by some mysterious process from the surface text—usually the alleged polar extremities occurring in it—are attributed a kind of double status, marking both the limits of the emic world in which they occur and being somehow mysteriously credited with also being the (etic?) bricks out of which that inward world of the culture in question has been constructed.'[17] ('Emic' and 'etic', in the terminology first proposed by Kenneth Pike, denote respectively the inside or native view of a given culture and the statements made about the same culture by independent outsiders—normally anthropologists.) To put it bluntly: the trouble with structuralism is that, for all its talk about identifying the basic elements of a culture's kaleidoscope, it does not deliver the goods, since at the end of the day there is no actual demonstration of generative mechanisms, no real formula for the mapped-out transformations; its reach remains far greater than its grasp.

It might be objected against Gellner's strictures that there are at least *some* structuralist theories in which a core structure is identified. An example comes readily to mind: 'narratology', the 'grammar' of narrative. Narratological equations from Propp to Bremond, Greimas and Todorov break down narratives into a few functional or sequential units belonging to a general—and generative—'code'. But then, narratology notoriously fails even minimally to come to grips with the wealth of connotation of fictional meaning. Small wonder its practitioners never tackled the moral and psychological complexities of the high art of the novel, from Cervantes to Musil. Thus, even when we do have a generative mechanism in non-linguistic structural theory, it produces only the most trivial revelations: the generative mechanism remaining too generic, its results too jejune.

As a rule, therefore, structuralisms, outside linguistics,

---

[17] Gellner, 'What is structuralisme?', in Gellner, *Relativism and the Social Sciences*, Cambridge 1985.

spawn classifications but no real transformational models. Now this failure can in turn be seen in two ways. One may regard it as *contingent* on the hitherto analytical performances of structuralism or as a *congenital* fault, resulting from the attempt to extend to unsuitable phenomena the core/surface model employed (arguably with success) in modern linguistics. Gellner himself, in his conclusion, hints at a structural flaw in structuralism. Elaborating on the same point, Perry Anderson deems the relation between *langue* and *parole* 'a peculiarly aberrant compass' for explaining the determination of cultural spheres other than language. Anderson lists three basic reasons for this inadequacy of the linguistic paradigm in social science. First, while the subject of speech is 'axiomatically individual', the relevant subjects in culture, as in the economy or the polity, are predominantly collectivities like nations, classes or generations. Second, whereas human activity in all these areas normally occurs within severe material constraints, speech knows no such limitation. Third, most linguistic structures evince a rate of change exceedingly slow in relation to the speed of alteration in other cultural spheres.[18]

To the epistemologically alert social scientist, this last argument sounds especially convincing. To the historian of ideas, it rings a familiar bell: it recalls one of the best points made against early conservative social theory. Early romantic conservatives, such as the jurist Friedrich Karl von Savigny, the leader of the 'historical school' fought by Hegel, relished organicist comparisons between law and language. But by the mid-century such analogies were being contradicted. Thus Rudolf von Jhering stressed that law was very *unlike* language, for while language undergoes no sharp conflicts, the legal frame of society—especially modern society—does. We need only to add: as with law, so with culture.

The question of the theoretical inadequacy of structuralism calls for some further comment. Structuralism, it is generally agreed, *deals with meaningful connections, not causes*. The only major exception to this seems to be the Marxist structuralism of Althusser, where talk of 'structural causation' is *de rigueur*. However, as far as causality is concerned, Althusserian structuralism notoriously takes with one hand what it gives with the

---

[18] Anderson, *In the Tracks of Historical Materialism*, pp. 44–45.

other. It tries to combine lip service to classical Marxism—
'economic determination in the last analysis', as the saying
goes—with a more flexible approach, less unpalatable to the
fastidious anti-reductionism of contemporary academic opinion
(Althusserianism, in Raymond Aron's immortal dictum, was
'Marxism for *agrégés de philo*').[19] No wonder, then, the
Althusserians never produced a major explanatory work which
could confirm their scholastic conceptual absurdities: how could
they, with such an equivocal, slippery notion as 'structural
causation' for a framework?

Now relinquishing the causal perspective altogether would
too heavily reduce the cognitive power—no matter how
spurious or incomplete up to now—of social science. To be
sure, as Lévi-Strauss wrote in *Elementary Structures of Kinship*,
'any culture may be looked upon as an ensemble of symbolic
systems, in the front rank of which are to be found language,
marriage, laws, economic relations, art, science and religion.' It
would be silly to deny that many a fruitful insight can be yielded
by such an approach to culture, based as it is on the search for
significant linkages ('symbolic systems' literal or otherwise)
instead of cause and effect relations. But it is hard to see how
this perspective could ever be generalized as a global recipe for
sociological enquiry. For such a way of looking at culture and
society is hardly fit for accounting for cultural change; and it so
happens that more often than not, in order to understand, let
alone explain, culture one simply has to understand change.
Now to understand change implies thinking in terms of causes.
Culture is not just made up of objects and norms—it also
consists of *events*, if only because important social and cultural
changes often occur, even when they are not upheavals; and
wherever you have events, you must have an objective causal
nexus—precisely what run-of-the-mill structural analyses never
offer.

I submit that the secret of the a-chronism of structuralism lies
in its lack of causal depth: in this and not in the unqualified

---

[19] R. Aron, *Marxisms and the Existentialists*, 1969, p. 78. For a slightly less
scholastic debate than the Althusserians' hair-splitting on 'structural causation',
see French anthropological theory since Maurice Godelier (the first Marxist-
structuralist to re-think the base-superstructure model as applied to primitive
societies). Cf. Godelier, *Horizons* and Maurice Bloch, ed., *Marxist Analyses
and Social Anthropology*, London 1975.

anti-historist stand usually but wrongly identified solely with structuralist theory. After all, from Fustel de Coulanges and Mommsen to the Annales school, western historiography had often shown that not all historical writing has a diachronic focus. This timely reminder comes from the doyen of historians of historiography, A. Momigliano, a mind so alien to the structuralist bias against change that he wisely warns: 'Because of change, our knowledge of change will never be final. . . . But our knowledge of change is real enough.'[20] For, in the past, the deepening and enriching of historical analysis with a synchronic focus by no means lead to a theoretical abhorrence of time, change or transition. While in *linguistic* theory there were remarkable attempts to supersede Saussure's ultra-synchronism, structuralist social theory was spellbound by spatial thinking. Jakobson chided Saussure for his failure to envisage a structural account of diachrony.[21] No such move ever occurred within sociological structuralism.

On the contrary: whenever structuralist, or rather *parastructuralist,* philosophy turned to history, either on a theoretical plane (Althusser) or on the level of actual historiographic work (Foucault), instead of an effort to grasp historical change all that issued was the sacralization of 'breaks', a useful notion put forward by the epistemologist Gaston Bachelard (1884–1962) but much overstated by both Althusser and his former pupil Foucault. Those two thinkers, fellow travellers of structuralism in the sixties, naturally showed a lofty contempt for those who accused them of sharing the structuralist *taedium historiae*: Althusser, after all, was eliciting the 'science of history' from Marxian theory, and Foucault protested that what he was studying was precisely change. Yet such disclaimers are far from convincing. Gerry Cohen, author of the best sustained effort at making sense of Marx's theory of history, opened the book of that name (1978) by confessing that though Althusser helped him sense that the truly important Marx is to be found in *Capital*, not in his youthful philosophizing, all he got from Althusser's own contributions to *Reading Capital* (1965) was a

[20] A. Momigliano, *Essays in Ancient and Modern Historiography*, Oxford 1975, pp. 368–69.
[21] Cf. Jakobson's report to the VIII International Conference of Linguists (Oslo 1975), chapter 3 of Jakobson, *Essais de Linguistique Générale*, Paris 1963.

sense of how elegantly and evasively the French language can be used.

To limit ourselves to the case of Foucault: in his masterpiece, *Les Mots et les Choses* (1966), he held that the discontinuities between epochal *'epistemes'*—the unconscious conceptual structures underpinning all the knowledge of an age—were perfectly 'enigmatic'. In his subsequent work on power configurations, notably in *Discipline and Punish* (1975), the stress on absolute historical caesuras is partly attenuated; but it is still obvious that Foucault is only interested in change *after the event*, in outcomes rather than in mechanisms of change. His 'archaeological' glance froze historical processes into successive strata utterly unrelated to each other. In Foucault's oeuvre, change is never shown *in fieri*. If its results are described, its roots are not even identified. In this sense, no *explanation* of history was attempted. Historiography as a rational discipline can hardly be expected to live on such a diet.

Thus, criticisms of structuralism began by blaming its scientism, only to conclude that it does not fit the scientific bill, lacking explanations where they are required. But there is another line of criticism liable to move in a similar full-circle. I mean the *ideological* critique proper, which purports to unmask structuralism as a piece of class ideology. It first became visible when Sartre, in the issue of the southern French review, *L'Arc*, dedicated to his work, jibed at structuralism as the last stand of the bourgeoisie against Marxism.

This kind of imputation is of course exceedingly difficult to substantiate. If the charge is, as Sartre's angry tone suggested, that the structuralists were consciously acting on behalf of bourgeois power, it may be promptly objected that the actual political leanings of the structuralist tetrarchy—not to mention Althusser—scarcely supported the accusation. Indeed, three of the tetrarchs—Lévi-Strauss, Barthes, Foucault—had had impeccable leftist credentials in the past—and nothing they said or published in the sixties could be construed as right-wing politics. If, on the other hand, the charge implied that structuralists, by preaching their ideas, were *unwittingly* helping capitalism, then we are entitled to ask how and why—but neither the manner nor the cause of the alleged link was ever satisfactorily demonstrated. The closest we came to this link was Goldmann's vague Lukácsian correlation between structuralist unhistorical rationalism and post-war affluence—which, on inspection, does not even explain why the supposed rationalism of structuralist theory would serve class interests instead of the general welfare (while we can understand, without necessarily endorsing, the link between an anti-historicist cast of mind and social conservatism, there is no obvious reason for postulating any ties between conservatism and rationalism).

Ironically, almost twenty years later, it was claimed that structuralism and post-structuralism were in league with socio-political radicalism—quite the obverse of Sartre's charge. Nothing less, in effect, is intended by Laurence Lerner, head of an anti-structuralist and anti-deconstructionist reaction based in the literary quarters of the University of Sussex. Professor Lerner is the first to admit that structuralism can very well be conservative; but he seems to think that deconstructionism—the textual theory of post-structuralism viewed as a sequel to structuralism—made the latter into a radical weapon.[22]

Lerner's thesis was derided in the TLS,[23] but in truth it deserves more qualification than rejection. True, Lerner makes the mistake of calling most of the practitioners of French literary criticism 'Marxists', so his TLS reviewer scores an easy point by recalling that: (a) deconstructionism is not structuralism but largely the latter's undoing; and (b) neither current is in any sense Marxist. However, (a) is at best half-truth and although (b) is true, it does not follow that a lot of structuralism and most of deconstructionism are not strewn with radical, if not Marxist, themes. If one takes the ideology of class struggle, the denunciation of bourgeois values and the anathema cast on modern civilisation, that is, liberal industrial society, to be central radical tenets, then both structuralist and post-structuralist theory exude radicalism—though of course its range and intensity vary a great deal with each main thinker (class struggle, for instance, is virtually absent from the writings of Lévi-Strauss, Lacan or Derrida).

A Modernist Invasion of Theory

There is indeed a large overlap between structuralism/post-

---

[22] L. Lerner, *Reconstructing Literature*, ed., Oxford 1983, pp. 2–3.
[23] 28 October 1983 (review by Imre Salusinszky).

structuralism and radical ideology—which is hardly surprising, given that several countercultural beliefs are nowadays espoused by the majority of humanist intellectuals. Indeed, from the viewpoint of the history of ideas, structuralism and its succession ought to be seen as the main forces in *a colonization of thought by the modernist idea* in literature and art. This is the source of the crypto-humanist streak in the epistemology of structuralism (for all its scientist façade); and of the wildly humanist ones in that of post-structuralism, a paradise of Nietzschean assaults on truth, logic and objectivity. At the heart of it there lies a deep agreement between the structuralist outlook on the nature of modern society and the humanist 'countercultural' ethos.

Now the idea of counterculture is a spiritual child of High Modernism. It represents, as stressed by Daniel Bell, the migration of antinomian ideas from the early twentieth-century humanist intelligentsia into the space of contemporary *social* culture.[24] What was once thought and symbolized by the avant-garde artist is now believed and acted out (at least in principle) by the declassed student rebel, the radical academic, in public happenings, and in punk sub-culture. To be sure, all these groups are still, in terms of number, a minority within the larger bourgeois and bourgeoisified society. *But, unlike the erstwhile avant-gardes, they are becoming the master public in high culture, thereby considerably strengthening the onslaught of modernism on modernity.* The structuralist temper was already marked by this overflowing of modernist revulsion against the official, liberal-rational values of modern society. Post-structuralism just takes it for granted. In many respects it is humanism gone berserk.

Incidentally, this might also explain the frequency with which those who masterminded the 'structural revolution' insisted on putting on a fundamentalist face (Lacan 'returns' to Freud; Althusser 'reads' Marx; Foucault never drops Marxism altogether, and so on). The point is that structuralism—and still less post-structuralism—did not aim to get rid of Marx and Freud—they were only exploring the many themes, motives and elements of a world view in Marxism, as well as in Freudianism, which are in deep agreement with the romantic mythology of the counterculture, despite the fact that both

[24] Bell 1976, pp. 46–54.

Marx and Freud saw themselves as heirs to the Enlightenment.
The roots of structuralist thought, therefore, lie in the aesthetic revolt (turned orgiastic of late) carried out by modernist
culture. French structuralisms, both classical and 'neo', aim at
providing a conceptual and axiological framework for a generalized anti-Enlightenment. That is why, in an ideological climate,
nonlinguistic structuralisms developed in tandem with the counterculture. Sometimes, structuralist stars are superb writers,
like Lévi-Strauss or Foucault. Sometimes, they are professorial
scribblers like Derrida. No matter: the essence of what is
'literary' and 'modernist' in the structuralist orbit is not a matter
of art but of world-view. It is rare for a work of structuralist
ancestry to adopt as openly 'experimental' a form as Derrida
did in *Glas* (1974).

Let's open *Glas* at random. Each page unfolds at least two
texts: down the left-hand column runs a whimsical commentary
on the concepts of family and absolute knowledge in the young
Hegel; the right-hand one contains a spotty, leaping reading of
Jean Genet. The whole text bristles with 'witty' puns whose
quality the reader may assess by knowing that on page 7 Hegel
is assimilated to an eagle because the French pronunciation
(egl'/aigle) uncannily captures something of the magisterial
coldness of the philosopher, 'an eagle caught in the ice'. This
goes on for almost three hundred pages.

Mercifully, however, the French *maîtres à penser* since the
sixties (including Derrida himself, up to the early seventies)
usually promote their curious 'literarization' of thought and
theory in far more conventional, linear prose. Both Lévi-
Strauss and Lacan were conversant with surrealism and, through
surrealism, with the culture of High Modernism, in their formative years [25]—Lacan alone was an athlete of the compulsive
pun.

Why on earth—it may be asked—did so 'literary' a

---

[25] On Lacan's momentous relationship with surrealism, see Sherry Turkle,
Psychoanalytic Politics: Freud's French Revolution, London 1979, and David
Macey's article in *Radical Philosophy*, 35, autumn 1983, pp. 1–9; on Lévi-
Strauss and surrealism, see the odd review of *Le Regard Éloigné* by Rodney
Needham (TLS, 13 April 1984). In a recent interview with Didier Eribon for *Le
Nouvel Observateur*, Lévi-Strauss 'accepted' (sic) Needham's characterization
of him a a surrealist. He and Breton became friends when they both worked for
Voice of America in New York during the war.

212

theoretical fashion put on a 'scientific' (semiotic) mask? We must consider at least two factors. First the sacralization of Method and the lavish use of jargon seem to have become staple defence mechanisms of the soft-brained humanities, increasingly corroded by inner doubts about their cognitive validity in our science-shaped world. Flaunt a method, proclaim a new theoretical paradigm, popularize some jargon and you may very well rise out of the ruck and become notable. Especially if, as in Paris, philosophers and social scientists were often expected to utter the High Talk of literary 'prophets' instead of plodding through the prosaic researches of mere experts, stolid craftsmen of specialized lores.

Is it all, then, at bottom, just a method or (less charitably) a jargon? Let us call it, rather, a mode of discourse, an intellectual tic essentially based on the systematic neglect of a (medieval) precept: *sit modus in analogia*—moderation in the use of analogy'. Structuralism, like deconstruction, is above all ana-logism with a vengeance. One might recall Loulou, the won-drous parrot in Flaubert's *'Un coeur simple'*. It had usurped the place of the Holy Ghost in the devotions of pious Félicité. Why? Since the church's symbol of the Holy Ghost was a dove, Loulou would do better: for, like the dove, it could fly—but then, it could also speak.

Over and again, structuralist rapprochements of the unexpec-ted, and structuralist pinpointing of 'symmetrical oppositions'— not to mention the deconstructionist mill of puns—beget whole sequences of free-wheeling comparisons of this kind, giving a similar impression of grotesque far-fetchedness. True, in trail-blazing minds such as Lévi-Strauss's this is often the price to pay for genuine illumination. But even here, the binarist eliciting of surface polarities yields more discovery than explanation; and far-fetchedness seems endemic to the 'method' itself. As Raymond Aron politely wondered: 'What guarantees of scientificity does structural analysis possess? Does it not risk always succeeding once the analyst has the genius of Lévi-Strauss?.'[26] In other words: the demon of analogy is no friend of falsifiable statements. The theory is bound to be more ingenious than rigorous; and the ingenuity is not at all a function of the

[26] Aron in Pouillon and Maranda, *Echanges et Communications*, II, p. 952. My translation.

method—it depends too much on the exceptional cleverness of the writer who handles it ('the genius of Lévi-Strauss').

Lévi-Strauss often shows an awareness of this, the most amusing example being his addition of a new strand to the structural interpretation of the plot of *Sarrasine*. Having read *S/Z* in his country home at Lignerolles in Bourgogne in early 1970, Lévi-Strauss sent a good-humoured letter to Barthes offering him *'une petite fantaisie'*: nothing less than the demonstration, by the demon of analogy, that, given the symmetries of male/female positions in Balzac's plot, the young Lanty siblings, Marianina and Filippo, are bound to be, *'par la force des choses'*, an incestuous couple.[27] Therefore Barthes's own overstress on castration is compounded with incest. The difference is that Lévi-Strauss does it in a spirit of quizzical self-mockery.

A Dismal Unscience: Deconstruction

> *Much was believ'd, but little understood,*
> *And to be dull was constru'd to be good.*
>
> Pope, *An Essay on Criticism*

As already intimated, such conceptual acrobatics, which still retained much heuristic power in structural anthropology, tend to become a stale and sterile norm (disguised as a feast of normlessness) in the writings of the deconstructionists. Deconstruction has proved to be the hegemonic form of post-structuralism and the ablest coloniser of discourse in the humanities outside its heartland in French philosophy. We should therefore take a look at its theoretical make-up by briefly considering some central aspects of the work of its founder, Jacques Derrida. All we have said about Derrida and his ideas up to now boils down to four points: (a) like most post-structuralists, he is a Nietzschean; (b) he seems to have inherited from, or to share with, Lacan the mystique of the primacy of the signifier over the signified; (c) he constructed a theory of the sign as radical difference by out-Saussureing

---

[27] The letter is reproduced in Levi-Strauss 1979, pp. 495–97.

Saussure; and finally (d) he somehow combined this radicalized sign-theory with the philosophy of Heidegger. Let us see how Derrida's thought feeds on this intersection of Lacan, Saussure and Heidegger, under the imposing shadow of Nietzsche.

Derrida conceives of philosophy as pre-eminently a critique, the object of which is *logocentrism*. What is wrong with the logos? According to Derrida, the snag is not so much in 'logos' as in 'centre'. Critical thinking, to his mind, demands 'the abandonment of all reference to a centre' (*Writing and Difference*, p. 286). A centre of meaning, of origin, of truth would imply form and identity—yet we ought to look, it will be remembered, not for form and identity but—having understood the crucial lesson of Nietzsche—for 'force' and 'difference'. Difference as deferment (différance) of meaning.

By definition, 'difference' cannot be given a local habitation and a name. If Derrida gives pride of place to the sign (thereby firmly attaching his own brand of post-structuralism to the semiotic outlook of classical French structuralist theory), it is precisely because *signs, by their very nature, invite us to distinguish between thought and things*: for a sign is what represents, what takes the place of something else—and to this extent, signs always point to a 'beyond' from the viewpoint of immediate reality, of being with a face. Signs imply an intellectual movement beyond immediate perception—and in any case, as he makes clear in the tenth essay of *Writing and Difference*, Derrida does not 'believe that anything like perception exists'. Therefore signs are symbols of difference at work. Grammatology—Derrida's first label for his own theory—is the theory of *traces*, of the invisible marks of ever-deferred, different meaning. As the positive side of deconstruction, grammatology is a theoretical weapon directed against all logocentrisms.

Logocentric theories, in Derrida's view, are always built on a pattern of *presence*. Logocentrism is the claim of truth as presence. One of his first major books, *Of Grammatology* (1967), criticizes models of presence as based on the mythical superiority attributed to voice (*phone*) over *writing*. Therefore, logocentrism is, to Derrida, 'phonocentrism'. Now 'voice' theories of meaning are wrong in that they impose on signs the ideal of a present, transparent, immediate meaning whereas the true life of the sign lies, as we saw, in meaning deferred and different (deferred because ever-different; self-differentiating because always deferred). From Plato to Rousseau (in his essay on the origin of languages) and Lévi-Strauss, western thought decreed writing to be inferior and dangerous: unfaithful to spoken meanings or a prop to social domination (as in the Lévi-Straussian likening of education to conscription). With the alphabet, says Socrates at the end of the *Phaedrus*, 'you will give your disciples not truth but the semblance of truth.' *Of Grammatology* purports to undermine this imperialism of phonocentrism. Derrida is delighted that, in French pronunciation, the difference between différance and différence is so hard to tell: if it cannot be heard, but just written and read, so much the better! (*Positions*, p. 16)

During the heyday of structuralism, Marshall McLuhan attacked the 'Gutenberg galaxy' (1962). He belittled the modern culture of print, which desiccated human communication by putting the written word well above the warmth of oral-aural community. McLuhan's own master, also a Canadian, Harold Innis (*The Bias of Communication*, 1951), had already sung the virtues of oral media as against writing and painting: oral traditions rest on interpersonal rather than impersonal forms of communication, local rather than centralized forms of authority; and they foster dialogue instead of a monopoly of information.

Derrida, who simply overlooks the Canadian school of media theory, will have none of this. His is a 'Protestant' not an agro-Catholic evaluation of writing. It is as though Jewish traditions in him upheld the culture of the Book against oral paradises, which are lacking in 'prophetic' restlessness. Writing is to him a metaphor of meaning set free; the oral-aural means subjection to the horror of horrors—the world of stable signifieds. In his view, the reign of *phone* spells order, form, identity.

No wonder phonocentrism has a Platonic pedigree. 'We must kill our Greek father', states Derrida in *Writing and Difference*: one has to overthrow every residue of the Theory of Forms, the last echo of Plato, the resilient rule of logos in our discourse. In terms of interpreting the content of Plato's doctrines, this insistence on a philosophy of forms is, of course, not only correct but traditional. Yet by sticking to it Derrida misses one of the best comments made in modern Plato scholarship (and published in the same year as *Writing and Difference*). I refer to Eric Havelock's *Preface to Plato* (1967), a fresh look at the philosopher's notorious attack on poetry in the *Republic*. Have-lock shows that Plato's rejection of poetry stemmed from his preference for an education, and therefore a society, based on literacy and knowledge as opposed to myth and oral tradition.

Thus Plato's historical position gives the lie to the phono-centric reading of Platonism, notwithstanding the unkind Socratic comments on writing. With supreme irony, Plato used the most oral of genres—the dialogue—to destroy the authority of oral culture by criticizing its kernel of wisdom: myth, as conveyed by national (Homeric) poetry. By demoting poetry from its educational role in Greek culture, Plato actually delivered a decisive blow against the roots of phonocentrism; for myth, and not logos, was the natural home of the *phone*.

Therefore Derrida's grand 'epochal' outlook, a direct de-scendant from Heidegger's equally portentous 'destruction of metaphysics' since Plato, sounds more impressive than it is. The idea that western thought has consistently held an oral model of language and communication, privileging speech over writing, hardly bears analysis. Indeed, one could very well argue the opposite view. 'From the medieval development of Aristotle's logic', writes John Searle, one of Derrida's best critics, 'through Leibniz's *Characteristica Universalis* through Frege and Russell and up to the present development of symbolic logic, it could be argued that exactly the reverse is the case; that by emphasizing logic and rationality, philosophers have tended to emphasize written language as the more perspicuous vehicle of logical relations. Indeed, as far as the present era in philosophy is concerned, it wasn't until the 1950s that serious claims were made on behalf of the ordinary spoken vernacular languages, against the written ideal symbolic languages of mathematical logic.'[28]

Nor could it be shown that the speech/writing distinction, in factual or valuational terms, plays any important role in main-stream philosophy, from Aristotle and Aquinas to Descartes, Hume or Kant. That is perhaps why Derrida often retreats to a sly redefinition of concepts, taking 'writing' to mean not just written language but an 'arch-writing',[29] an Ur-writing

---

[28] Searle, 'The word turned upside down' (a review of Jonathan Culler's *On Deconstruction*), *New York Review of Books*, 27 October 1983, p. 75.

[29] J. Derrida, *Of Grammatology*, Baltimore 1976, pp. 56–57.

conceived of as the essential differential nature of all signs and language, prior to any external manifestation. Naturally, once writing is redefined in this fashion, as an all-pervasive semiotic essence, then it becomes possible for him to state that 'there never has been anything but writing'[30]—but, as is to be expected, the concept loses in grasp what it acquires in breadth.

Derrida's phonocentric charge against western thought is just a piece of rhetorical macro-*Kulturkritik*, hardly defensible if one cares for an accurate portrait of cultural evolution in general or the history of philosophy in particular. *The trouble with phonocentrism is that it is phoney history.* Ultimately what makes deconstruction tick is not the formidable ghost of Plato but the beckoning of a far more recent figure: Dr Lacan, the paladin of the free signifier. 'Phonocentrism' really amounts to an unfelicitous (because too idiosyncratic) 'epochal' metaphor for logocentrism; but logocentrism in turn is only condemned because the rule of the logos stifles the wondrous, uncanny creativity of language, the gorgeous play of unattached signifiers. Like Lacan, Derrida sets out to extol the signifier as a purely referentless sign, divested of reference even to its own signified.

However, despite his debt to the Lacanian hypostasis of the signifier, Derrida has criticized Lacan for his 'phallogocentrism'—his Freudian obsession with an Oedipal, and therefore phallic, view of libido, law and language. In Lacan's egregious—and untranslatable—pun: *'le nom du père/le non du père'*; the father's name is paternal prohibition; Oedipus is the core of the symbolic as a law prior and superior to every subject and its desire—something that enjoyed for Lacan a kind of preternatural verity. To Derrida, this reeks of identity-theory, all the more regrettable in a thinker so keen on the free-floating of signifiers. In his little book *Positions* (1972) Derrida chides Lacan for his alleged attachment to a model of presence. Why his own battle-cry of 'kill our Greek father' should sound less Oedipal than Lacan's desexualised phallic symbolic, he does not stoop to explain.

Derrida always makes a point of sternly accusing the thinkers on whom he is most dependent—Saussure, Lacan, Husserl, Heidegger—of one form of phonocentrism or another. Like

[30] Ibid., p. 159.

218

Figaro, Derrida serves more than one master and mocks them all. Such rituals of appropriation/repudiation have earned him great glory in literature departments. Normally illiterate in philosophy, the latter are increasingly colonized by theoretical literary criticism in a frantic search for a *weltanschauliche* pedigree. Trained philosophers such as Searle usually protest when they read literary critics like Culler who, in their enthusing over Derrida, overlook the importance to him of Husserl or Heidegger. Few realize—as did Luc Ferry and Alain Renaut[31] —that Derrida's originality is at bottom merely rhetorical, an enterprise of relentless symbolization of Heidegger's theme of the 'ontological difference'. The protest is clearly well-founded but—sociologically speaking—a bit naïve. For deconstruction is acclaimed in philosophically unskilled quarters precisely because it got rid of argumentative rigour while providing the pathos of an apocalyptic *Weltanschauung*. The first thing liberated by the Liberation of the Signifier movement is the right to wild philosophizing—an outcome blessed frivolously by Derrida's own *destruction* of the difference between logos and mythos, best expressed in his famous plea for 'white mythologies'.[32]

Killing our Greek father means to Derrida—as it did to Heidegger—primarily a confrontation with the text of Plato. Heidegger's key work in this connection came in 1947, with *Platons Lehre von der Wahrheit* (Plato's Theory of Truth). Derrida's is the first, long essay in *Dissemination* (first published in *Tel Quel*), *'La pharmacie de Platon'*. It quickly became a paradigm of deconstructive reading. Derrida returns to the *Phaedrus* and its Socratic condemnation of writing. In Plato's dialogue, writing is said to be a *pharmakon*—meaning both 'remedy' (for instance, a medicine for failures of memory) and 'poison'. Socrates thinks that writing, a gift from Kadmos to mankind and intended as a remedy, is in fact a dangerous poison. The ambiguity is ironically reflected in Socrates's own life, since he dies by taking a poison (*pharmakon*) which is the sole remedy for his fate as a sentenced 'sorcerer' (*pharmakeus*). Then Derrida brings in another word: *pharmakos*, the 'scape-

[31] L. Ferry and A. Renaut, *La Pensée 68—essai sur l'anti-humanisme contemporain*, Paris 1985, pp. 185, 191.
[32] In *Marges de la Philosophie*, Paris 1972.

goat'. The expulsion of scapegoats purges the polis, just as the exclusion of 'poisonous' writing in Socrates's speech in the *Phaedrus* aimed at purifying thought by keeping it close to the immediacy of speech. Nevertheless, in order to be a proper *pharmakos*, one has to be cast out *from within* the polis. Thus in a sense the *pharmakos* blurs the boundaries between inside and outside. Similarly, writing, declared 'secondary' and 'treacherous' to speech, is already 'within' spoken language insofar as the latter is made up of signs. Why? Because sign is difference, and difference is division—like the severance of writing from speech.

Our summary is grossly schematic but it does not do violence to the thrust of Derrida's argument. The latter is, of course, infinitely more fanciful than cogent. Moreover, a Plato expert might (if Plato experts were interested in Derrida's pretentious readings) object that these analogies do little to respect the logic of Plato's text. But Derrida has a prompt reply. He contends that the 'chain of significations' around *pharmakon* has nothing whatsoever to do with 'the intentions of the author known by the name of Plato'; connections are established 'by the play of the language' alone.[33] In plain English, this means that deconstruction, for all its stress on the text, cares nothing for the textual context. Instead texts become mere pretexts for daring speculations based on rickety etymologies—a spurious habit introduced into continental philosophy by Heidegger (but then, even the term 'deconstruction' is itself a refraction of the Heideggerian 'destruction' of metaphysics). But the whole technique becomes intelligible (if not justifiable) when one becomes familiar with Derrida's views on what interpretation amounts to. This in turn is perhaps best understood by casting a glance at the evolution of his work.

Schematically, 'grammatology' is Derrida Phase I, or Derrida 1967 (the year of *Of Grammatology* and *Writing and Difference*). 'Deconstruction' is Derrida II, or vintage 1972 (the year of *Dissemination* and *Marges de la Philosophie*). Deconstruction is at once the 'method' of grammatology as the theory of difference and a further stage in Derridean thought—a stage which finally did away with even the relatively austere sign-problematic of the grammatological period. Now everything,

---

[33] Derrida, *Margins of Philosophy*, Chicago 1982, p. 96.

including semiotics (however radicalized), joins in the cosmic 'play' of a Nietzschean 'innocence of becoming' in 'a world of signs which has no truth, no origin, no nostalgic guilt, and is proffered for active interpretation.' This statement, fraught as it is with Nietzschean formulae (the world-play; the joyous acceptance of Dionysian becoming; active interpretation instead of truth), comes at the close of the essay by Derrida most quoted in humanities departments—"Structure, sign and play in the discourse of the human sciences".[34] It was triumphantly received as a brief for *activist misinterpretation* as the sacred duty of pretentious, pseudo-epistemological literary criticism.

Indeed, as a worship of writing, deconstruction could only turn out to be a theory of *text*. 'There is no outside-the-text' (*il n'y a pas d'hors-texte*): This is, in Derrida's own words, the 'axial proposition' in *Of Grammatology*. A diktat whose chief casualty is, to the dismay of many of his critics, history. The third interview in *Positions*, enlarging on some hints in *Marges*, attacks the 'metaphysical concept of history', the idea of history as a linear unfolding of meaning. As Culler notes, Derrida uses history against philosophy whenever philosophy is essentialist (in his view, quite often); but he also uses *philosophy against history*. Replace 'also' by 'mainly' and you have a still truer picture. Culler himself stresses that the deconstructionist rejection of the metaphysics of history does not stop at the removal of linear and teleological assumptions: it takes on the entire 'historical approach', for the latter relies on 'historical narratives' whose authority to certify bygone meanings is in itself far from established: 'A historical approach appeals to historical narratives—stories of changes in thinking and of the thoughts or beliefs appropriate to distinguishable historical periods—in order to control the meaning of rich and complex works by ruling out possible meanings as historically inappropriate. These historical narratives are produced by interpreting the supposedly less complex and ambiguous texts of a period, and their authority to authorize or control the meaning of the most complex texts is certainly questionable.'[35]

There are scores of epistemological difficulties involved in

[34] Derrida, *Writing and Difference*, chapter x.
[35] J. Culler, *On Deconstruction: Theory and Criticism after Structuralism*, Ithaca 1982, p. 129.

ascertaining the historical truth of meanings. Anachronism, for one, is a Protean demon, breeding several fallacies that often fatally mislead the interpreter of historical texts. In his essay, "Meaning and understanding in the history of ideas" (1969), Quentin Skinner, now a well-known Cambridge luminary, lucidly identified the common 'mythologies' to which practitioners of intellectual history succumb. Skinner's well-honed analysis of conceptual errors underlying historiographic misinterpretation rightly came to enjoy the status of a classic in this important department of the theory of social science. The whole point of Skinner's critical examination is to identify the pitfalls of historical knowledge. But the moral of the exercise is clear: the remedy for bad history is more, and better, history— a far cry from wholesale distrust, let along ditching, of the 'historical approach', on the reckless a priori assumption that all historical narratives are equally unwarranted because they can be questioned. This piece of Derrideanism, like so many others, amounts to little more than a sweeping *rhetoric* of cavalier scepticism. The 'historical approach' cannot be dispatched in one page of unargued assertion in a cursory interview with the Master of Deconstruction, let alone by epigonic pot-shots from his literary critical disciples. So long as history refuses to be swallowed by 'textuality', the odds are against our dispensing with the historical approach. And it must be said that the deconstructionist's dismissive rejection of the historical approach is far less sophisticated than the anti-historicism of classical French structuralism.

The roots of Derrida's mystique of the text lie in his *pan-semioticism*—in which reality is engulfed by the sign. From the assumption, which he has never bothered to prove, that every 'embodied' meaning leads directly to what *Of Grammatology* spurns as the 'transcendental signified', Derrida infers, in that same seminal book, that 'from the moment there is meaning there are nothing but signs'. Texts, of course, are clusters of signs. It follows that 'there is nothing outside the text'—the saying that so infuriated Foucault. But then, there is no text either—there is just 'textuality'. As he explains in 'Living On: Border Lines', his lengthy contribution to *Deconstruction and Criticism* (1979), the text, in deconstruction, is 'no longer a finished corpus of writing, some content enclosed in a book or its margins, but a differential network, a fabric of traces referring endlessly to something other than itself, to other differential traces.' So, after all, there is at least one *hors-texte*: the pan-text of textuality, that is, of the signifier let loose.

Such an apotheosis of the text could hardly fail to enthral many of those in charge of textology, namely, those professional interpreters who teach (or used to teach) literature, past or present (especially present: for the others use the poor 'historical approach' as a crutch to go about their business). All the more so since, at first sight, deconstruction seems to relish interpretation. For deconstruction—let it never be forgotten—is no destruction. What the Lord of signs taketh away, he promptly giveth back. Derrida always makes plain that he 'dismantles the metaphysical and rhetorical strucures' of a text *not* to reject them (since they are inherent in language itself) but just *'to reconstitute them in another way'*. One cannot speak outside the logos of language; all that can be done is to 'erase', not to annul, the presence of signifieds and the signs of presence. However, if deconstruction, a necessarily immanent method, 'falls prey to its own work' by continuously inverting, subverting signifieds, then it only destabilizes logocentric readings through a cascade of reinterpretations *'en abîme'*. No meaning escapes the hidden spell of its contrary, so that the end result of text-deciphering can but be be *aporetic* (from the Greek *aporia*, puzzle)—a raising of problems without offering any stable solutions. Deconstruction has turned infinite regression from a philosophical vice into an interpretive virtue; in practice, it operates as the euphoria of aporia. It is this abyss-effect, the ultimate bottomlessness of its readings, that appears to turn deconstruction into a paroxysm of over-interpretation. Interpretation forever on the move is not a bad description of the art of deconstruction (in fact, Derrida's translator, Gayatri Spivak, insists on this ever-dynamic character in her introduction to *Of Grammatology*).

Nevertheless, deconstruction has proven to be the undoing of hermeneutics. It is not hard to see why. Mesmerized by the play of difference, interpretation must bask in the ultimate 'undecidability' of texts, which is not at all a nice consequence of polysemy, of the peaceful accumulation of meaning, but is on the contrary a playful *dissemination*, a *dispersion* of unstable sense (bow to the ghost of Bataille). No art of interpretation could bear such high pressure for *indeterminate* meaning.

Derrida, a philosopher by training, more familiar with Husserl and Heidegger than with Saussure, insists on placing his revolutionary anti-hermeneutics within the framework of ontology—the theory of being. From the outset, his aim has been to revise Saussure with the help of Heidegger's critique of metaphysics, from Plato to Nietzsche. Derrida, it is true, makes a point of breaking with Heidegger's own nostalgia of Being (so patent in this capital letter): instead, he extols the aggressive Dionysian pathos of Nietzsche, the hero of post-structuralism. He definitely thinks of deconstruction as a powerful counter-cultural weapon, but does not strike the typical Heideggerian note, at once wistful and messianic, that once led the Master to state solemnly that 'we moderns arrived too late for the gods and too soon for Being.' Nevertheless, for all their discrepancies in temperament, Derrida owes Heidegger the very structure of his *Fragestellung*.

Nowadays the chief disciples of Heidegger, like Hans-Georg Gadamer (*Truth and Method*, 1960), are primarily theorists in *hermeneutics*—the stubborn response of German culturalism to the scientistic tradition of critical epistemology that stretches from Hume and Kant to Popper and Quine. Derrida is no exception: his praise of sign as difference is as concerned with meaning (where Heidegger was with being) as Gadamer is with the reconstruction of the concept of tradition. But Derrida condemned post-structuralism to feed on the problématique of French structuralism by grafting the Heideggerian element onto theoretical semiotics, on the reflection on the sign. Derrida's grammatology employs Saussurean concepts such as 'difference' and 'signifier' to convey Heideggerian tenets. Thus Saussure's 'difference', which in the *Course in General Linguistics* humbly denotes the diacritical nature of linguistics signs, was converted into a portent of ever-delayed meaning based on a pun on *différence* (*différance*, a mix of differing and deferring): a modest scientific conceptual tool became burdened with an unexpected metaphysical load, quite alien to the original empirical analysis of semiotic phenomena.

These metaphysical conceits turn deconstruction into a kind of blank mysticism. Difference theory beckons to a nowhere, a desert of being that is deemed to supersede all reality. To Mikel Dufrenne, it all comes down to an ontology of the void that recalls Plotinus: 'Because there is nothing in the One, all things derive from it; (for) in order for being to be, the One cannot be being, but the breeder of being' (Enneads, v,2,1). Dufrenne also reminds us that in the history of ancient thought this fascination with nothingness has been interpreted as a clash between Greek intellectualism and eastern theology. Oriental religions had proposed the idea of a supreme Being beyond the grasp of language. But Greek thinkers were so wont to identify the real and the conceivable with *what can be said* that they dared not state there is an unintelligible reality; therefore, they made it into a non-being, thus originating the *ontology of absence* whose latest versions are Heidegger's Being (always placed beyond all positive existence) and its semiotic child, Derridean difference or 'trace', forever avoiding presence and identity.[36]

The usefulness of such comparisons is that they show that, for all the novelty of his terminology, the thought-structure of Derrida is a philosophical antique with a more theological than epistemological origin—something that may remain concealed to those who broach deconstruction theory as though it were just a conceptually sharpened semiotics.

Theological sources were indeed conspicuous in the formative, grammatological period of Derrida's thought. A good deal of *Writing and Difference* consists of a dialogue with Jewish thought of unabashedly theological and messianic, as well as openly anti-philosophical, intent. Thus one chapter in that 1967 *recueil* is devoted to praising the work of the Sephardic poet Edmond Jabès (b. 1912), whose messianic verses describe Judaism as pre-eminently a passion for writing. For the homeless Jew, says Jabès, the Book is a fatherland. Home is a holy Writ, and its text is sacred precisely because it replaces home by hope. Here at last we find a cultural habitation for Derrida's apotheosis of text and writing.

Nor was Jabès the only seminal Jewish writer for the young Derrida. His indictment of the 'ocular' metaphysics of presence, which he identified with the philosophical tradition, was not just a reprise of Heidegger's sweeping rejection of metaphysics from Plato to Hegel (and, in his view, even Nietzsche): it owed much to the work of the Lithuanian-born Jewish thinker

---

[36] M. Dufrenne, *Le Poétique*, Paris 1973, pp. 23–4. The historian of ancient philosophy quoted by Dufrenne is Emile Bréhier.

Emmanuel Levinas (b.1905), a former pupil of Husserl and Heidegger on whose work Derrida comments lengthily in an essay in *Writing and Difference* entitled "Violence and Metaphysics".[37] Levinas criticized Husserl in the thirties for enslaving phenomenoloy in a 'visual' model of intuition as opposed to the auditory pattern of man's relationship with the biblical God (the concept of *'intuitus'*, like 'theory', echoes its visual etymons). This critique of 'theoreticism' and of the 'optical' cognitive model harks back to Nietzsche and to the young Heidegger, who used St Paul, St Augustine and Luther in order to buttress a more 'existential' notion of knowledge.[38] But after the war Levinas turned against Heidegger and the whole philosophical tradition for yielding the Other to the sway of the Same. According to Levinas, it was not enough to condemn, like Heidegger, the ontological oblivion of technological civilization: one should also stop looking for being as such, for every ontology brings about a tyranny of sameness; all theory of being is violent, both because it is 'theory' and because it deals with 'being', with the One as a mask of the Same. The only way to save a true respect for the other(s) is to insist on ethics, the realm of duty towards others, instead of pursuing ontology—a point missed by Heidegger because, with his 'pagan' peasant roots, he remained ensnared in the cautious, possessive love for sameness characteristic of agrarian culture, and therefore had no grasp of the value of infinite alterity so strong in Jewish piety and in the Jew's long experience of exile and outsiderness.

Now one may quibble over Levinas's portrayal of Heidegger's 'fundamental ontology'. I have no fondness for it, but even so I very much doubt that a book like *Identität und Differenz* (1957) can be construed in terms of a reduction of otherness to a stubborn sameness; rather, its clear leitmotiv is the 'non-identity of the same'. Heidegger was too sly a fox to be caught in Levinas's rigid characterization. Be that as it may, this is not where Derrida departs from Levinas. Typically, he qualifies Levinas's ethical eschatology by pointing out that for all its

---

[37] For good short accounts of the links between Derrida, Levinas and Jabès, see A. Megill, *Prophets of Extremity: Nietzsche, Heidegger, Foucault, Derrida*, Berkeley 1985, pp. 305–11 and 316–20.

[38] For this theme in the young Heidegger, see O. Pöggeler, *Der Denkweg Martin Heideggers*, 1963, chapter II, 2.

priceless worth the Hebraic sense of respect for otherness is
bound to speak 'Greek', that is, the language of logos. The
moment it expresses itself in words, the most Jewish of cultural
traits—the sacredness of ethics—becomes unavoidably per-
meated by the pagan logic of thought. For this reason Derrida
caps his essay on the anti-Greek Levinas with a nod to Matthew
Arnold's celebrated recipe for a nice balance between Hebra-
ism and Hellenism, conscience and spontaneity. Derrida's
qualification of Levinas clearly reminds one of his criticism of
Foucault: that the discourse on madness, however sympathetic
to its object, must of necessity side with reason. Yet the tenor of
Derridean philosophy shares with Heidegger's a dangerous
proclivity towards the bombastic translation of problems of
being and knowledge into strident moral dilemmas. Like the
cosmic drama of Being repressed by being in Heidegger,
Derrida's protest against phonocentrism sounds more like lay
sermonizing than genuine analytical argument. These manichaean dichotomies—Being versus being, 'writing' versus
phoné—betray a religious pattern of thought that leaves
Derrida—for all his reticence regarding eschatology—infinitely
closer to the prophet Levinas than to the cool-headed practitioners of philosophy as analysis.

Once removed from this original 'theological' and mystical
framework, the Derridean ontology of absence makes for an
irrationalist philosophy, as was the case with Heidegger. Hence
its blatant non-sequiturs. Let me mention one which Vincent
Descombes identified in Derrida's critique of Husserl, *Speech
and Phenomena* (1967). In his first *Logical Investigation* (1900)
Husserl claims that the presence of a signified object is necessary for any given signifying *intentio* to be fulfilled. Nonsense,
says Derrida: nobody needs actually to see a spectacle in order
to understand an account of it; the life of meaning is quite used
to meaningfulness without presence. Thus the sentence, contrary to Husserl's claim, does not put its reader into any relation
with presence, either of the subject or of the object of what is
said. So far so good. But Derrida insists on inferring from this
that the sentence, and in fact every signifying process, necessarily relates us to an *absence* (of subjects, objects). As
Descombes wryly comments: it is as though, having received an
anonymous letter, I concluded that it was written by a non-
existent person; or as if the fact that a sentence might not be

true meant automatically that it is necessarily false.[39] Logical jumps are dictated by the obsessional nature of *dramatic* philosophy; by a kind of philosophy, that is, where the glamour of a manichaean grand-guignol (Presence the baddie versus Absence the goodie) is substituted for analytical rigour.

It is this manichaean cast of mind, with its attendant anathema on a whole cultural tradition, that keeps Derrida, despite all disclaimers, in the murky waters of Heidegger's stream. In her *Dialectic of Nihilism*, Gillian Rose has shrewdly noticed that Derrida's theory of difference rehearses Hegel's argument about the insufficiency of representation only to turn it against Hegel's idea of philosophy: for whereas Hegel conceived of philosophy as a knowledge beyond representation, Derrida *equates* philosophy with representation.[40] Yet what lies at the bottom of this wilful, nearly perverse demotion of philosophical reason but the powerful imprint of Heidegger's 'destruction' of Western logos from Plato to Hegel? No wonder Heidegger's thought is said to be, in Derrida's *Positions*, 'incontournable'—impossible to bypass.

However, one deep difference remains. Heidegger employed his negative ontology in an avowed soteriological enterprise; he wanted to rescue humanity by summoning it to a respectful expectation of the epiphany of Being. Derrida, who has no discernible positive programme, harnesses the ontology of absence to a quite different task. His leitmotiv is not the appeal to an uncanny salvation but the relentless undermining of the western code of values. Hence the paradoxically parasitical status of deconstruction: it feeds on the text of tradition, from Plato and Rousseau to Freud, Husserl and Saussure. Yet it has no theory other than the systematic reversal of western thought—'a complete overturning of cultural domination'.[41] Deconstruction is *Kulturkritik* in the form of corrosive commentary; it is the art of lethal paraphrase.

This 'civilizational' range is just what its fast-growing American branch—almost entirely confined to rampantly theoretical literary criticism—tends to downplay. In the noisy, boisterous attacks of transatlantic deconstruction against

---

[39] V. Descombes, Grammaires d'Objets en Tous Genres, Paris 1983, pp. 71–79.

[40] G. Rose, *Dialectic of Nihilism: Post-Structuralism*, Oxford 1984, p. 160.

[41] Derrida, *Positions*, Chicago 1981.

previous critical persuasions, *Kulturkrisis* often comes as an upbeat. Textual theory sounds much more technical, as when the late Paul de Man insisted that texts never say exactly what they mean because they are caught in a ceaseless shuttle between 'blindness and insight': in a text, major statements are constantly undermined by rhetorical drives beyond their control; and as with text, so with criticism: critics err most precisely where they display their fullest conceptual mastery.[42] This is every bit as dogmatic and aprioristic as the diktats of Derrida himself; yet it is also, in a quaint way, much more down-to-earth, closer (at least in intention) to the text than to cosmic dramas of cultural fate. Thus, instead of the Derrida-versus-Plato match, we get textual issues, however slanted by the deconstructionist bias. Again, Jonathan Culler argues that 'to deconstruct a discourse is to show how it undermines the philosophy it asserts, or the hierarchical oppositions on which it relies, by identifying in the text the rhetorical operations that produce the supposed ground of argument, the key concept or premiss.'[43] The confident 'methodological' tone betrays none of the sophisticated fudging of Derrida's High Equivocation—and none of its epochal ontological stakes. American deconstruction theory has become merely a technique for unreading texts. In the original Deconstructor, by contrast, *Kulturkrisis* always gets the upper hand. The hermeneutic manoeuvres are merely a pretext for uprooting history with a capital H. As in Foucault or Deleuze, the ultimate focus is always on a demonstrative countercultural move.

We will say more about the theme of *Kulturkrisis* in our concluding pages. For the moment, we can sum up the situation of mainstream deconstruction by pointing out that while in literary criticism, where it has a growing constituency, deconstruction now operates basically as a *technique* for showing—for the umpteenth time—that all literature is self-subversive, in Derrida's hands, it has become increasingly quaint in style and apocalyptic in content. In most later essays by Derrida, oracular assertion by dint of jocular or half-jocular pun-juggling has come to replace argument almost completely.

[42] Cf. P.de Man, *Blindness and Insight: Essays in the Rhetoric of Contemporary Criticism*, London 1983, especially ch. VII (originally published in 1971, it is de Man's major statement on Derrida).

[43] Culler, *On Deconstruction*, p. 86.

But this does not mean that the spread of deconstruction is confined to the literary province. Despite the growing distance between Derrida's own stylistic self-indulgence and that modicum of argumentative rigour normally expected from philosophical discourse—even when the latter comes from beyond the pale of the analytic tradition—there have been some gallant attempts to stress the relevance of deconstruction to some central issues in modern philosophy. Perhaps the best was that recently made by Christopher Norris. In chapter 7 of *The Deconstructive Turn* (1983), he claims that Derrida's work brought French theory 'in the wake of Saussure' surprisingly close to Anglo-American linguistic philosophy.

In Norris's view, what links Saussurean theory to linguistic philosophy is the principle, classically formulated by Frege, that *meaning determines reference*. Frege, launching a line of thought subsequently adopted by Russell and Wittgenstein, tried to show that our very identification of referents depends on a whole set of linguistic and logical criteria. Word and concept, logic and language, shape our ability to grasp referents. Naming—our chief means of pointing to reality 'out there'—encapsulates semantic definitions resting on rules of predication. To that extent, 'reference' depends on 'meaning'.

Now, according to Norris, meaning precedes reference in Saussure, too. Like Frege, Saussure and the structuralists 'acknowledge this primacy of the signifying process'. Wittgenstein believed that the limits of one's language are also the limits of one's world. Norris remarks how well this squares with 'the structuralist emphasis on language as the omnipresent mediating element in all existing orders of knowledge and representation.'[44]

Norris knows that whereas analytic philosophy from Frege to the early Wittgenstein strove to build a logical semantics that could purge natural languages of their ambiguities, and thereby achieve a precise universe of reference based on solid conceptual grounds, Saussure on the other hand never envisaged anything of the kind. Yet *The Deconstructive Turn* also states that 'certainly it follows from the structuralist argument that thought is necessarily constrained by certain regularities of

---

[44] C. Norris, *The Deconstructive Turn: Essays in the Rhetoric of Philosophy*, London 1983, pp. 144–45.

language which semiological theory seeks to explain.'[45] It is none too easy to understand Norris's argument at this crucial point. He seems eager to equate, in this respect, the structuralist enterprise with the semantic epistemology of Fregean descent; still, being too sophisticated to ignore that Saussure's own aims were by no means epistemological, he seems a bit uneasy about the rapprochement he has achieved; hence he hedges each sentence by pointing, with careful qualifications, to a supposed link between Frege and Saussure, always acknowledging *differences* between Saussure and Fregean theory. Nevertheless, the reader is given the persistent impression that: (a) although Fregeans, unlike Saussureans, are interested in adding an epistemological filter to the postulate that meaning determines reference, (b) both groups do share the latter claim, that is, both hold that reference is a function of meaning.

Now (a) is hardly disputable: there is no doubt that Saussure never contemplated replacing the ambiguous semantics of natural languages with a logical idiom devised to ensure univocal reference. And once we grant (b), it becomes hard not to agree with Norris's elegant thesis that, thanks to the neo-Saussureanism of Derrida, the convergence between the semiotics stemming from the *Course in General Linguistics* and post-Fregean analytic philosophy becomes all the more striking. For, just as Saussure tended to concur with Frege in holding that meaning determines reference, so Derrida converges with Quine and Rorty in raising doubts about the possibility (Quine) or even the need (Rorty) of building watertight logical languages which ensure clear-cut reference. If Quine is an anti-Fregean, who gets rid of the fetish of an a priori logical necessity in the grounding of knowledge, Derrida, the heir to Nietszche, is the thinker who has delivered the soul of structuralism from any such temptation.

However, I am not sure we can accept (b). After all, Norris's claim presupposes that Saussure was talking about the same subject as Frege: the relation between logic, as expressed in language, and reality—the meaning/reference problematic. But it can certainly be argued that Saussure was *not* dealing with this. He did not distinguish between signified (the 'concept' of the signifier) and reference in order to talk about, let

[45] Ibid.

alone grapple with, the latter. Rather, he wanted to circum-
scribe the area of linguistic theory regardless of the thorny problems of general epistemology. We misrepresent his purpose whenever we make Saussure sound like Sapir or Whorf, the linguist-
anthropologists who held that differently structured natural
languages articulate a mapping of the world *radically distinct*
from ours. Significantly, Norris hints at a 'parallel' between the
alleged Frege/Saussure link and the Sapir-Whorf hypothesis.

Saussure sets out to conceptualize a proper way of describing
language, not the relation of language to reality. Consequently,
he can hardly provide a linguistic pedigree to Derrida's
philosophizing about that relation. As to the language-bound
character of thought, it may well 'follow from the structuralist
argument'—but it was never asserted by Saussure, and therefore
it cannot be used to prop up a dubious analogy between him
and Frege. The analogy would be spurious even if it obtained,
because for structuralism the language-bound nature of thought
refers to the peculiarities of natural languages (as in the Sapir-
Whorf thesis), while in the Fregean tradition whatever linguistic
element constrains thought is of an essentially *logical*, and
therefore *universal*, nature. Fregeans, like good logicians, are
universalists who think of language as a human attribute; Sapir-
Whorf's 'structuralists', by contrast, are by definition *relativists*
who see no language—just *languages*, each one of them being an
attribute of a particular culture, incommensurate with all the others.

Now the culturalist belief in radically different language-
bound world pictures or 'conceptual schemes' has not passed
philosophical muster (see Davidson, 1984, chapter 3). But was
it Saussure's idea? Culler would have us believe that Saussure
not only held to the arbitrariness of signifiers but that he also
thought that 'each language produces a different set of signifieds', that 'it has a distinctive and thus "arbitrary" way of
organizing the world into concepts or categories.'[46] But,
as Robert Scholes[47] has pointed out, this is rather hard to square
with the well-known fact that Saussure himself in the *Course*
stresses that the 'same signified' exists both for French *'boeuf'*

[46] J. Culler, *Saussure*, p. 23. For a critique on Whorfianism, see Mounin,
1975, chapter xi.

[47] R. Scholes, *Textual Power: Literary Theory and the Teaching of English*,
New Haven 1985, pp. 89–90.

and for German '*Ochs*'. If indeed the same concept works both sides of the Rhine, could it be by dint of a translinguistic reference to the same animal, which insists on grazing outside the world made of Whorf's (but not Saussure's) signifieds?

The truth of the matter seems to be that Saussure, despite acknowledging that thought without language is shapeless (*Course*, pp. 111–12), never went beyond the sensible recognition that, to a certain extent, natural languages vary in their 'charting' of reality. To take an oft-quoted example from the *Course*: English 'sheep' differs from French '*mouton*' on two accounts—(a) their signifiers are wide apart; and (b) they also have different 'values', since 'sheep', while translating '*mouton*', also contrasts, within English, with 'mutton' (you raise sheep but you eat mutton), whereas in French there is no such contrast. Therefore Saussure fully realized that each natural language tends to delimit areas of meaning in its own different way.

But does it really amount to asserting the arbitrariness of *signifieds* as well as of signifiers? Not if we care to remember the context of Saussure's discussion of 'values'. He addresses the contrast between French '*mouton*' and English 'sheep'/'mutton' in the course of his central theorization of the need for a synchronic grasp of language as a system, dominated by paradigmatic relations of inclusion/exclusion (thus 'eat' goes along with 'mutton' but not with 'sheep').[48] In other words, when he came to consider the phenomenon of the different areas of meaning staked out by each natural language, Saussure was dealing with meaning rather than with knowledge. His point was a semantic, not an epistemological one. On the 'knowledge' plane, of course, English 'sheep' does correspond, in Saussure's own terms, to French '*mouton*': they share the same translinguistic signified, however different their intralinguistic values. It follows that one should not saddle Saussure with a philosophical outlook, and in particular a culturalist overstatement, of which he is innocent: the suggestion that language not only 'charts' but moulds or creates reality. Is it not telling that while we know by heart Saussure's dicta on the normally arbitrary signifier, no general statement of his has yet been adduced that

[48] For Saussure's stress on the paradigmatic, see G. Sampson, *Schools of Linguistics: Competition and Evolution*, London 1980, pp. 48–49.

can be taken to assert a normal arbitrariness of signifieds?

To Norris, Derrida's philosophical merit lies in his Nietzschean surpassing of the 'foundational' dreams of the Fregean. Yet one can turn the tables on such a claim. For one might say that, far from rejecting the foundationalist outlook, Derrida offers a mirror-image of it. In fact, precisely this charge was levelled at Derrida by an elder statesman of American criticism, M. H. Abrams. In a remarkable article in *Partisan Review*, "How to do things with texts" (1979), Abrams points out that Derrida's urge to deconstruct meaning is based on a curious non sequitur. From the fact that language lacks an ultimate ground, Derrida concludes that the work of meaning can only be deceptive. Texts may be legible, but they are not truly intelligible, since meaning is 'undecidable'. Thus in the end Derrida shares the belief that for determinate meanings to obtain, language must have an absolute foundation. Derrida, says Abrams, is 'an absolutist without absolutes'. Unlike the later Wittgenstein, he cannot bring himself to trust language games that do not have a bedrock of ultimate meanings. In a curious negative way, a belief in foundational meaning seems to have survived, in his thought, the demise of the transcendental signified. As so often, radical scepticism, about meaning as about almost everything else, is at bottom just a disappointed absolutism.

A possible line of defence would be to argue that Derrida is *no* knock-down sceptic. Norris himself, in a previous book, *Deconstruction: Thought and Practice* (1982), has argued this way. There he warns that Derrida's own deconstructionism—unlike some of his disciples'—is not a licence to play havoc with texts by wantonly misreading them, but a 'long and strenuous process', 'a hard-won position sustained by arguments' that bear and deserve close scrutiny.[49]

Yet it would seem that Norris finds his own ascription of such a philosophical work ethic to the playful Nietszschean Derrida slightly out of tune with the gist of Derrida's work. For no sooner has he asserted his hero's argumentative efforts than he takes an entirely different tack. Siding with Richard Rorty's influential thesis about the gulf between two rival traditions in modern philosophy, analytic and continental, he now suggests

---

[49] C. Norris, *Deconstruction: Theory and Practice*, London 1982, pp. 127–29.

that Derrida is best understood as a vigorous member of the second league, that is of the disparate group of European thinkers who, eschewing the ideal of 'a rational dialogue of minds pursued . . . in the quest for communicable truth', thrive on style and paradox and evince a 'rooted scepticism about ultimate truth and method'.[50]

Much as I agree with Norris's characterization of Derrida, who more and more came to rely on blunt paradox and avant-garde 'style' (and whose earlier work, though admittedly more argumentative, had far less sustained reasoning than Norris suggests), I see no way of reconciling the Master of Paradox and *ad libitum* verbal play with his pious picture of the hard-working theorist. Obviously we must choose either the image of an ascetic reasoner or the blithe Dionysian. The real Derrida cannot be both at once. Surely the Rortyan portrait is a truer rendering of the intellectual personality of Jacques Derrida. But mark: if Derrida is really a 'rooted sceptic' with little time or taste for rational dialogue and the hardships of sustained argument, then Abrams is basically right. Instead of viewing him as a Nietszchean Quine, rationally trying to surpass the foundationalist stance in modern epistemology, we should indeed see him as a crypto-absolutist, 'an absolutist without absolutes'. Which is scarcely surprising, since few things suit an apocalyptic prophet better than an all-or-nothing philosophical outlook. Apocalyptic visions make short shrift of relative truths; and deconstruction is pre-eminently a scholastic way of spelling doom for enlightened culture under the pretext of making 'theory'.

To be sure, the Master of Deconstruction is too clever to *proclaim* an apocalyptic view—not even an apocalyptic pathos, as Heidegger did. Far from it: one of his favourite deconstructions is, quite predictably, the deconstruction of Apocalypse. It has an extra irony about it, as shown in the title of a recent essay, *"D'un ton apocalyptique adopté naguère en philosophie"* (1981), where we are invited to welcome 'an apocalypse without apocalpyse, an apocalypse without vision, without truth, without revelation'. But it is always the same trick: what is denied is at once affirmed, what is denounced survives in the very gesture of denunciation. We are not to get any apocalyptic vision, but

---

[50] Ibid.

neither are we to have anything short of an apocalyptic cast of mind. Deconstruction is an art of reluctant denial and perverse reassertion.

Well before the death of Foucault, deconstruction had already conquered a dominant position in post-structuralism. Its growing spate of texts, ever fulminating against 'Western logocentrism' in all forms, constitutes a glaring confirmation that the chief commitment of recent French new thought is an onslaught on the critical rationalist ethos of the Enlightenment tradition. Critical thinking is victimized by lofty proclamations of Kulturkrisis; *crisis theory declares war on the rigours of critique.* Such is the final consequence of the surrender of philosophy to the literary ideology forged by High Modernism. Every concern with objective knowledge is thrown overboard: no more of truth, reason, evidence or reference—they were just ploys of a repressive civilization . . . Yet nobody bothers to prove the point.

Deconstructionism may be used less as a licence for theoretical pyrotechnics than as a yardstick for contradictions in highly theoretical readings. Thus Yales' Barbara Johnson in *The Critical Difference*, has skilfully identified blindspots in the interpretive moves whereby Derrida outwitted Lacan's analysis of Poe's short story 'The purloined letter' under the pretext of deconstructing famous deconstructive readings. But critical bite is achieved at the expense of theoretical bark in such enterprises, which hardly belong to the school in any positive philosophical sense. Ms Johnson may have been one of Derrida's translators—as a critic, she is mercifully free from the burden of most of his theses. As a widespread practice signalling the triumph of 'text and theory'—an appallingly uncritical mix of wild philosophizing, truistic semiotics, unexamined Lacanese, and occasional bits of ill-digested social science—deconstruction is a drab neo-structuralist scholastics.

Its location in the literary academy is itself further evidence of the 'literarization of thought' we have already noted, and serves as an ecological niche for a very significant retreat: the apotheosis of 'textuality' marks a clear defeat for the ambition to conquer the social sciences, the cognitive drive that animated structural theory between Saussure and Lévi-Strauss, and inspired a small but impressive number of genuinely pathbreaking researches in several scholarly fields. In the hands of a Lévi-Strauss or of, say, a Vernant, a Louis Dumont or a Duby, the inspiration of classical structuralism helped to chart new ground, and to that extent, to achieve or to adumbrate new knowledge.

Deconstruction, on the other hand, seems content to undo meaning instead of trying to make knowledge. Its theory of the text is not only anti-empiricist but downright anti-empirical. At heart, it relishes the starkest intellectual anarchism. Feyerabend abolished only the hierarchy of contending scientific theories. Derrida goes far beyond this: he wants to suppress order among meanings, not just among theories. Feyerabend and his like, the anarchists of epistemology, remain logocentric squares: anarchy must free signification, not just knowledge.

Yet when all is said and done, the general result belies the exaggerated claims of the whole current of thought. For all its official Nietzschean alacrity, deconstruction invariably sounds pretty dull: a vastly repetitive and overpredictable strategy, a tiresome 'demonstration' that everybody always says the very opposite of what they mean. In its obsessive reductionism, deconstruction turns out to be a rather melancholy business—the dismal unscience of our time.

'Nietzschean alacrity' without the Nietzschean temper would indeed be an accurate description of the Derridean mood. Derrida's homage to Nietzsche as the greatest master of post-structuralism is as warm as Foucault's. He discards Heidegger's well-known attempt to charge Nietzsche with metaphysical blindness by construing the will-to-power as an arch-instance of erroneous ('ontic' or 'positive') ontology. Like Foucault, he underscores Nietzsche's freedom from the vain pursuit of truth and objectivity, his launching of consciously fictional philosophy. In *Spurs* (1978), Nietzsche's inauguration of 'the epochal regime of quotation marks' is pointedly contrasted with Heidegger's pet notion of truth as unveiling (*alétheia*).[51] Nevertheless, no true reader of Nietzsche will miss an essential difference between him and his self-appointed deconstructionist heir. The author of the *Genealogy of Morals* was a master of *Kulturkritik* but not of nihilist irony, of relentless denial. The *Lebensphilosophie* might have flattened much of Nietzsche's prismatic vision, but at least it was right in securing his wide-

[51] Derrida 1979, p. 107.

spread reception as a prophet of vitality, not of despair or unbelief. This prophetic quality of the optimist *malgré tout* in Nietzschean thought seems quite lost to contemporary thinkers indebted to him. Foucault, like Adorno, borrowed much from Nietzsche's *Kulturkritik*, but added to it something altogether foreign to him: *Kulturpessimismus*, the very element that Nietzsche so loathed in Schopenhauer.[52]

As for Derrida, his own addendum—quickly imparted to all his school—was not a direct statement of pessimism, for *any* direct statement is against the first law of deconstruction: perpetual equivocation. His way of unnerving the original Nietzschean temper used not despair but radicalized unbelief. Yet in the end the result is pretty much the same as in Adorno or Foucault: a *Kulturkritik* conspicuously lacking positive horizons, constructive alternatives, in a word—*historical optimism*, however prudently qualified. So one might say that whilst Nietzsche was a tragic but not a pessimist thinker, Derrida is a non-tragic yet a (crypto-) pessimist one. The name of the difference is, of course, Nietzsche's old foe: decadent nihilism. And that is what makes deconstruction, the unscience of the decadent humanities, so dismal in performance.

Nihilist Irrationalism in Thought as 'Modern Art'

'Advanced' continental thought nowadays presents two main faces. In Germany, 'critical theory' continues to argue that modern culture is strained by serious legitimacy gaps. Yet, thanks to Habermas, a sense of universal values—including truth—has been restored within the framework of an emancipatory ideal of man and society. In France, by contrast, chiefly in the schools of Foucault and Derrida, the antinomian stance vis à vis the culture of modernity broke with every vestige of anthropological optimism, with every positive appreciation of humanity or polity. Antinomianism without Utopian ingredients became the rule. Moreover, in the view of French post-structuralist doctrine, 'critical theory', its challenger across the

---

[52] I have dwelt on this contrast between Nietzsche and modern thought elsewhere: for Nietzsche, see Merquior, *Foucault*, London 1985, pp. 99–101; for pessimism in Western Marxism, see my *Western Marxism*, London 1986.

Rhine, is not that advanced. It has a backward epistemology based on universal truth-claims, and as such is far less well-equipped to grapple with the depth of our cultural crisis.

Foucault and Derrida have not just transmuted the disillusionment of the structuralist world-view into nihilism—they have also directed nihilism against truth. As a result, the countercultural idea is no longer just a romantic vision—it is also an openly irrationalist *idiom of thought*. But there is a difference. While in Foucault, a post-structuralist without a proper structuralist background, irrationalism was a question of Nietzschean premises and conclusions that did not affect the style of exposition, in Derrida, it manages to engulf his very language. His learned American convert, Geoffrey Hartman, called him 'Monsieur Texte'—only to have to admit that *Glas* may well be a piece of 'Derridadaism'.[53] An epigonic echo of *Finnegans Wake*, *Glas* entirely replaces the argumentative style of philosophy with perpetual pun-making. Chance meetings between words—such is its (paranomastic) law. '*La glu de l'aléa fait sens*' (the glue of chance creates meaning), Derrida writes, and if you are clever you will note that all the letters of '*glas*' got into that gnomic proposition . . . Deconstruction, after all, as the undoing of meaning, is a parasite of language: it wages war on meanings by means of a relentless technique of word-stretching. Panofsky said that Hegel's dialectic was a boa-constrictor. Now, each age getting the Hegel it deserves, we have our boa-deconstructor and are none the wiser for it.

Between them, Derrida and Foucault, the two caudilloes of post-structuralism, reoriented French philosophy away from the last semblance of sustained argument. Both sound decidedly 'literary' compared to their Anglo-Saxon or German counterparts. They made a vice out of a necessity: since mainstream continental philosophy had a pretty poor analytical performance, why not jettison the rites of careful analysis? But from this point their paths diverge. They do so in content: whereas Foucault, cast in the Sartrean role of the Thinker-as-

[53] Hartman 1981, chapter 1 and p. 33. Monsieur Texte is of course a wink at Valéry's *Monsieur Teste*. Jonathan Culler (*On Deconstruction*, p. 137), who is as little amused by the wild wordplay of *Glas* as he was by the later Barthes's hedonist heresies, reprehends Hartman for this blithe 'art-history' perspective on Derrida's studious work. Culler always reminds me of those whom Nietzsche described as the 'conscientious of mind'.

Rebel, catered to radical taste with a (largely mythical) ana-lytics of power, regarding his main philosophical histories as the building blocks of a critical 'history of the present', Derrida stuck to the priestly posture of the hermeneut, the Semiocrat, the Knower-of-Signs, the exegete, not of an Ur-meaning, but of an Un-meaning disseminating differences galore, all opaque. And by the same token, they begat different ways of 'super-seding' philosophy as rational argument. Foucault replaced it with dramatic historiography, the rhetoric of *histoire à thèse*. Derrida did it in a subtler way. He kept the genre or format of conventional philosophy only to subvert it from inside. He shuns the burning issues of insanity, punishment and sexuality and remains abstract and theoretical, endlessly commenting not only on the 'hot' topicalities of Nietzsche or Freud (as in *La Carte Postale*, 1980) but also on the arduous ruminations of Husserl, Hegel or Kant (as in 'Economimesis', 1975). Alas, the laborious cogitations of prior philosophers are to him little more than pretexts for embarking on long, loose chains of conceptual jokes, as though great and vexed questions of knowledge and signification could be settled by the obiter dicta of a wanton scepticism that increasingly substitutes verbal witticisms for argument and analysis.

From the viewpoint of genuine argumentative philosophy, the difference between the topical strategy of Foucault and the subtle subversion accomplished by Derrida looks minimal. Put either of them beside Michael Dummett's re-examination of the epistemological issues visited on western thought since Frege, a century ago, started probing the logical foundations of mathe-matics; or again, read whole chapters of Foucault and entire essays of Derrida after just a page of Donald Davidson on the problem of truth, meaning and interpretation: you shall feel bound to conclude that calling Derrida on the one hand, and Dummett and Davidson on the other, 'philosophers' cannot possibly mean the same thing, since they are conspicuously not playing the same game. In fact, whatever there is in common between the baroque deconstruction of the former and the bold but thoroughly staid cogitations of the latter two seems scarcely more relevant than the fact that all three bear family names starting with the same letter.

To claim, as does Richard Rorty in his influential books, that the difference between these two widely disparate styles of thought-writing is not also a difference in value—of cognitive power or at the very least of rational control—would imply too great a debasement of the standards we have a right to expect from skilled critical thinking. Denis Donoghue said of a foremost English critic (Christopher Ricks) that 'he puns to think'. I wish I could say the same of the deconstructionists, who seem to pun *instead* of thinking.

The kind of theory represented by Derrideanism must be treated less as philosophy *stricto sensu* than as a new style of free-wheeling, essayistic cultural criticism with an apocalyptic spirit. Its content is not a set of arguments but an axiom of debunking—the indictment of modern culture; and its method consists in pinpointing crises in the latter's main assumptions about truth and knowledge. Modern culture is deemed to be in crisis because its mental set is 'shown' to be fallacious; *Kulturkritik* presupposes a *Kulturkrisis*.

However, what if one turns the table against it? What if the crisis, too, has no referent? For it may well be that behind the cultural void and trash alleged by advanced nihilist thought there is nothing to be apprehended. *The crisis, then, would be less an object than a product of countercultural thought.* Post-structuralist theory is *the modern art of thought*: it basks in its own stubborn anti-figurativeness. It amounts to an intellectual (as opposed to literary-artistic) High Modernism, thriving on the same odium against modernity in its historico-social sense. By the same token, post-structuralist theory should be prepared to accept the possibility that its One Big Thesis—the massive rottenness of our culture—is a creative fake. Hence the invariable phoniness of its thundering against Western (that is modern, enlightened) values: it must sound hollow, since it is all a construct rather than a record of a real situation. In any case, how can such a school of thought, embattled as it is against all notions of objective truth, ever convince us that its picture of our cultural predicament is the *right* one?

Karl Kraus wryly dubbed psychoanalysis the illness for which it purports to be a cure. Similarly, nihilist theory might be described as that cultural crisis of which it deems itself to be a diagnosis. The drama of 'non-figurative' thought is that it dramatizes a portrait which, according to its own principles, it cannot even begin to paint. And the irony of it is that *post-structuralism has converted thought to modernism precisely when modernism in the arts had become irrevocably exhausted*. In his brilliant essay, 'The ideology of the text', Fredric Jameson tried to connect this shrivelling of late modernism to the spread of consumer capitalism. We can question his analysis and yet subscribe to his contention that today's modernisms *'no longer represent . . . the conquest of new materials'*.[54] Now the same goes for modernism as for theory: textual theory, with all its talk of crisis, shows no grasp of new realities. Hence the intensification of what we called the mantic pathos in modern French thought: the systematic, utter deletion of reference and meaning.

Few interpretations of post-structuralism ever broach such large historico-philosophical issues as the exact role of crisis theory in French thought from Sartre to Derrida. Yet without this large framework we may be tempted to take for granted the main assumptions of post-structuralist ideology. A worthy partial exception to this interpretive diet is Allan Megill's *Prophets of Extremity*, a study of Nietzsche, Heidegger, Foucault and Derrida.

Megill correctly detects an *aestheticist* sensibility in all these thinkers, taking aestheticism not in the usual sense of artistic insularity but in the romantic, expansionist sense of so stretching the aesthetic mode, or experience, as to embrace the whole of reality. But modern aestheticism, founded by Nietzsche, is aestheticism with a vengeance. Whereas a romantic like Schelling saw art as the summit of thought because art alone yielded genuine insight into reality, Nietzsche gives pride of place to the aesthetic precisely because it is free from cognitive claims. We are thus already at the threshold of the ironical suspension of truth in deconstruction theory. The post-romantic Nietzsche redefined art and myth away from all ties with 'things'.[55] Deconstruction takes this derealizing drive deep into the core of meaning itself.

Megill sees the rise of Nietzschean aestheticism as a result of

[54] Jameson, in *Salmagundi*, 31/32, Fall 1975–Winter 1976, p. 246. Two other thought-provoking recent reflections on the current predicament of modernism are Marshall Berman's book *All that is solid melts into air*, London 1982, and Perry Anderson's critical article on it, 'Modernity and Revolution', *New Left Review*, 144, March–April 1984, pp. 96–113, followed by Berman's reply, pp. 114–23.

[55] See Megill, *Prophets of Extremism*, especially pp. 50, 63, 78, 90 and 100. For a partly convergent analysis, see Habermas 1985.

the fall of historicism, of the belief in a (normally good) logic, or direction, of history. Again he is right. And he also mentions the kinship between the aestheticist anti-historicism of modern thought and the sense of cultural crisis embodied in most modernist, avant-garde art. No doubt his four thinkers are all *Kulturkritiker*—opponents of the social culture of modernity.

Unfortunately, however, this is where Megill's historico-philosophical analysis stops. Following Richard Rorty, he sees Nietzsche, Heidegger, Foucault and Derrida as just so many reactions against the Enlightenment and progressive tradition, the tradition that classical Marxism still represents, and which embodies a Cartesian faith in science, a Kantian faith in humanity and a Hegelian faith in history. Its collapse landed us in crisis. But although Megill is shrewd enough to realise that 'the problem with the crisis notion is that it can only speak in vague generalities'[56]—which is music to our ears—he actually swallows a great deal of the *Kulturkrisis* myth and does not see that Derrida's nihilistic equivocations, including his underrating of crisis theory itself, are a cure still worse than the illness. Briefly, Megill's able characterization of crisis thinking as aestheticism falls short of the crucial critical step: it balks before the acknowledgement that the *Kulturkritik*—be it 'prophetic' (Heidegger), rebel-like (Foucault) or cynical-ironic (Derrida) —is not a mimetic but a productive concept, a theory that begets its own object and then lays it in a humanist mind only too eager to hatch it, as an insignia of its self-important wisdom. Post-structuralist thought marks the ultimate intellectual decay of this vacuous ideological posturing; and within it, deconstruction, the tame pseudo-Nietzscheanism of academe, is a gloomy histrionics passing for theoretical insight.

Michel Foucault, in his polemic with Derrida (for example his afterword to the second edition of *Histoire de la Folie*) singled out the 'pedagogic authoritarianism' of the deconstructors as a model of 'obscurantist terrorism' built on Derrida's resoundingly dogmatic dictum, 'there is nothing outside the text'. Foucault was right in attacking the navel-gazing of the ideologues of the text, still more so in denouncing the snooty abstruseness of most deconstructionists. But even when post-structuralism is not obscurantist it lacks true cognitive power

[56] Ibid., p. 347.

because, as in Foucault's own oeuvre, its neo-modernist flight from reality thwarts any broader grasp of historical dynamics. Too much is sacrificed on the altar of countercultural romance. Hence the mantic, inward-looking mannerisms of all post-structural thought. The mantic look is a romantic outlook—and as such it is, in its impotent ritual fury against the social culture of modernity, evidence of the exhaustion of what Borges likes to call 'the subromanticisms of our age'.

Post-structuralism essentially makes gestures towards an apocalyptic sense of a crisis largely of its own invention. The whole thing clearly belongs to the kind of problem analysed by Frank Kermode in a crucial chapter ('The modern apocalypse') of his book *The Sense of an Ending* (1967). Kermode's point was to distinguish between early and late modernisms, showing how the latter, having rekindled 'eschatological pressures', breathes an ethos of 'schismatic nihilism'; but he acknowledged that 'the sense of an ending' is 'as endemic to . . . modernism as apocalyptic utopianism is to political revolution'; then—à propos of Pound's fascist leanings—he spoke of 'a failure' or 'betrayal' of clerical scepticism.[57]

Building on this we could say that when, via post-structuralism, modernist ideology invades philosophy (in which we called the literarization of thought), the 'modern apocalypse' turns overtly nihilistic. As for the new *trahison des clercs*, it consists less in embracing spurious political millenarisms than in *betraying critique through crisis-mongering*; it is a betrayal of *critical scepticism in that* it abandons critical argument and shuns debate.

As Jacques Bouveresse has recently noted, it is as if this form of philosophy deliberately advanced further and further towards amateurism and frivolity—precisely what those who are concerned with scientific or argumentative standards blame much continental philosophy for. Not surprisingly, this *fuite en avant* from intellectual responsibility reaches unheard-of heights of conceptual laxity: question-begging, fallacies and non-sequiturs reign unimpeded. For instance, in their Nietzschean epistemology, the post-structuralists eagerly uphold the idea that there are no thoroughly neutral independent facts, all observations being already theory-laden and thus bound to a prior interpre-

[57] See especially Kermode 1967, pp. 98, 109, 114 and 122.

tation of reality. But the same thinkers seem keen to conclude, from the premiss that one needs a theory whenever one knows a fact, that facts are actually *created* by our theories. However, it does not in the least follow that because our knowledge of the world presupposes interests and values the world itself is therefore but a product or a projection of those values and interests.[58]

Literary Theory: from Hubris to Self-Criticism

As was only to be expected, literary theory hastened to build variants of such crass non-sequiturs into the current dogmas of critical wisdom. Robert Scholes, always nimble in expounding or exposing the structuralist doxa, caught the gist of the matter. In olden times, claims Scholes, it was believed that fiction was about life and criticism about fiction. Now we know better: we have come to realise that all fiction is criticism (because it is about other fictions); and criticism proper is only about the impossibility of 'aboutness': its real subject is 'the impossibility of its own existence'. As Scholes succinctly puts it: 'there is no mimesis, only poesis.'[59]

One could hardly say it more elegantly. But consider for a moment the kind of argument commonly used to justify the sacking of mimesis. The underlying assumption is that what we naively call correspondence to reality rests on no more than shared language which imposes on things a conformist adjustment to unconscious or manipulated social meanings rather than grasping their real nature (which is merely in any case a function of our 'active interpretations'). The trouble is, it does not follow from this premiss that 'there is no mimesis'. As Gerald Graff very sensibly remarks in that brave piece of critical dissent, *Literature Against Itself* (1979): 'It is true that the idea of a "natural correspondence" between language and reality has often been used to justify the view of reality held by those wielding political power. But one can reject the ideological

[58] J. Bouveresse, *Le Philosophie chez les Autophages*, Paris 1984, pp. 25–26, 54–65 and 108–115.
[59] R. Scholes, 'The fictional criticism of the future', *Tri Quarterly*, 34, Fall 1975; quoted by G. Graff, *Literature Against Itself: Literary Ideas in Modern Society*, Chicago 1979, p. 72.

bias of such a justification without rejecting the principle of correspondence itself. Indeed, one can argue that the established ideology fails to correspond to reality, and go on to present an alternative view which corresponds more closely. In a similar way, the fact that our shared linguistic contracts often conceal ideological mystifications favorable to the interests of the ruling class is an argument for exposing these particular linguistic formulations, not for attacking the very concept of shared formulations.'[60]

The real progress of modern criticism has been the increase in our sense of the meaningfulness of form. The advantage of its sundry methods of close reading was that they enhanced our grasp of complex patterns of literary meaning and in so doing improved our ability to detect poetic or fictional value and gauge its degree. Yet nothing in the critical experience of meaningful form implied a denial of the relation between literature and life or its basic reference to the world. For this reason, the latest challenger of the formalist orthodoxy, A. D. Nuttall, is absolutely right in my view when he observes that the superiority of 'transparent criticism', of criticism alive to the mimetic dimension of literature, over the formalist pieties of 'opaque criticism' is partly a matter of inclusiveness, since 'the Transparent critic can and will do all the things done by the Opaque critic but is willing to do other things as well.'[61] In other words: transparent criticism will *both* pay attention to form *and* will look through the text to the world of human experiences from which art takes its ultimate worth and most of its meaning.

The theoretical situation generated by 'structuralist philosophy' is a comic reversal of the old positivist Utopia of knowledge. Once upon a time, there was the positivist chimera of introducing into philosophy and social science the concept of truth and the scientific patterns found in hard science. Today, a growing number of 'radical' thinkers dream of a dogmatic transposition into the realm of science of the indiscriminate scepticism about truth and objectivity that pervades the humanities. But Bouveresse, for one, thinks the game is not worth a candle. Indeed, he is sick and tired of this *Salonskeptizismus*. He prefers

[60] Graff, *Literature Against Itself*, p. 89.
[61] A. D. Nuttall, *A New Mimesis: Shakespeare and the Representation of Reality*, London 1983, pp. 80–98.

to say loudly 'something that a relativist' (all post-structuralists being, obviously, fierce relativists) 'is well placed to understand, namely, that I have no sympathy at all with the kind of "progress" allegedly represented, in the view of certain (French) maîtres à penser, by the gradual liquidation of fundamental cognitive values such as coherence, truth, validity, objective confirmation or justification and I see no reason to accept as a historical fate what is, in reality, but the product of the historicising and historicist conformism in which we live and moreover constitutes too local and parochial a cultural phenomenon.'[62]

Nowhere more parochial than in the literary tribe of the humanities. For the literarization of thought created a climate of utter smugness in academic literary quarters. Listen, for instance, to the orotund self-satisfaction with which acolytes of the deconstructionist rite gravely aver that, in the ongoing surge of 'theory', 'it would not be inappropriate for *literary* theory to play the central role.'[63] Not *a* role, not even a central role: nothing less than *the* central role. After all, if philosophy itself turned fictional, why should the literary clerisy stick to old boundaries and keep literature in its (admittedly very important) place? All one can do is denounce this and other pieces of guild paranoia as manoeuvres within 'a struggle for academic power' in which a 'literary-critical imperialism' (in A. Megill's phrase) increasingly raises its silly head.[64] Moreover, their small smattering of philosophy only increases the gullibility of teachers and students in modern literature departments when reacting to the fallacies and absurdities 'theory' has come to indulge.

Those academic critics who have profited from structuralism without surrendering the rights of reason or sacrificing the intellect, as is so often required by post-structuralism, tend to be less enthusiastic about the present state of the art. Thus David Lodge has suggested that literary criticism has been damaged by the gulf between everyday language and technical

---

[62] Bouveresse, *Philosophie chez les Autophages*, p. 117 (my translation).

[63] Culler, *On Deconstruction*, p. 10. Emphasis added.

[64] Megill, review of Culler's *On Deconstruction*, in *Philosophy and Literature*, Fall 1984, pp. 285–89.

discourse[65]—a gulf that the more jargon-laden brands of structuralese and post-structuralitis have widened into a chasm. Jargon has now made much of the humanities anything but humane—and the gain in knowledge is far from being, as a rule, substantial.

The post-structuralist literarization of thought has been accompanied by an overrating of the scope of literary theory. Departments of literature have become intellectual looms relentlessly weaving theoretical texts that are far from restricted to literary matters: their wild flux of standard theorizing—a veritable *theorrhea*—normally ploughs the open sea of loose but exceedingly ambitious philosophizing. Credulous inmates or naive bystanders of the literary academe may think that this theoretical boldness is a spillover from the power of literary theory at work on texts—but this is a pious illusion. Keener observers of contemporary literary criticism would agree with Arthur K. Moore: in our time, 'if analytical criticism has surpassed rank impressionism, the gains have been owing more to improved reading than to improved theory: for theory has most evidently provided a pretext rather than a regulative principle.[66] The theorrhea of academic literati is not a projection of methodological success but an imperialist extension of humanist ideology.

In their boundless theoretical pontification, many literary theorists do not balk, as we have seen, at assigning a dominating role to their trade. Jonathan Culler, a successful apostle of deconstruction, tells us that this is only too natural, for three reasons: (a) Literary theorists are open-minded thinkers. Why? Because they are better placed—as outsiders—to welcome challenges to 'the assumptions of orthodox contemporary psychology, anthropology, psychoanalysis, philosophy, sociology, or historiography'. (b) Literary theory is self-conscious. Why? Because it 'inexorably' explores 'problems of reflexivity and metacommunication, trying to theorise the exemplary self-reflexiveness of literature'. (c) Given that 'literature takes as its subject all human experience' and its interpretive articulation,

---

[65] David Lodge, 'Avoiding the double bind', (a review of Bernard Sharratt's *Reading Relations*), *Times Literary Supplement* 23 April 1982, p. 458.

[66] A. Moore, *Contestable Concepts of Literary Theory*, Baton Rouge 1973, p. 218.

theory normally finds literature very instructive: 'the comprehensiveness of literature makes it possible for any extraordinary or compelling theory to be drawn into literary theory.'[67]

Even the most perfunctory examination shows this threefold claim to be a piece of appallingly poor thinking. Granted that literary theorists can look, as unprejudiced outsiders, at new ideas in a host of human sciences; but 'psychologists, anthropologists, psychoanalysts, philosophers, sociologists, historians', as non-literary researchers, can also look, without the bias of craft, at 'contemporary literary theory'. Seriously to suggest that the relationship is one-way, to the sole benefit of the literati, requires a touching leap of faith in the higher wisdom of the theory of literature—but that is grotesquely question-begging, for the entitlement of literary thinking to 'the central role' was precisely what Culler was trying to justify in the first place. Either *all* the tribes in the humanities have their own craft-bound biases and (in principle) can look afresh at theoretical developments outside their purview or they haven't and cannot—but if the first alternative is true, then the obvious upshot is a general trade-off, not a privileged insight accruing to literary theorists.

Culler's second balloon can be popped even more easily, for claim (b) simply *takes for granted* the formalist-deconstructionist myth of literariness as self-reflexiveness. To equate theoretical acumen with a compulsive quest for aporia, alleged to be the quintessence of literature, is a very tall order but it is certainly not sufficient grounds for giving modern literary thought the throne of Theory.

What about Culler's third (in his own list, emphatically the first) claim, namely, that literary theory must rule because literature deals with 'all human experience'? Prima facie, the premiss seems reasonable. Literature does indeed encompass all human experience. However, it does not follow that its comprehensiveness provides a clear-cut basis for a body of knowledge, let alone of *ruling* knowledge. For it is far from easy to transform the range of literature from a warrant of relevance and significance into a basis for theoretical cognition.

Nor does the matter end with the problem that literature's comprehensiveness, in terms of human relevance, is not readily

[67] Culler, *On Deconstruction*, pp. 10–11.

translatable into theoretical cognition. The problem becomes still more complex or elusive because, while it is true that literature embodies comprehensive truth about the human condition, normally it is only (good) literature *as a whole* that does so. Consequently there is little point in suggesting that literary theory qualifies as higher knowledge simply because it deals with an art whose object is human experience: for literary truth (or, for that matter, literary beauty) cannot be predicated unconditionally of any single given work.[68] Therefore criticism cannot be invoked as a stable basis for literary theory as a knowledge of all matters human.

Humanist prophets such as Matthew Arnold used to think that, in his famous words, 'more and more mankind will discover that we have to turn to poetry to interpret life for us.'[69] In their theoretical fervour deconstructionists seem eager to bestow this prerogative upon their overblown literary theory. They already see literary thought—a thought, incidentally, now only tangentially related to literature—as the dominating brand of Theory. Can one help seeing this, in turn, as an ill-founded attempt at domination? Lest this be reckoned an exaggeration, I hasten to recall that Paul de Man, the late godfather of the deconstructionist mafia in America, did not balk (in *Blindness and Insight*) at casting the net of the textual ideology wide enough to annex history itself to the rarefied realm of the suicidal meaning, the gist of self-reflexive literature. Coupling an axiomatic assertion that literature is endless aporia with a Nietzschean perspectivism ('no facts, just interpretations'), de Man hinted, to the apparent delight of avant-garde literary departments, that wars and revolutions are not empirical events (there is no such thing) but 'texts' masquerading as facts.[70]

This book does not purport to discuss in any detail the fate of post-structuralism in America, although it is in America, from Yale deconstructionists to Californian Foucaldians, that Anglophone post-structuralism is strongest. My title is *From*

[68] The point is perspicuously discussed by Moore, *Contestable Concepts*, pp. 212–14.
[69] Arnold, 'The Study of Poetry' (1880), reprinted as the opening essay in his *Essays in Criticism, Second Series* (posth., 1888).
[70] de Man, *Blindness and Insight*, p. 165.

Prague to Paris, not *From Paris to New Haven*. Suffice it then to say that de Man's preposterous reduction of history to a textual puzzle did not go unchallenged. The main challenger, Frank Lentricchia, earned prominence as a historian of criticism for whom—as he made clear in *After the New Criticism* (1980)—both structuralism and deconstruction originally contained radical promises belied and betrayed by their transatlantic acclimatization. Yet on close inspection the 'radical' structuralism Lentricchia seems to have in mind is chiefly the work of Barthes in the *Mythologies* phase, still basically pre-structuralist, as we saw; and his claim that Derrida's dismantling of meaning is far more rigorous than its American counterparts[71] cries out for substantiation. American deconstruction, says Lentricchia, 'tends to be an activity of textual privatization',[72] marking the critic's retreat from the social fray. But did we not see Foucault raise the same charge against Derrida himself? No wonder the tone of Lentricchia's objections got harsher in his next book, *Criticism and Social Change* (1983), where de Man plays villain to the hero, Kenneth Burke, who features as an American Gramsci. Then he stresses the 'Prufrockian mood of current critical sophistication',[73] an enterprise contrasted with the pugnacity of Foucault's new kind of social critique.

Much as I share Lentricchia's impatience with the ritualistic puzzle-mongering of deconstruction, I fail to see how post-structuralism qua genealogy (Foucault) can kill the virus of post-structuralism qua exegesis (Derrida). As Terence Hawkes notes, Foucault's idea of history is vulnerable to more than one of the strictures levelled against Derrida's way of wreaking anarchy upon texts[74]—scarcely surprising, in view of their common Nietzschean stance in regard to knowledge and truth. Some Foucaldians, as is well known, set the avowed Nietzscheanism of their idol against Marxism, as an alternative form of critique. Others, however, tipsy on the Marxo-Nietzschean cocktail, deem Foucault's microphysics of power/knowledge to be the best way of rescuing Marxism from scientism or science

[71] F. Lentricchia, *After the New Criticism*, London 1980, p. 209.
[72] Ibid., p. 186.
[73] F. Lentricchia, *Criticism and Social Change*, Chicago 1983, p. 51.
[74] Terence Hawkes, review of *After the New Criticism*, in TLS 17 April 1981.

tout court.[75] Lentricchia, who does not blush in equating 'Marx without science' with 'Marx without Stalin', and is happy to follow Richard Rorty in an attack on 'a past of epistemological repression',[76] obviously aligns himself with the Marxo-Nietzschean Foucaldians—to no visible analytical gain.

Fortunately, one can resist the spell of deconstruction—and the paranoid philosophizing of criticism as 'theory'—without falling into rival irrationalisms; and I should like to end my remarks on the current predicament of literary theory by pointing to what looks like a case of mature self-criticism by an ex-structuralist: Tzvetan Todorov. We left him, many many pages ago, as a true believer in 'linguisticism', a virulent form of formalist structuralism. Todorov has gone through much soul-searching since the days of his 'structural analysis of narrative' and other similiar ventures. In a recent book, *Critique de la Critique* (1984), he devotes the entire concluding essay to questioning the unexamined assumption of his erstwhile theorizing. In a nutshell, he confesses to having embraced structuralism, in early sixties Paris, because as a Bulgarian he was fed up with the ideological appropriation of literature usually prevalent in the socialist countries. 'Discovering about me a literature enslaved to politics, I believed in the need for breaking all ties and keeping literature free from all contact with everything else.' Hence his espousal of an 'immanent' criticism coupled with the idea, of romantic ancestry, that literature is a language that finds an end in itself: immanent criticism—that is structuralism—was adopted in order to account for an autotelic verbal art.[77]

But Todorov now realises that this might lead to as blind an alley as the narrowness of 'dogmatic' criticism, be it Christian or Marxist.[78] After all, he says, literature deals with human life: it is a discourse geared towards truth and ethics. Sartre was right to call it an unveiling of humanity and the world. If literature does not just mirror ideologies, it is because it is itself an ideology, a statement about reality; and the critic's task is to

[75] For brief comments on this issue among Foucault interpreters, see Merquior, *Foucault*, pp. 142–43.

[76] Lentricchia, *Criticism and Social Change*, pp. 13 and 17.

[77] T. Todorov, *Critique de la Critique: Un Roman d'Apprentissage*, Paris 1984, p. 188 (my translation).

[78] Ibid., p. 192.

analyse works without turning a deaf ear to such a statement, but without being afraid of contradicting it either. Above all criticism must recognize that, being caught up in the world, it, too, speaks about life and the conflict of values. Therefore, it should not be ashamed of a humanism conceived of as an 'attempt to ground science and ethics in reason'.[79] All that matters is that the attempt be conducted in a liberal, tolerant, judicious yet at the same time judicative way: for whereas dogmatic criticism ends in a critic's monologue, and immanent criticism in an author's monologue, humanist criticism proceeds through *dialogue* (the humanism Todorov opposes to the ellision of world and subject in deconstruction has learned from Bakhtin's stress on dialogism, as well as from Paul Bénichou's concern for the ideological, as against the formal, element in literature).[80]

Todorov is aware that to a large extent he is re-discovering long-found Americas temporarily hidden by the conceptual fog of structuralist bigotry and by the hysterical denial of reference and reality promoted by post-structuralism. But this makes his self-criticism no less healthy, nor less apposite. That such a leading figure in the formalist revival and the establishment of structuralism has decided to withstand the cacophony of post-structuralitis on grounds of reason and humanity, without in the least dropping the lucid, urbane style of his impressive previous output, is something to be welcomed wholeheartedly.

At most, one wishes that his plea for a new rational humanism in literary criticism were more sympathetic towards historical approaches, and less derogatory about Marxism. As a non-Marxist critic myself, I feel reasonably well placed to say that Todorov takes too unilateral a view in equating Marxism with relativism (in both knowledge and morals) on the grounds that it replaces reason with history, and is therefore no better than Foucault's Nietzschean dismissal of universal values.[81] Whatever its many shortcomings, Marxism—classical Marxism at least—

[79] Cf. Todorov, 'All against humanity', *Times Literary Supplement*, 4 October 1985.

[80] Todorov refers to Bénichou's masterpiece of literary history from the viewpoint of ideology: *Morales du grand siècle*, Paris 1948, *Le Sacre de l'écrivain*, Paris 1973 and *Le Temps des prophètes*, Paris 1977; pp. 143 to 177 of *Critique de la Critique* contain a long interview with Bénichou.

[81] See 'All against humanity', p. 1094.

has a core of strong universalist tenets, and an Enlightenment and Hegelian background, irreducible to the unabashed histor-ist relativism of the post-structuralist masters. Moreover, if we are to recover a sense of literature as a worldly discourse, and hence of the author's voice (conscious as well as unconscious), we shall also need to grasp the voice of the age, not as a lofty *Zeitgeist* but as a sum, often contradictory, of historical pre-suppositions and concrete conditions of literature. Historical materialism remains, as a powerful heuristics, the best available programme for this necessary if not sufficient dimension of analytical criticism. To dare to judge without prejudice, a discipline of historical piety is mandatory; but it was the impact of historical materialism that taught us that the best historical piety is not an exercise in blind nostalgia, a romance of wistful empathy, but an intelligent grasp of the changing limits and constraints imposed on human experience.

But for all their deficiences neither Todorov's anti-Marxism nor Lentricchia's pro-Marxism prevent them from contributing cogently to the supersession of the formalist environment re-vamped by the assault of deconstruction. Significantly, the model critics they propose—Burke, Bakhtin, Bénichou—represent seminal strands of analysis very distant from the cult of contentless forms and blank signifiers. Their joint revival would provide a natural antithesis to the influence of the main formalist axes: the lines of Shklovsky-Jakobson and Blanchot-Barthes. And it is no less instructive that none of the three mistook theoretical range (quite wide in all of them) for a licence to treat texts as pretexts for wanton philosophizing in arcane jargons. In their different ways, Todorov and Lentricchia, together with critics like Jameson, Scholes, Graff or Compag-non, are currently building a basis for effective dissent from a formalist orthodoxy disguised as rampant avant-gardism. For the moment, they lead the overdue rescue of literary theory from hubris and unreason.

Towards a Sociology of Theorrhea

Post-structuralism has been the seat of theorrhea in the human-ities—ambitious 'theory' as a pretext for sloppy thinking and little analysis, fraught with anathemas against modern civilisation.

But how could the humanities be so hospitable to such an unpalatable scribbling? Here I can only sketch some suggested explanations. The trouble is that the humanities, outside of their natural fields of scholarship—history, philology, ethnography—have for too long felt insecure in the face of the growth of hard science. Humanist intellectuals, heirs of the ancient possessions of higher knowledge and literacy skills, nowadays face a society in which literacy is universal and world-shaping knowledge is beyond their ken. Little wonder if these displaced 'artisans of cognition', as E. Gellner calls them,[82] fall for the kinds of lore and language that sound like their private property, and that may therefore enhance their status and self-image in an increasingly narcissistic academic world.

If, in addition, the new skills revolve around *language*, so much the better. Language was the oldest flame of the humanist soul. Linguistics, after all, was virtually the only area in which humanists managed to produce decent science (as opposed to scholarship or erudition, best typified by history). Moreover, with the continuing 'linguistic turn' of philosophy (Wittgenstein and Austin, Heidegger and hermeneutics), what could be more apposite than the advent of structuralisms, the brainchildren of Saussure? Logocracy held sway over the humanist guild. Humanity was no longer seen as lord of the logos, a sovereign *homo loquens*, but as the language-bound animal. However, something is amiss. As Roger Shattuck perceived, we don't really like surrendering everything to Mistress Language. We have therefore taken a subtle, hidden revenge on her spell. In order quietly to vindicate some sense of choice and individuality, we have embarked on an absurdist lusting after fantasy and rule-breaking. Our myths of transgression help us to bear the anonymous rule of language. Hence our latest cultural kit: the metaphysical picaresque.[83] The label seems tailor-made for grasping the essence of Lacan, Derrida or Deleuze as well as the anti-realist novelists Shattuck has chiefly in mind. But it goes without saying that theoretical clowning, for all its wilful unruliness, turns into the rule. After all, it is just a mirror-image

[82] See his essay on the crisis in the humanities in E. Gellner, *The Devil in Modern Philosophy*, London 1974 (quote, p. 29).

[83] R. Shattuck, *The Innocent Eye: On Modern Literature and the Arts*, New York 1984, pp. 332–36.

of logocracy. Dada theory, too, works as a language game.

Now in such a context, to say, as Paul de Man did as late as 1982,[84] that the 'terrorism' of 'ruthless theory' would be an anti-establishment academic drive, could only be sheer rhetoric[85] or downright disingenousness. For the spate of 'theory' nurtured in literature departments may go on voicing its rhetoric of dissent and deviancy as loud as it pleases; the plain fact is that this noisy talk of transgression has become enormously ritual-ized—as ritualized as the stale avant-gardist breaks in the modernist-ridden artworld that the new humanities chose to copy.

If I may stress the main point: as a cluster of intellectual mores, the structuralist/post-structuralist wave may pass for a theoretical avant-garde, but in reality it is rooted in strictly parochial traits of the humanities system. In a pithy recent es-say[86] the sociologist, Raymond Boudon, has sketched an interes-ting explanation of the aestheticization of knowledge normally associated with what he dubs 'the Freudian-Marxian-Structur-alist movement' (FMS) in France. In a nutshell, Boudon accounts for the wilful opacity of most masters of FMS by means of an institutional model of a specific kind of academic world that lacks some patterns of interaction usually present in centres of higher learning. In order for constant orientation toward sober knowledge-building to prevail, he claims, some institutional conditions have to be met, in social as well as natural science. These conditions imply a number of consequences for the role social scientists play: they impose a set of obligations to be clear and to comply with acceptable standards of objectivity. As they are supposed to address themselves primarily to their peers, authors in a cognitively oriented social science will normally try to abide by impersonal rules when justifying their theses or their findings: there is no question of suggesting that they are true just because the author is more clever or gifted than fellow experts. And, last but not least, academic advancement in each

[84] Paul de Man, 'Professing Literature', *Times Literary Supplement*, 10 December 1982, pp. 1355-6.

[85] As noted by M. Felperin, *Beyond Deconstruction: The Uses and Abuses of Literary Theory*, Oxford 1985, p. 141.

[86] Raymond Boudon, 'The Freudian-Marxian-Structuralist (FMS) Movement in France: variations on a theme by Sherry Turkle', *Revue Tocqueville*, vol. II, 1, Winter 1980, pp. 5-23.

specialty depends on the observance of such codes of cognitive conduct.

Boudon submits that these institutional constraints have been very weak in the case of *French* social science, with the exception of history. The symbolic rewards and material resources available to the community of social scientists have been too restricted, the degree of differentiation between universities too low to foster social climbing through intellectual achievement. Hence theories that legitimize epistemological relativism (and not only methodological pluralism) thrive on the humanist side of French academe: for epistemological relativism (asserted with a vengeance by thinkers like Lacan, Barthes, Derrida or Foucault) is just the ideological pendant to the lack of a true, self-conscious and rule-bound cognitive community. And given the lack of a satisfactory social science system, the actual receivers of 'social science' or literary theory are often not the equals of its senders. Rather they are a motley crowd of humanist intellectuals only loosely connected with the particular disciplines from which the new theoretical trends are coming: thus the *average* (and not just the occasional) reader of Lacan tends not to be a psychoanalyst, nor the reader of Foucault or Derrida a philosopher, and so on. As a result, the producer/consumer relationship becomes too asymmetrical, with the latter unable to assess the bibles of new thought with a modicum of competence. What is more, given such diffuse, unskilled audiences, the senders of theoretical messages are not likely to be penalized for indulging in opacity or intellectual permissiveness: on the contrary, their receivers are quite prepared to countenance their obscurity and arbitrariness, interpreting them as further evidence of their inferiority in relation to their chosen gurus.

In such circumstances, what tempts the gifted academic is not the career of an expert but the triumph of a prophet. But Boudon adds another perceptive remark. He notes that unlike, say, Marshall McLuhan or Wilhelm Reich (or Ivan Illich), the FMS gurus do not address themselves as authors directly to the public at large, over the heads of academic specialists. Hence a curious effect: the FMS masters, Lacan, Althusser, Barthes, and so on churned out a highly aestheticized theory, one at a far remove from the stern rules of clarity and cogency demanded by institutionalized social science—and yet, they insisted on

Science with a capital letter, flaunting their output as an arcane model of theoretical and methodological 'rigour'. The paradox of 'aesthetic' knowledge wrapped up in scientistic guise is again explained by the social situation of the FMS masters—experts by origin but 'prophets' by behaviour (this paradox, in turn, accounts for the eventual shifts from scientism or near-scientism to open relativism in such authors as Barthes, Althusser and Foucault). Only the nouveaux philosophes chose to behave like Reich or McLuhan, and therefore opted for a pop philosophy that retained the same degree of irresponsible intellectual bravado, but dropped opacity as the trademark of 'creative' thinking. As for the FMS stardom, it is as esoteric as it is self-indulgent. 'Theory' comes close to being no more than the diktats of abstruse gurus; theoretical revolutions strangely resemble logorrheic revelations. The main target is always the same: modern society and its values. The actual victim, however, is the quality of rational intellect.

Post-structuralism and Kulturkritik

These sociological remarks help us to understand why theorrhea—sweepingly self-important theory—found fertile ground in a particular kind of academic culture, the burgeoning new humanities. But our own analysis is concerned less with the *why* than with the *what* of structuralist, and especially post-structuralist, theory. Accordingly, we should return at last to its ideological tenor. What wine is served in the opaque bottles of the new humanities?

As we saw in our brief discussion of Allan Megill's gallery of the masters of *Kulturkritik* (pp. 241–42), most versions of post-structuralism stem from the radical aestheticism of Nietzsche. In a long and important recent work, *Der philosophische Diskurs der Moderne*, published in the same year (1985) as Megill's *Prophets of Extremity*, Jürgen Habermas, too, dwells on the Nietzschean heritage. He sees in Nietzsche the chief forerunner of 'postmodern' reactions against the spirit of modern culture, the turning point in the history of our entry into a postmodern world.[87] Coming of age philosophically after the failure of the

---

[87] Habermas, *Der philosophische Diskurs der Moderne*, Frankfurt 1985, pp. 104 sq.

1848 revolutions, Nietzsche renounced the historicist belief in the emancipatory power of philosophy (the gist of Hegel's 'reason in history'). In addition, he rejected the compensatory role of high culture under capitalism—the idea of culture as, so to speak, the comforting sigh of society, what Bergson later called *un supplément d'âme*, allegedly desperately lacking in our technological society.

Given the failure of historicism, claims Habermas, Nietzsche found himself torn between the following theoretical alternatives: *either* he was to undertake an 'immanent critique' of philosophical reason, in an attempt to rescue it from the shortcomings of historicist thought (a fair description of Habermas's own endeavour) *or* he could ditch philosophy's rational programme altogether. Nietzsche chose the latter course. He adopted a paradoxical strategy of subverting reason. Boldly flaunting an uncompromising irrationalism, he denounced reason as a form of will-to-power and deprived value judgements of all cognitive force.

In so doing Nietzsche was not only the first to give a conceptual form to modernist aesthetics as a ludic, Dionysian mode of change and self-denial: he also built an alluring *aesthetocentric* redefinition of thought. Theory itself disparaged sustained logical analysis for the sake of 'life' and wild insight. Whilst *logos* was played down, 'myth' was given a free hand. Unlike Wagner, however, for whom myth became increasingly Christian and nostalgic, in Nietzsche the mythical element is given a futurist thrust, pledged against decadence and the repression of instinct. But this privileging of the aesthetic in turn contradicted the very spirit of the project of modernity. For the logic of western culture since the Enlightenment is predicated on the strict, Kantian autonomy of the three spheres of thought —knowledge, art and morality. Science, artistic creation and ethics are supposed to operate within well-defined boundaries, however unstable the balance between them. By inflating aesthetic values into a resounding challenge to the very aims of knowledge (the sphere of truth) and morals (the sphere of duty), Nietzsche canonized *Kulturkritik*—the refusal of modernity—as a structure of thought in its own right.

Nietzsche himself often shifted between two courses in this supersession of rationalism. On the one hand, he contemplated the possibility of a new, sceptic history, a starkly critical genealogy of morals freed from every illusion about objective truth. On the other hand, he countenanced a critique of metaphysical assumptions that was still faithful to the idea of philosophy as a higher knowledge.

Nietzsche's posterity among the *Kulturkritiker* reproduces this bifurcation. Foucault (like Bataille before him) took the first path—of sceptical, openly irrational history; Heidegger, and nowadays Derrida, represent the second—the way of anti-metaphysical philosophy.

In Heidegger this antilogos takes the form of a hermetic wisdom, an arcane renewal of ontology with a mystical accent. Derrida's version is far less assertive and soteriological: Being is no longer emphasized; meaning is forever shifting and ambiguous. Instead, all difference between logic and rhetoric is abolished: the aesthetic imposes its law on all concepts and categories. The distinction between concept and image, theory and art, still so dear to the negative dialectics of the first Frankfurt school, is swamped by the strange combination of 'Nietzschean' perspectivism without the slightest hint of an anti-decadent animus—the main motive of Nietzsche's thought.

Habermas's particular diagnosis of the centrality of the aesthetic is up to now the best discussion of postmodern and post-structuralist theory. Its advantage over those who correctly note the aestheticist nature of *Kulturkritik*, but leave it at that, is that unlike them Habermas sees that aestheticism, as far as cognitive standards go, is more of a problem than a solution. Moreover, as he is at pains to stress, aesthetocentric thought, whether in Nietzsche himself or in Heidegger, Foucault or Derrida, over-looks the positive rational potential of modern culture—its humanizing, emancipatory horizon. In Habermas, the gallant attempt to reinstate reason as dialogue and 'communicative action'[88] walks hand in hand with a qualified acceptance of the 'modern project'—something very different from the wholesale repudiation of modernity to be found among the Nietzschean *Kulturkritiker*. (In the same way, he undertakes a stern critique of Horkheimer and Adorno's Nietzschean unmasking of the Enlightenment in their *Dialektik der Aufklärung*.)

Nevertheless, mere questioning of aesthetocentrism is far from enough. For it takes issue with a *response* to the crisis of

[88] For an overview of Habermas's oeuvre, see my *Western Marxism*, pp. 163–85.

modernity but scarcely examines the validity of the concept of crisis itself, as applied to modern culture. Habermas sensibly rejects the dismissal of cultural modernity root and branch; yet his own diagnosis gives pride of place to the idea of a 'legitimation crisis' inbuilt in late capitalist culture. We can go further, and question the whole 'humanist' claim that there is something basically wrong with modern *culture* as it actually is, in the developed, liberal capitalist societies of our time.

By stating that Foucault's anti-Enlightenment philosophical history, as well as Derrida's brand of irrationalism, are not only instances of a literarization of thought but also *a surrender of thought to modernist ideology*, that is, to the pious counter-cultural worldview of most modern art, I meant to stress how questionable are the assumptions that gave birth to the radical tradition within *Kulturkritik*. Do the many failures and short-comings of modern culture actually warrant such a massive indictment of modernity's achievements? Can we really say that the historicist appraisal and approval of an industrial order, where knowledge, art and morals work as separate though obviously not wholly unrelated spheres, has been convincingly shown to be erroneous? Are there not sufficient grounds to present a case for what Hans Blumenberg has called *'die Legitimität der Neuzeit'*?[89] That a deep cultural crisis is endemic to historical modernity seems to have been much more eagerly assumed than properly demonstrated, no doubt because, more often than not, those who generally do the assuming—humanist intellectuals—have every interest in being perceived as soul doctors to a sick civilization. Yet is the medicine that necessary, or the sickness that real? Perhaps we should be entertaining second thoughts about it all.

[89] H. Blumenberg, *The Legitimacy of the Modern Age*, Cambridge, Mass., 1983 (1st German ed., 1966).

Bibliography

AA. VV. *The Critical Moment: Literary Criticism in the 1960s*. London: Times Literary Supplement, 1963.

Aarsleff, Hans. *From Locke to Saussure: Essays on the Study of Language and Intellectual History*. Minneappolis: Minnesota Univ· Press, 1982.

Adorno, Theodor W. *Aesthetische Theorie*. Ed. Gretel Adorno and Rolf Tiedemann. Frankfurt: Suhrkamp, 1970.

Aguiar e Silva, Victor Manuel. *Teoria da Literatura*. Coimbra: Almedina, 1983 (5th ed.).

Allemann, Beda. *Literatur und Reflexion, 1973*. Spanish tr., Buenos Aires: Alfa, 1975.

Althusser, Louis. *For Marx*. London: Allen Lane, 1969. Translated by Ben Brewster. (*Pour Marx*. Paris: Maspero, 1965)

— *Reading Capital*. London: New Left Books, 1970. Translated by Ben Brewster. (*Lire le Capital*, with E. Balibar and others. Paris: Maspero, 1965, 2 vols.)

Ambrogio, Ignazio. *Formalismo e Avanguardia in Russia*. Rome: Riuniti, 1968.

Anderson, Perry. *In the Tracks of Historical Materialism*. London: Verso, 1983.

Argan, Giulio Carlo. *Salvezza e Caduta Nell'Arte Moderna*. Milano: Il Saggiatore, 1964.

Aron, Jean-Paul. *Les Modernes*. Paris: Gallimard, 1984.

Aron, Raymond. *Marxism and the Existentialists*. New York: Harper, 1969. (Translation of part of *D'Une Sainte Famille à L'Autre: Essai sur les Marxismes Imaginaires*. Paris: Gallimard, 1969).

Augé, Marc. *Symbole, Fonction, Histoire: les Interrogations de l'Anthropologie*. Paris: Hachette, 1979.

Bachelard, Gaston. *Le Nouvel Esprit Scientifique*. Paris: PUF, 1934.

— *La Poétique de l'espace*. Paris: PUF, 1957.

Badcock, G. R. *Lévi-Strauss: Structuralism and Sociological Theory*.London: Hutchinson, 1975.

Bakhtin, Mikhail. 1978. *Esthétique et Théorie du Roman*. Paris: Gallimard.

Tr. of *Voprosy Literatury i Estetiki,* Moscow, 1975.
— *Problems of Dostoevsky's Poetics.* Minneapolis: Univ. of Minnesota Press, 1984. Translated by Caryl Emerson. (*Problemy poétiki Doestoevskogo,* Moscow, 1963 (1st ed., Leningrad, 1929)).
Barthes, Roland. *Michelet par lui-même.* Paris: Seuil, 1954.
— *On Racine.* New York: Hill and Wang, 1964. Translated by Richard Howard. (*Sur Racine.* Paris: Seuil, 1963.)
— *Critique et Vérité.* Paris: Seuil, 1966
— *Writing Degree Zero.* London: Cape, 1967. Translated by Annette Lavers and Colin Smith. (*Le Degré Zéro de l'Ecriture.* Paris: Seuil, 1953.)
— *Elements of Semiology.* London: Cape, 1967. Translated by Annette Lavers and Colin Smith. (*Eléments de Sémiologie.* Paris: Seuil, 1964.)
— *Système de la Mode.* Paris: Seuil, 1967. (English translation 1985.)
— *Mythologies.* London: Cape, 1972. Partial translation by Annette Lavers. (*Mythologies.* Paris: Seuil, 1957.)
— *Critical Essays.* Evanston: Northwestern University Press, 1972. Translated by Richard Howard. (*Essais critiques.* Paris: Seuil, 1964.)
— *S/Z.* London: Cape, 1975. Translated by Richard Miller. (*S/Z* Paris: Seuil, 1970.)
— *The Pleasure of the Text.* London: Cape, 1976. Translated by Richard Miller. (*Le Plaisir du Texte.* Paris: Seuil, 1973.)
— *Sade/Fourier/Loyola.* London: Cape, 1977. Translated by Richard Miller. (*Sade/Fourier/Loyola.* Paris: Seuil, 1974.)
— *Roland Barthes by Roland Barthes.* London: Macmillan, 1977. Translated by Richard Howard. *Roland Barthes par Roland Barthes.* Paris: Seuil, 1975.
— *Image, Music, Text.* London: Fontana Paperbacks, 1977. Essays selected and translated by Stephen Heath.
— *Sollers écrivain.* Paris: Seuil, 1979.
— *A Lover's Discourse: Fragments.* London: Cape, 1979. Translated by Richard Howard. (*Fragments d'un discours amoureux.* Paris: Seuil, 1977.)
— *New Critical Essays.* London: Cape, 1980. Translated by Richard Howard (*Nouveaux essais critiques.* Paris: Seuil, 1972.)
— *Le Grain de la Voix. Entretiens 1962–1980.* Paris: Seuil, 1981.
— *Empire of Signs.* New York: Hill and Wang, 1982. Translated by Richard Howard. (*L'Empire des signes.* Geneva: Skira, 1970.)
— *Camera Lucida: Reflections on Photography.* London: Cape, 1982. Translated by Richard Howard (*La Chambre Claire: note sur la photographie.* Paris: Gallimard and Seuil, 1980.)
— *L'Obvie et l'Obtus-Essais Critiques III.* Paris: Seuil, 1982. Translated by R. Howard as *The Responsibility of Forms.* Oxford: Blackwell, 1986.
— *Barthes: Selected Writings.* Ed. by Susan Sontag. London: Cape, 1982
— *The Grain of the Voice* Translated by Linda Coverdale, London: Cape, 1985
Bastide, Roger, ed. *Sens et Usage du Mot Structure.* The Hague: Mouton, 1962.
Bataillon, Marcel. *Défense et Illustration du Sens Littéral.* Modern Humanities Research Association (pamphlet). Leeds, 1967.
Bateson, Gregory. *Naven: A Survey of the Problems suggested by a Composite Picture of the Culture of a New Guinea Tribe drawn from three points of view.* Stanford, California: Stanford University Press, 1936.

Baudrillard, Jean. *Le Miroir de la Production—l'Illusion Critique du Matérialisme Historique.* Paris: Casterman, 1974.

Béguin, Albert. *Balzac Visionnaire,* Geneva: Skira, 1946; repr. in *Balzac Lu et Relu,* Paris: Seuil, 1965.

Bell, Daniel. *The Cultural Contradictions of Capitalism.* London: Heinemann, 1976.

Benjamin, Walter. *Illuminations.* Ed. and introduced by Hannah Arendt. Translated by Harry Zohn. London: Fontana, 1973.

— *Das Passagenwerk* (Gesammelte Schriften v), 2 vols ed. by Rolf Tiedemann. Frankfurt: Suhrkamp, 1982.

Bennett, Tony. *Formalism and Marxism.* London: Methuen, 1979.

Benoist, Jean-Marie. *La Révolution Structurale.* Paris: Grasset, 1976.

Benveniste, Emile. *Problems in General Linguistics.* Miami: Miami University Press, 1971 (Fr. original, Paris: Gallimard, 1966).

Bergson, Henri. *Oeuvres.* Paris: PUF, 1959.

Berlin, Isaiah. *Four Essays on Liberty.* Oxford: OUP., 1969.

Berman, Marshall. *All That is Solid Melts Into Air: The Experience of Modernity.* New York: Simon and Shuster, 1982 and London: Verso, 1983.

Blanchot, Maurice. *La Part du Feu.* Paris: Gallimard, 1949

— *L'Espace Littéraire.* Paris: Gallimard, 1955

— *L'Entretien Infini.* Paris: Gallimard, 1969

Bloch, Maurice, ed. *Marxist Analysis and Social Anthropology.* London: Malaby Press, 1975.

Blumenberg, Hans. *The Legitimacy of the Modern Age.* Translated by Robert M. Wallace. German original, Frankfurt: Suhrkamp, 1966, 1976.

Bobbio, Norberto. *Existentialism.* Oxford: Blackwell, 1948.

Boon, James. *From Symbolism to Structuralism: Lévi-Strauss in a Literary Tradition.* New York: Harper and Row, 1972.

Boudon, Raymond, *A quoi sert la notion de "structure"? Essai sur la signification de la notion de structure dans les sciences humaines.* Paris: Gallimard, 1968.

Boudon, Raymond and Bourricaud, François: *Dictionnaire Critique de la Sociologie.* Paris: Presses Universitaires de France, 1982.

Bourdieu, Pierre. *Outline of a Theory of Practice.* Translated by Richard Nice. Cambridge: CUP, 1977.

Bouveresse, Jacques. *Le Philosophe chez les Autophages.* Paris: Minuit, 1984.

Bradbury, Malcolm and McFarlane, James, eds. *Modernism 1890–1930.* Harmondsworth: Penguin, 1976.

Bühler, Karl. *Sprachtheorie.* Jena: Fischer, 1934. Spanish translation Madrid, 1950.

Burke, Kenneth. *Philosophy of Literary Form.* Baton Rouge: Louisiana State University, 1941.

Butler, Christopher. *After the Wake. An Essay on the Contemporary Avant-Garde,* 1980.

— *Interpretation, Deconstruction and Ideology.* Oxford: Clarendon, 1984.

Calvet, Louis-Jean. *Roland Barthes: Un Regard Politique sur le Signe.* Paris: Payot, 1973.

Cardinal, Roger and Short, Robert. *Surrealism: Permanent Revelation.* London, 1970.

264

Cardoso de Oliveira, Roberto. *Enigmas e soluções*. Rio de Janeiro: Tempo Brasileiro, 1983.

Carrouges, Michel. *André Breton et les données fondamentales du surréalisme*. Paris: 1967.

Caruso, Paolo. *Conversazioni con Claude Lévi-Strauss, Michel Foucault, Jacques Lacan*. Milan: Mursia, 1969.

Charbonnier, Georges. *Conversations with Claude Lévi-Strauss*. London: Cape, 1969 (French original, 1961).

Chatman, Seymour (ed). *Literary Style: A Symposium*. Oxford: OUP, 1971.

Chomsky, Noam. *Aspects of the theory of syntax*. Cambridge, Mass: MIT, 1965.
— *Cartesian Linguistics*. London: Harper and Row, 1966.
— *Language and Mind*. New York: Harcourt, Brace and World, 1968.
— *Reflections on Language*. London: Temple Smith, 1976.
— *Language and Responsibility. Hassocks, Sussex: Harvester Press, 1979.* Translated by John Viertel. *Dialogues avec Mitsou Ronat*. Paris: Flammarion, 1977.

Clair, Jean. *Considérations sur l'état des Beaux-Arts: critique de la modernité*. Paris: Gallimard, 1983.

Clairmont, Christoph W. *Die Bildnisse des Antinous—ein Beitrag zur porträtplastik unter Kaiser Hadrian*. Rome: Schweiyerisches Institut, 1966.

Clark, K. and Holquist, M. *Mikhail Bakhtin*. Cambridge, Mass: Harvard University Press, 1984.

Clastres, Pierre. *La Société contre l'État*. Paris: Minuit, 1974.

Clément, Catherine. *Vies et Légendes de Jacques Lacan*. Paris: Grasset, 1981.

Compagnon, Antoine. *La Troisième République des Lettres: De Flaubert à Proust*. Paris: Seuil, 1983.

Coseriu, Eugenio. *Tradición y Novedad en la Ciencia del Lenguaje: estudios de historia de la lingüística*. Madrid: Gredos, 1977.

Coutinho, C. N., *O Estruturalismo e a Miséria da Razão*. Rio: Paz e Terra, 1972.

Coward, Rosalind and Ellis, John. *Language and Materialism: Developments in Semiology and the Theory of Subject*. London: RKP, 1977.

Culler, Jonathan. *Structuralist Poetics: Structuralism and the Study of Literature*. London: Routledge and Kegan Paul, 1975.
— *Saussure*. London: Fontana, 1976.
— *The Pursuit of Signs: Semiotics, Literature, Deconstruction*. London: Routledge and Kegan Paul, 1981.
— *On Deconstruction: Theory and Criticism after Structuralism*. Ithaca: Cornell University Press, 1982.
— *Barthes*. London: Fontana, 1983.

Curtius, Ernst Robert, *Balzac*. Bern: Francke, 1952 (translation, Milan: Mondadori, 1969).

Da Matta, Roberto. *Ensaios de Antropologia Estrutural*. Petrópolis: Vozes, 1973.

Davidson, Donald. *Inquiries into Truth and Interpretation*. Oxford: Clarendon, 1984.

De Dieguez, Manuel. *L'Ecrivain et son Langage*. Paris: Gallimard, 1960.

De George, Richard and Fernande, eds. *The Structuralists from Marx to Lévi-Strauss*. Garden City: Doubleday, 1972.

De Heusch, Luc. *Pourquoi l'épouser? et autres essais*. Paris: Gallimard, 1971.

Deleuze, Gilles and Guattari, Félix. *L'Anti-Oedipe: Capitalisme et Schizophrénie*. Paris: Minuit, 1972.

De Man, Paul.*Blindness and Insight: Essays in the Rhetoric of Contemporary Criticism*. London: Methuen, 1983 (1st ed. 1971).

Derrida, Jacques. *Speech and Phenomena and Other Essays on Husserl's Theory of Signs*. Evanston: Northwestern University Press, 1973. Translated by David B. Allison. (*La Voix et le phénomène: introduction au problème du signe dans la phénoménologie de Husserl*. Paris: Presses Universitaries de France, 1967.)

— *Glas*. Paris: Galilée, 1974.

— *Of Grammatology*. Baltimore: Johns Hopkins University Press, 1976. Translated by Gayatri Spivak. (*De la Grammatologie*. Paris: Minuit, 1967.)

— *Writing and Difference*. Chicago: Chicago University Press, 1978. Translated by Alan Bass. (*L'Ecriture et la différence*. Paris: Seuil, 1967.)

— *Spurs: Nietzsche's Styles*. Bilingual edition. Chicago: Chicago University Press, 1979. Translated by Barbara Harlow. (*Eperons: Les Styles de Nietzsche*. Paris: Flammarion, 1978.)

— *La Carte Postale de Socrate à Freud et au-delà*. Paris: Aubier-Flammarion, 1980. One of the essays, "*Le Facteur de la Vérité*", translated as *The Purveyor of Truth* by Willis Domingo, James Hulbert, Moshe Ron and Marie-Rose Logan in *Yale French Studies*, 52, 1975, pp. 31–113.

— *Dissemination*. Chicago: Chicago University Press, 1981. Translated by Barbara Johnson. (*La Dissémination*. Paris: Seuil, 1972.)

— *Positions*. Chicago: Chicago University Press, 1981. Translated by Alan Bass. (*Positions*. Paris: Minuit, 1972.)

— *Margins of Philosophy*. Chicago: Chicago University Press, 1982, Translated by Alan Bass. (*Marges de la Philosophie*. Paris: Minuit, 1972.)

Descombes, Vincent. *Modern French Philosophy*. Cambridge: CUP, 1980. (French edition *Le Même et L'Autre*, Paris: Minuit, 1979).

— *Grammaire d'objets en tous genres*. Paris: Minuit, 1983.

Doubrovsky, Serge. *The New Criticism in France*. Chicago: Chicago Univ. Press, 1973. Translated by Derek Cottman. (*Pourquoi la nouvelle critique?* Paris: Mercure de France, 1966.)

Douglas, Mary. *Purity and Danger, an analysis of concepts of pollution and taboo*. London: Routledge and Kegan Paul, 1976 (1st ed. 1966).

Duby, Georges. *Les Trois Ordres ou l'Imaginaire du Féodalisme*. Paris: Gallimard, 1978.

Ducrot, Oswald, ed. *Qu'est-ce que le structuralisme?* Paris: Seuil, 1968.

Dufrenne, Mikel. *Le Poétique*. Paris: PUF, 1973.

Eco, Umberto. *A Theory of Semiotics*. Bloomington: Indiana Univ. Press, 1976.

Ehrlich, Victor. *Russian Formalism: History–Doctrine*. The Hague: Mouton, 1955.

Ehrmann, Jacques, ed. *Structuralism*. New York: Doubleday, 1970 (originally *Yale French Studies*, 36–37, October 1966).

Eichenbaum, Boris. *Il giovane Tolstoy. La Teoria del Metodo Formale*. Bari: De Donato, 1968 (Russian original, 1926).

Eliade, Mircea. *Cosmos and History*. New York: Harper, 1959.

Elster, Jon. *Sour Grapes: Studies in the Subversion of Rationality*. Cambridge: CUP, 1983.

Evans-Pritchard, E. E. *Social Anthropology*. London: Routledge and Kegan Paul, 1972. (1st ed. 1951).

— *Essays in Social Anthropology*. London: Faber, 1962.

Felperin, Howard. *Beyond Deconstruction: The Uses and Abuses of Literary Theory*. Oxford: Clarendon, 1985.

Ferry, Luc and Renaut, Alain. *La Pensée 68—essai sur l'anti-humanisme contemporain*. Paris: Gallimard, 1985

Finas, Lucette, ed. *Écarts, Quatre Essais à propos de Jacques Derrida*. Paris: Fayard, 1973.

Fodor, Jerry A. and Katz, J. eds. *The Structure of Language: Readings in the Philosophy of Language*. Cambridge, Mass: MIT, 1964.

Fokkema, D. W. and Kunne-Ibsch, Elrod. *Theories of Literature in the Twentieth Century: Structuralism, Marxism, Aesthetics of Reception, Semiotics*. London: Hurst, 1977.

Foucault, Michel. *The Order of Things: an archaeology of the human sciences*. London: Tavistock, 1970. (*Les mots et les choses*. Paris: Gallimard, 1966.)

— *Madness and Civilization: A History of Insanity in the Age of Reason*. London: Tavistock, 1971 Translated by Richard Howard. (*Histoire de la folie à l'âge classique*. Paris: Gallimard, 1964; 1st ed., 1961.)

— *The Archaeology of Knowledge*. London: Tavistock, 1972. Translated by A. M. Sheridan Smith. (*L'Archéologie du Savoir*. Paris: Gallimard, 1969.)

— *Power/Knowledge: Selected interviews and other writings 1972–1977*. Brighton: Harvester, 1980

Fox, Robin. *Kinship and Marriage: An Anthropological Perspective*. Harmondsworth: Penguin, 1967.

Frank, Manfred. *Was ist Neostrukturalismus?* Frankfurt: Suhrkamp, 1983.

Freeman, Donald C. *Linguistics and Literary Style*. New York: Holt, Rinehart and Winston, 1970.

Frye, Northrop. *Anatomy of Criticism: Four Essays*. Princeton: Princeton Univ. Press, 1957.

Galan, František, *Historic Structures: The Prague School Project, 1928–1946*. London: Croom Helm, 1985.

Gardner, Howard. *The Quest for Mind: Piaget, Lévi-Strauss and the Structuralist Movement*. London: Quartet Books, 1976 (1st ed. New York: Knopf, 1972).

Garvin, Paul L. *A Prague School Reader on Aesthetics, Literary Structure and Style*. Washington DC: Georgetown Univ. Press, 1964.

Geertz, Clifford. *The Interpretation of Cultures*. London: Hutchinson, 1975.

Gellner, Ernest. *Words and Things: An Examination of, and an attack on, Linguistic Philosophy*. London: Routledge and Kegan Paul, 1959.

— *Cause and Meaning in the Social Sciences*. London: Routledge and Kegan Paul, 1973.

— *The Devil in Modern Philosophy*. London: RKP, 1974.

— *Spectacles and Predicaments: Essays in Social Theory*. Cambridge: CUP, 1979.

— *Relativism and the Social Sciences.* Cambridge: CUP, 1985.
Gellner, E., ed. *Soviet and Western Anthropology.* New York: Columbia UP, 1980.
Genette, Gérard. *Figures I.* Paris: Seuil, 1966.
— *Figures II.* Paris: Seuil, 1969.
— *Figures III.* Paris: Seuil, 1972.
— *Introduction à l'architexte.* Paris: Seuil, 1979.
Gilbert, K. and Kuhn, H. *A History of Aesthetics.* New York: Dover, 1972 (1st ed. Indiana UP, 1939).
Glucksmann, Miriam. *Structuralist Analysis in Contemporary Social Thought.* London: RKP, 1974.
Godel, R. *Les Sources manuscrites du 'Cours de Linguistique Générale' de F. de Saussure.* Geneva, 1957.
Godelier, Maurice. *Horizon, trajets marxistes en anthropologie.* Paris: Maspero, 1977 (2 vols; 1st ed. 1973).
Goldmann, Lucien. *The Hidden God.* London: Routledge and Kegan Paul, 1964. (*Le Dieu caché.* Paris: Gallimard, 1959).
— *Pour une sociologie du roman.* Paris: Gallimard, 1964.
Gombrich, E. H. *The Sense of Order.* Oxford: Phaidon, 1979.
Graff, Gerald. *Literature Against Itself: Literary Ideas in Modern Society.* Chicago: Chicago Univ. Press, 1979.
Granger, Gilles Gaston. *Pensée Formelle et Sciences de l'Homme.* Paris: Aubier, 1967.
Greimas, A. J. *Sémantique Structurale.* Paris: Larousse, 1966. *Du Sens.* Paris: Seuil, 1970.
Gurvitch, Georges and Moore, Wilbert, eds. *Sociology in the Twentieth Century.* New York: Philosophical Library, 1945.
Habermas, Jürgen. *Der Philosophische Diskurs der Moderne.* Frankfurt: Suhrkamp, 1985.
Harman, Gilbert, ed. *On Noam Chomsky: Critical Essays.* New York: Anchor, 1974.
Harris, Marvin. *The Rise of Anthropological Theory.* New York: Crowell, 1968.
Harris, Roy. *The Language Myth.* London: Duckworth, 1981.
Hartman, Geoffrey H. *Beyond Formalism: Literary Essays 1958–1970.* New Haven: Yale Univ. Press, 1970.
Hawkes, Terence. *Structuralism and Semiotics.* London: Methuen, 1977.
Hayes, E. Nelson and Tanya, eds. *Claude Lévi-Strauss: The Anthropologist as Hero.* Cambridge, Mass.: MIT Press, 1970.
Heath, Stephen. *Vertige du déplacement: Lecture de Barthes.* Paris: Fayard, 1974.
Heidegger, Martin. *The End of Philosophy.* Translated from Vol. II of *Nietzsche* (Pfullingen, 1961) by Joan Stambaugh. New York: Harper and Row, 1973.
— *Identität und Differenz.* Pfullingen: Neske, 1957. (Eng. tr., New York: Harper, 1969).
Hegel, Georg Wilhelm Friedrich. *The Philosophy of History.* Introd. by C. J. Friedrich. New York: Dover, 1956.
— *Phenomenology of Spirit.* Translated by A. V. Miller. Oxford: OUP, 1977.
Hjelmslev, Louis. *Prolegomena to a Theory of Language.* Madison: Wisconsin

Univ. Press. 1961. Translated by Francis J. Whitfield from the Danish original, Copenhagen, 1943.

Holenstein, Elmar. *Jakobson ou le structuralisme phénoménologique*. Paris: Seghers, 1974.

Holub, Robert C. *Reception Theory—A Critical Introduction*. London: Methuen, 1984.

Homans, George Caspar. *Social Behaviour: Its Elementary Forms*. New York: Harcourt, Brace and World, 1961.

Honneth, Axel. *Kritik der Macht*. Frankfurt: Suhrkamp, 1983.

Honour, Hugh. *New-Classicism*. Harmondsworth: Penguin, 1968

— *Romanticism*. Harmondworth: Penguin, 1979.

Hyman, Stanley, Edgar. *The Armed Vision: A Study in the Methods of Modern Literary Criticism*. New York: Knopf, 1948.

Ivanov, V. V. et al. Michail Bachtin. *Semiotica, teoria della letteratura e marxismo*. Bari: Dedalo, 1977.

Jakobson, Roman. *Essais de Linguistique Générale*. Tr. from the English by Nicholas Ruvet. Paris: Minuit, 1963.

— *Questions de Poétique*. Paris: Seuil, 1973.

Jakobson, Roman and Halle, Morris. *The Fundamentals of Language*. The Hague: Mouton, 1956.

Jameson, Fredric. *The Prison-House of Language: A Critical Account of Structuralism and Russian Formalism*. Princeton: Princeton Univ. Press, 1972.

— *Marxism and Form*. Princeton: Princeton Univ. Press, 1971.

— *The Political Unconscious—Narrative as a Socially Symbolic Act*. London: Methuen, 1986.

Jarvie, I. C. *The Revolution in Anthropology*. Chicago: Gateway, 1969. (1st ed. London: Routledge and Kegan Paul, 1964).

Jenkins, Alan. *The Social Theory of Claude Lévi-Strauss*. London: Macmillan, 1979.

Johnson, Barbara. *The Critical Difference: Essays in the Contemporary Rhetoric of Reading*. Baltimore: Johns Hopkins Univ. Press, 1980.

Jones, Robert Emmet. *Panorama de la nouvelle critique en France: de Gaston Bachelard à Jean-Paul Weber*. Paris: Sedes, 1968.

Juranville, Alain. *Lacan et la philosophie*. Paris: Presses Universitaires de France, 1980.

Kermode, Frank. *Romantic Image*. London: Routledge and Kegan Paul, 1957.

— *The Sense of an Ending: Studies in the Theory of Fiction*. Oxford: OUP, 1967.

Klossowski, Pierre. *Les derniers travaux de Gulliver suivi de Sade et Fourier*. Montpellier: Fata Morgana, 1974.

Korn, Francis. *Elementary Structures Reconsidered: Lévi-Strauss on Kinship*. London: Tavistock, 1973.

Kristeva, Julia. *Sémiotiké: Recherches pour une Sémanalyse*. Paris: Seuil, 1969.

— *La Révolution du Langage Poétique*. Paris: Seuil, 1974.

Kroeber, A. L. *Anthropology: Culture, Patterns and Processes*. New York: Harbinger, 1963.

Kuper, Adam. *Anthropologists and Anthropology: The British School 1922-72*. Harmondsworth: Penguin, 1975. (1st ed. London: Allen Lane, 1973).

Kurzweil, Edith. *The Age of Structuralism: Lévi-Strauss to Foucault*. New York:

Columbia Univ. Press. 1980.

Lacan, Jacques. *Ecrits: A Selection*. Translated by A. Sheridan-Smith. London: Tavistock, 1977. (Fr. original, Paris: Seuil, 1966).

— *The Language of the Self: the Function of Language in Psychoanalysis*. Tr. by A. Wilden (also a selection from *Ecrits*). Baltimore: Johns Hopkins University Press, 1978.

— *The Four Fundamental Concepts of Psychoanalysis*. (*Le Séminaire, livre XI: Les Quatre Concepts fondamentaux de la psychanalyse*, ed. Jacques-Alain Miller; Paris: Seuil, 1973.) London, Hogarth Press, 1978.

Lardreau, Guy and Jambet, Christian. *L'Ange (Ontologie de la Révolution, I)*. Paris: Grasset, 1976.

Leach, Edmond. *Rethinking Anthropology*. London: Athlone Press, 1961.

— *Lévi-Strauss*. London: Fontana, 1970.

— *Culture and Communication: The logic by which symbols are connected. An introduction to the use of structuralist analysis in social anthropology*. Cambridge: Cambridge University Press, 1976.

Leach, Edmond, ed. *The Structural Study of Myth and Totemism*. London: Tavistock, 1967.

Leaf, Murray. *Man, Mind and Science: a history of anthropology*. New York: Columbia University Press, 1978.

Leitch, Vincent B. *Deconstructive Criticism: An advanced introduction*. New York: Columbia Univ. Press, 1983.

Lemaire, Anika. *Jacques Lacan*. London: RKP, 1977 (Translated and revised by David Macey. Brussels: Charles Denart, 1970).

Lemon, Lee T. and Reis, Marion J. *Russian Formalist Criticism: Four Essays*. Lincoln: Nebraska Univ. press. 1965.

Lentricchia, Frank. *After the New Criticism*. London: Athlone, 1980.

— *Criticism and Social Change*. Chicago: Univ. of Chicago Press, 1983.

Lepschy, Giulio C. *La Lingustica Strutturale*. Torino: Einaudi, 1966.

Lerner, Laurence. ed. *Reconstructing Literature*. Oxford: Blackwell, 1983.

Levin, Harry. *The Gates of Horn:* A Study of Five French Realists. New York: Oxford University Press, 1963.

Lévi-Strauss, Claude. *Race and History*. Paris: Unesco, 1952. Simultaneously published in French: *Race et Histoire*, Paris, 1952.

— *Structural Anthropology*. New York: Basic Books, 1963. (*Anthropologie Structurale* Paris: Plon, 1958.)

— *Totemism*. Boston: Beacon Press, 1963. Translated by Rodney Needham. (*Le Totémisme d'aujord'hui*. Paris: Presses Univ. de France,. 1962.)

— *The Savage Mind*. Chicago: Chicago Univ. Press, 1966. (*La pensée sauvage*. Paris: Plon, 1962.)

— *The Scope of Anthropology*. London: Cape, 1967. Translated by Sherry Ortner Paul and Robert A. Paul. (*Leçon inaugurale*, Collège de France. Paris: Gallimard, 1960.)

— *Elementary Structures of Kinship*. Boston: Beacon Press, 1969. Translated by James Bell, John von Sturmer and Rodney Needham. (*Les structures élémentaires de la parenté*. Paris: Presses Univ. de France, 1949.)

— *The Raw and the Cooked*. New York: Harper and Row, 1969. Translated by John and Doreen Weightman. (*Mythologiques, I. Le Cru et le Cuit*. Paris: Plon, 1964.)

270

— *Tristes Tropiques*. London: Cape, 1973. (Penguin ed., 1976). Translated by John and Doreen Weightman. (*Tristes Tropiques*. Paris: Plon, 1955. repr. (in the 10/18 series) 1966.)
— *From Honey to Ashes*. New York: Harper and Row, 1973. Translated by John and Doreen Weightman. (*Mythologiques II. Du miel aux cendres.* Paris: Plon, 1966.)
— *Structural Anthropology II*. New York: Basic Books, 1976. (*Anthropologie Structurale*. Paris: Plon, 1973.)
— *Mythologiques III, L'origine des manières de table.* Paris: Plon, 1968. (*The Origin of Table Manners*. London: Cape, 1978. Translated by John Weightman.)
— *Myth and Meaning*. London: Routledge and Kegan Paul, 1978.
— *Claude Lévi-Strauss*. Texts of and on Claude Lévi-Strauss. Edited by Raymond Bellour and Catherine Clément. Paris: Gallimard, 1979.
— *Mythologiques IV. L'Homme nu.* Paris: Plon, 1971. (*The Naked Man.* London: Cape, 1981. Translated by John and Doreen Weightman.)
— *The Way of the Masks*. London: Cape, 1983. Translated by Sylvia Modelski. *La Voie des Masques*. Geneva: Skira, 1975.)
— *Paroles Données*. Paris: Plon, 1984
— *The View From Afar*. New York: Basic Books, 1985. Translation by Joachim Neugroschel and Phoebe Hoss. (*Le Regard Eloigné*. Paris: Plon,1983.)
— *La Potière Jalouse*. Paris: Plon, 1985.
Lewis, I. M. *Social Anthropology in Perspective*. Harmondsworth: Penguin, 1976.
Lodge, David. *Working with Structuralism: Essays and Reviews on Nineteenth and Twentieth Century Literature.* London: Routledge and Kegan Paul, 1981.
Lotman, J. M. *La Struttura del Testo Poetico*. Milan: Mursia, 1972. (Translated from *Struktura Chudozestvennogo teksta*. Moscow: Iskusstvo, 1970). *The Structure of the Artistic Text.* Tr. by Ronald Vroon. Ann Arbor: Michigan Slavic Contributions, 1977.
Lowie, Robert H. *Primitive Society*. New York: Boni and Liveright, 1920.
Löwith, Karl. *Meaning in History*. Chicago: Chicago U.P., 1949.
Lukács, Georg. *The Historical Novel*. New York: Humanities Press, 1965. Translated by Hannah and Stanley Mitchell. (A történelmi regény. Budapest: Hungaria, 1947.)
— *Studies in European Realism: A Sociological Survey of Stendhal, Zola, Tolstoy, Gorki and others.* London: Hillway, 1948. *Essays über Realismus*. Berlin: Aufbau).
Lyotard, Jean-François. *Economie Libidinale*. Paris: Minuit, 1974.
— *La Condition Post-Moderne*. Paris: Minuit, 1979.
Macchia, Giovanni. *Il Paradiso della ragione: L'ordine e l'avventura nella tradizione letteraria francese*. Turin: Einaudi, 1960.
Macherey, Pierre. *A Theory of Literary Production*. London: NLB, 1978. (Fr. original, Paris: Maspero 1966).
Macksey, Richard and Donato, Eugenio, eds. *The Structuralist Controversy: The Languages of Criticism and the Sciences of Man.* Baltimore: Johns Hopkins U.P. 1970.
Magny, Claude-Edmonde. *Les Sandales d'Empédocle—essai sur les limites de la littérature,* Paris: Payot, 1945.

Malmberg, Bertil. *Les Nouvelles Tendances de la Linguistique*. Paris: PUF, 1966. Translated by Jacques Gengoux of *Nya Vagar Inom Sparkforskningen—En orientering i modern lingvistik*. Stockholm: Svenska Bokförlaget, 1962.

Mandelbaum, Maurice. *History, Man and Reason: a study in nineteenth century thought*. Baltimore: Johns Hopkins UP, 1971.

Manners, Robert A. and Kaplan, David, eds. *Theory in Anthropology—A comprehensive sourcebook of classic and contemporary views of anthropological theory, covering its definition, development, application and confirmation*. Chicago: Aldine, 1968.

Marino, Adrian. *La critique des idées littéraires*. Paris: PUF, 1977.

Martinet, A. *Éléments de linguistique générale*. Paris: A. Colin, 1960.

Martinet, A. et al., *To Honour Roman Jakobson*. The Hague: Mouton, 1967.

Matamoro, Blas. *Saber y literatura: Por una epistemología de la critica literaria*. Madrid: Ediciones de la Torre, 1980.

Matejka, Ladislau and Pomorska, Krystyna, eds. *Readings in Russian Poetics: Formalist and Structuralist Views:* Cambridge Mass. MIT, 1971.

Matejka, Ladislau and Titunik, I. R., eds. *Semiotics of Art*. Cambridge, Mass.: MIT, 1976.

Mauss, Marcel. *Sociologie et Anthropologie*. Paris: Presses Univ. de France, 1950.

— *The Gift*. London: Routledge and Kegan Paul, 1969. Translation of *Essai sur le Don*, 1925.

McConnell, R. B., ed. *Science and Human Progress*. London: John Murray, 1983.

Megill, Alan. *Prophets of Extremity: Nietzsche, Heidegger, Foucault, Derrida*. Berkeley: California Univ. Press, 1985.

Merleau-Ponty, Maurice. *Phenomenology of Perception*. Translated by C. Smith. London: RKP, 1962. (Fr. ed., Paris:Gallimard, 1945.)

— *Signs*. Translated by R. McCleary. Evanston, Illinois: Northwestern Univ. Press, 1964. (Fr. ed., Paris: Gallimard, 1960).

Merquior, J. G. *Formalismo e Tradição Moderna*. Rio de Janeiro: Forense Universitária, 1974.

— *L'Esthétique de Lévi-Strauss*. Paris: Presses Univ. de France, 1977.

— *The Veil and the Mask: Essays on Culture and Ideology*. London: Routledge and Kegan Paul, 1979.

— *As idéias e as formas*. Rio de Janeiro: Nova Fronteira, 1981.

— *Foucault*. London: Fontana, 1985.

— *Western Marxism*. London: Paladin, 1986.

Merton, Robert K. *Social Theory and Social Structure*, enlarged edn. New York: Free Press, 1968 (1st ed., 1949).

Meschonnic, Henri. *Pour la poétique*. Paris: Gallimard, 1970.

— *Le signe et le poème*. Paris: Gallimard, 1975.

Momigliano, Arnaldo. *Essays in Ancient and Modern Historiography*. Oxford: OUP, 1975.

Montefiore, Alan, ed. *Philosophy in France Today*. Cambridge: CUP, 1983.

Moore, Arthur K. *Contestable Concepts of Literary Theory*. Baton Rouge: Louisiana State Univ. Press, 1973.

Morin, Edgar and Piattelli-Palmarini, Massimo, eds. *L'Unité de l'homme:*

272

invariants biologiques et universaux culturels. Paris: Seuil, 1974.

Morot-Sir, Edouard. *La Pensée Française d'Aujourd'hui*. Paris: PUF, 1971.

Mounin, Georges. *Introduction à la Sémiologie*. Paris: Minuit, 1970.

Mounin, Georges, *Saussure ou le structuraliste sans le savoir*. Paris: Seghers, 1968.

— *Linguistique e philosophie* Paris: Presses Universitaires de France, 1975.

Mukařovsky, Jan. *Aesthetic Function, Norm and Value as Social Facts*, translated by Mark Suino. Ann Arbor: Univ. of Michigan Press, 1970 (Czech original, Prague 1934).

— *The Word and Verbal Art*. (selected essays). Translated and edited by John Burbank and Peter Steiner. New Haven: Yale Univ. Press, 1977.

— *Structure, Sign and Function* (selected essays). Translated by John Burbank and Peter Steiner. New Haven: Yale Univ. Press, 1978.

Nadeau, Maurice. *History of Surrealism*. London: 1968 (Fr. ed., Paris, 1964).

Nadel, S.F. *The Foundations of Social Anthropology*. London: Cohen and West, 1951.

— *The Theory of Social Structure*. London: Lowe and Brydone, 1957.

Needham, Rodney. *Structure and Sentiment: A Test Case in Social Anthropology*. Chicago: Chicago Univ. Press., 1962.

Nochlin, Linda. *Realism*. Harmondsworth: Penguin, 1971.

Norris, Christopher. *Deconstruction: Theory and Practice*. London: Methuen, 1982.

— *The Deconstructive Turn: essays in the rhetoric of philosophy*. London: Methuen, 1983.

Novotny, Fritz. *Painting and Sculpture in Europe 1780 to 1880*. Harmondsworth: Penguin, 1960.

Nuttal, A. D. *A New Mimesis: Shakespeare and the Representation of Reality*. London: Methuen, 1983.

Pace, David. *Claude Lévi-Strauss: The Bearer of Ashes*. London: Routledge and Kegan Paul, 1983.

Panofsky, Erwin. *Studies in Iconology*. Oxford: OUP, 1939.

— *Meaning in the Visual Arts*. New York: Doubleday, 1955.

Papineau, David. *Theory and Meaning*. Oxford: Clarendon, 1979.

Passmore, John. *Recent Philosophers:* London: Duckworth, 1985.

Paz, Octavio. *Claude Lévi-Strauss: An Introduction*. Ithaca: Cornell UP, 1970. Translation of *Claude Lévi-Strauss o el Festín de Esopo*, Mexico, 1968.

Peacock, James L. *Consciousness and Change: Symbolic Anthropology in Evolutionary Perspective*. Oxford: Blackwell, 1975.

Peirce, Charles Sanders. *Collected Papers* (8 vols.). Edited by Charles Hartshorne, Paul Weiss and Arthur W. Burks. Cambridge, Mass: Harvard Univ. Press, 1931–58.

Perowne, Stewart. *Hadrian*. Westport, Connecticut: Greenwood Press, 1960.

Pettit, Philip. *The Concept of Structuralism*. London: Macmillan, 1976.

Piaget, Jean. *Structuralism*. New York: Basic Books, 1970. (Translated and edited by Chaninah Maschler from *Le Structuralisme*. Paris: Presses Universitaires de France, 1968).

— *The Essential Piaget—An Interpretative Reference and Guide*. Edited by Howard Gruber and Jacques Vonèche. London: RKP. 1972.

Pike, Chris. ed. *The Futurists, The Formalists and the Marxist Critique*. London:

Ink Links, 1979.

Podro, Michael. *The Manifold in Perception: Theories of Art from Kant to Hildebrand.* Oxford: Clarendon, 1972.

— *The Critical Historians of Art.* New Haven: Yale UP, 1982.

Pöggeler, Otto. *Der Denkweg Martin Heideggers.* Pfüllingen: Neske, 1963.

Pomorska, Krystyna. *Russian Formalist Theory and Its Poetic Ambiance.* The Hague: Mouton, 1968.

Popper, Karl. *The Poverty of Historicism.* London: RKP, 1957.

Poster, Mark. *Existential Marxism in Postwar France: from Sartre to Althusser.* Princeton UP, 1975.

Pouillon, Jean and Maranda P., eds. *Echanges et Communications.* The Hague: Mouton, 1970.

Prado Coelho, Eduardo. Os universos da crítica. Lisboa: Edições 70, 1982.

Praz, Mario. *The Romantic Agony.* Translated by Angus Davidson. New York: Meridien, 1956 (2nd ed., Oxford, 1952).

Propp, V. I. *Morphology of the Folktale.* Austin: Texas Univ. Press 1958. (2nd ed. revised and edited by Louis A. Wagner, 1968). 1st Russian ed., Leningrad, 1928.

Putnam, Hilary. *Meaning and the Moral Sciences.* London: Routledge & Kegan Paul, 1978.

Quine, Willard van Orman. *From a Logical Point of View.* New York: Harper and Row, 1963 (1st ed. 1953).

Radcliffe-Brown, A. R. *Structure and Function in Primitive Society.* London: Cohen and West, 1952.

Raimondi, Ezio. *Techniche della critica letteraria.* Turin: Einaudi, 1967.

Ray, William. *Literary Meaning: From Phenomenology to Deconstruction.* Oxford: Blackwell, 1984.

Remotti, Francesco. *Lévi-Strauss. Struttura e Storia.* Turin: Einaudi, 1971.

Rex, John, ed. *Approaches to Sociology: An Introduction to Major Trends in British Sociology.* London: RKP, 1974.

Riffaterre, Michael. *Essais de stylistique structurale.* Paris. Flammarion, 1971.

Robey, David, ed. *Structuralism. An Introduction.* Oxford: Clarendon, 1973.

Rorty, Richard. *Consequences of Pragmatism.* (Essays 1972–1980) Minneapolis: Minnesota Univ. Press, 1982.

Rose, Gillian. *Dialectic of Nihilism: Post-Structuralism and Law.* Oxford: Blackwell, 1984.

Rossi, Ino, ed. *The Unconscious in Culture: The Structuralism of Claude Lévi-Strauss in Perspective.* New York: Dutton, 1974.

Rotenstreich, Nathan. *Philosophy, History and Politics: Studies in Contemporary English Philosopy of History.* The Hague: Martinus Nijhoff, 1976.

Ryan, Michael. *Marxism and Deconstruction: a Critical Articulation.* Baltimore: Johns Hopkins UP, 1982.

Sampson, Geoffrey. *Schools of Linguistics: Competition and Evolution.* London: Hutchinson, 1980.

Sapir, Edward. *Selected Writings.* Berkeley: California UP, 1934.

Sartre, Jean-Paul. *What is Literature?* Translated by B. Frechtman. London: Methuen, 1950. (*Situations II.* Paris: Gallimard, 1948).

— *Being and Nothingness.* London: Methuen, 1959. Translated by H.

274

Barnes. (*L'Etre et le néant: essai d'ontologie phénoménologique*. Paris: Gallimard, 1943)

— *Saint Genet, Actor and Martyr*. London: W. H. Allen, 1964. Translated by B. Frechtman. (*Saint Genet comédian et martyr*. Paris: Gallimard, 1952)

— *Critique of Dialectical Reason: Theory of Practical Ensembles*. London: New Left, 1976. Translated by Alan Sheridan-Smith. (*Critique de la Raison dialectique: Vol. I. Théorie des ensembles pratiques*. Paris: Gallimard, 1960)

Saussure, Ferdinand de. *Course in General Linguistics*. London: Fontana 1974. Translated by Wade Baskin. (*Cours de Linguistique Générale*. ed. Charles Bally, Albert Sechehaye with Albert Riedlinger, 1916)

Schiwy, Gunther. *Der französische Strukturalismus*. Reibbek: 1969. (Spanish translation by Urs Jaeggi, *El Estructuralismo como método y moda*. Caracas: Monte Ávila: 1972.)

Scholes, Robert. *Structuralism in Literature: An Introduction*. New Haven: Yale University Press, 1974.

— *Textual Power: Literary Theory and the Teaching of English*. New Haven: Yale University Press, 1985.

Seabra, José Augusto. *Poética de Barthes*. Oporto: Brasília Editora, 1980.

Sebeok, Thomas A., ed. *Style in Language*. Cambridge, Mass.: MIT, 1960.

— *Current Trends in Linguistics vol. III: Theoretical Foundations*, 1966.

— *Approaches to Semiotics*. The Hague: Mouton, 1969.

— *Current Trends in Linguistics vol. XII: Linguistics and Adjacent Arts and Sciences*. (3 vols.) The Hague: Mouton, 1973.

— *The Tell-Tale Sign. A Survey of Semiotics*. Lisse: De Ridder, 1975.

Sedlmayr, Hans. *Die Revolution der Modernen Kunst*. Munich: Rowohlt, 1955.

Selden, Raman. *Criticism and Objectivity*. London: George Allen and Unwin, 1984.

Segre, Cesare. *Semiotics and Literary Criticism*. The Hague: Mouton, 1973. Translated by John Meddemmen. (*I Segni e la Critica*. Turin: Einaudi, 1969.)

Serres, Michel. *Hermès I: La Communication*. Paris: Minuit, 1968.

Shattuck, Roger. *The Innocent Eye: On Modern Literature and the Arts*. New York: Farrar, Strauss, Giroux, 1984.

Shalvey, Thomas. *Claude Lévi-Strauss: Social Psychotherapy and the Collective Unconscious*. London: Harvester Press.

Simmel, Georg. *Philosophie der Mode*. Berlin: Pan, 1905.

Skinner, Quentin, ed. *The Return of Grand Theory in the Human Sciences*. Cambridge: Cambridge Univ. Press, 1985.

Skorupski, John. *Symbol and Theory*. Cambridge: CUP, 1979.

Sloterdijk, Peter. *Kritik der Zynischen Vernunft* (2 vols). Frankfurt: Suhrkamp, 1983.

Sontag, Susan. *Against Interpretation*. London: NLB, 1967.

Sperber, Dan. *Rethinking Symbolism*. Cambridge: CUP, 1975. Translated by Alice L. Morton; French original Paris: Hermann, 1974.

Spink, J. S. *French Free-Thought From Gassendi to Voltaire*. New York: Greenwood, 1960.

Steiner, George. *Extraterritorial: Papers on Literature and the Language Revolution*. Harmondsworth: Penguin, 1975 (1st ed. 1971).

— *After Babel: Aspects of Language and Translation.* Oxford: OUP, 1975.

Strickland, Geoffrey. *Structuralism or Criticism? Thoughts on how we read.* Cambridge: CUP, 1981.

Sturrock, John, ed. *Structuralism and Since: from Lévi-Strauss to Derrida.* Oxford: OUP, 1979.

Thévenaz, Pierre. *De Husserl à Merleau-Ponty: Qu'est-ce que la Phénoménologie?* Neuchatel: Baconnière, 1966.

Thody, Philip. *Roland Barthes: A Conservative Estimate.* London: Macmillan, 1977.

Thomson, Ewa. *Russian Formalism and Anglo-American New Criticism.* The Hague: Mouton, 1971.

Thuillier, Jacques. *Peut-on parler d'une peinture 'pompier'?* Paris: Presses Univ. de France, 1983.

Thurley, Geoffrey. *Counter-Modernism in Current Critical Theory.* London: Macmillan, 1983.

Todorov, Tzvetan. *Introduction à la littérature fantastique.* Paris: Seuil, 1969.

— *Poétique de la Prose.* Paris: Seuil, 1974.

— *Théories du symbole.* Paris: Seuil, 1977.

— *Les Genres du Discours.* Paris: Seuil, 1978.

— *Mikhail Bakhtine, le principe dialogique, suivi de Ecrits du Cercle de Bakhtine.* Paris: Seuil, 1981.

— *Critique de la critique: Un roman d'apprentisage.* Paris: Seuil, 1984.

Todorov, Tzvetan, ed. *Théorie de la Littérature.* (Texts of the Russian formalists.) Paris: Seuil: 1965.

Toledo, Dionísio, ed. *Círculo Linguístico de Praga: Estruturalismo e Semiologia.* Porto Alegre (Brazil): Globo, 1978.

Tomashevsky, Boris. *Teoria della Letteratura.* Milan: Feltrinelli, 1978 (tr. from the Russian).

Trubetzkoy, Nikolai. *Principles of Phonology.* Berkeley: California UP, 1969. (*Grundzüge der Phonologie*, Prague, 1939).

Turkle, Sherry. *Psychoanalytic Politics: Freud's French Revolution.* London: Burnett, 1979.

Turner, Victor. *The Forest of Symbols: Aspects of Ndembu Ritual.* Ithaca: Cornell University Press, 1967.

Tynyanov, Yuri. *Il problema del linguaggio poetico.* Milan: Il Saggiatore, 1968 (Russian original: *Problema stichotvornogo jazyka*, Leningrad, 1924).

— *Avanguardia e tradizione.* Bari: Dedalo, 1968. (Russian original: *Archaisty i novatory*, Leningrad, 1929).

— *Formalismo e storia letteraria.* Turin: Einaudi, 1973.

Ungar, Steven. *Roland Barthes: The Professor of Desire.* Lincoln: Nebraska University Press, 1983.

Vachek, Josef. *The Linguistic School of Prague.* Bloomington: Indiana University Press, 1966.

Wahl, François, ed. *Qu'est-ce-que le Structuralisme?* Paris: Seuil, 1968.

Weimann, Robert. *Structure and Society in Literary History: Studies in the History and Theory of Historical Criticism.* London: Lawrence and Wishart, 1977.

Wellek, René. *Concepts of Criticism.* New Haven: Yale Univ. Press, 1963.

— *A History of Modern Criticism 1750–1950. Vol. 4. The Later Nineteenth*

Century. London: Cape, 1966.
— *The Literary Theory and Aesthetics of the Prague School.* Ann Arbor: Michigan Univ. Press, 1969.
— *Discriminations: Further Concepts of Criticism.* New Haven: Yale University Press, 1970.
Wellek, Réné and Warren, Austin. *Theory of Literature.* New York: Harvest, 1942.
Wienold, Götz. *Semiotik der Literatur.* Frankfurt: Athenäum, 1972.
Wilden, Anthony. *System and Structure: Essays in Communication and Exchange.* London: Tavistock, 1972.
Wimsatt Jr., W. K. and Brooks, Cleanth. *Literary Criticism: A Short History.* New York: Knopf, 1957.
Wittkower, Rudolf. *Sculpture—Processes and Principles.* London: Allen Lane, 1977.
Wollheim, Richard. *On Art and the Mind.* London: Allen Lane, 1973.

Landmarks in Structuralism
and Post-structuralism

1960   Jakobson: 'Linguistics and poetics'
       Martinet: *Eléments de Linguistique Générale*
1961   Foucault: *Madness and Civilisation*
1962   Lévi-Strauss: *The Savage Mind*
       Lévi-Strauss: *Totemism*
1963   Barthes: *On Racine*
       Foucault: *The Birth of the Clinic*
       Klossowski: *Un si funeste désir* (with a lecture on Nietzsche)
1964   Lacan founds the Ecole Freudienne de Paris
       Lévi-Strauss: *Mythologiques I*
       Barthes: *Critical Essays*
1965   Barthes: *Elements of Semiology*
       (Todorov, ed.: *Théorie de la Littérature*)
1966   Barthes: *Critique et Vérité*
       Lacan: *Écrits*
       Althusser: *For Marx*
       Foucault: *The Order of Things*
       Greimas: *Sémantique structurale*
       Benveniste: *Problems of General Linguistics*
1967   Barthes: *Système de la Mode*
       Dumont: *Homo Hierarchicus*
       Granger: *Pensée Formelle et Sciences de l'Homme*
       Derrida: *Writing and Difference*
       Derrida: *Of Grammatology*
1968   (Chomsky: *Language and Mind*)
       Eco: *La Struttura Assente*
       Poulantzas: *Political Power and Social Classes*
       Deleuze: *Différence et Répétition*
1969   Foucault: *The Archaeology of Knowledge*
       Serres: *Hermès I* (La Communication)
       Kristeva: *Semiotike*
       Klossowski: *Nietzsche ou le Cercle Vicieux*
1970   Foucault enters the Collège de France
       Barthes: *S/Z*
1971   Lévi-Strauss: *Mythologiques IV*
       de Man: *Blindness and Insight*
1972   Deleuze and Guattari: *L'Anti-Oedipe*
       Derrida: *Dissemination*
       Derrida: *Marges de la Philosophie*
       Girard: *La Violence et le Sacré*
       Détienne: *The Gardens of Adonis*
1973   Lacan: *Le Séminaire*, book XI
       Barthes: *The Pleasure of the Text*
       Baudrillard: *The Mirror of Production*
1974   Lyotard: *Economie Libidinale*
       Derrida: *Glas*
       Sperber: *Rethinking Symbolism*
1975   Foucault: *Discipline and Punish*

1976   Lardreau and Jambet: *L'Ange*
       Barthes enters the Collège de France
       Foucault: *History of Sexuality*, 1
       Leach: *Culture and Communication*
       (Chomsky: *Reflections on Language*)
1977   (Glucksman: *The Master Thinkers*)
       (B.-H. Lévy: *La Barbarie à Visage Humain*)
1979   Lyotard: *La condition postmoderne*
1980   death of Barthes
       Lacan dissolves the Ecole Freudienne de Paris
1981   Bourdieu: *La Distinction*
       Deleuze: *Mille Plateaux*
1982   death of Lacan
1983   Lévi-Strauss: *The View From Afar*
1984   death of Foucault

Index

J. G. MERQUIOR

FROM PRAGUE TO PARIS

A CRITIQUE OF STR[...]
POST-STRUCTU[...]

H 149.9609

3 DL
Fardon
July 94

FROM PRAGUE TO PARIS
A Critique of Structuralist and
Post-Structuralist Thought
J. G. MERQUIOR

From Prague to Paris is above all a critique of French structuralism. But it is also an exercise in the wider history of ideas, showing that structuralism had already matured significantly prior to its adoption in France. Far from being a methodological high-road, the route from Prague in the 1930s to Paris in the 1960s was complicated by various ideological biases. Merquior argues that Parisian structuralism was notably *formalist*, and that this was not the only option open to it -- as the work of the Prague School shows.

J. G. Merquior was a participant in the intellectual milieu of Parisian structuralism during its rise, and here focuses on three key figures of its heyday: Lévi-Strauss, Barthes and Derrida. The first remains the master of classical structuralism, the second its most distinguished apostle — and then apostate — in literary criticism, while Derrida currently leads the revolt against the rational elements of the philosophical tradition from which it springs.

While its decline in France itself is now obvious, the (post-) structuralist style of thought has conquered influential strongholds in the Anglo-Saxon world. *From Prague to Paris* offers an assessment of its results that is at once scholarly and uninhibited — an irreverent but impeccably researched assault on the citadels of fashionable ideology. It will be useful to students and general readers alike, and no familiarity with the jargon of structuralism is assumed.

J. G. Merquior's previous books include *Rousseau and Weber*, *L'Esthetique de Lévi-Strauss*, *Foucault* and *Western Marxism*.

ISBN 0 86091 860 2

VERSO

UK: 6 Meard Street, London W1V 3HR
USA: 29 West 35th Street, New York, NY 10001-2291
Cover design by Paul Burcher.
The cover illustration is *Mirror with Skeletons* by James Ensor